XML For Dummies 4th Edition

The First (and Last) Word on Valid versus Well-Formed

A *valid document* must conform to the rules in its DTD or schema, which define what elements can appear in the document and how elements may nest within one another. A *well-formed* document must have these characteristics:

- All beginning and ending tags match up. In other words, opening and closing parts must always contain the same name in the same case: `<tag>` . . . `</tag>` or `<TAG>` . . . `</TAG>`, but not `<tag>` . . . `</TAG>`.
- Empty elements follow special XML syntax, for example, `<empty_element/>`.
- All attribute values occur within single or double quotation marks: `<element id="value">` or `<element id='value'>`.

Rules for Creating DTD Elements

You may create many rules in your DTD that govern how elements can be used in an XML document.

Symbol	Meaning	Example
`#PCDATA`	Contains parsed character data or text	`<element (#PCDATA)>`
`#PCDATA, element-name`	Contains text and another element; `#PCDATA` is always listed first in a rule	`<element (#PCDATA, child)*>`
`, (comma)`	Must use in this order	`<element (child1, child2, child3)>`
`| (pipe bar)`	Use only one element of the choices provided	`<element (child1 | child2 | child3)>`
`element-name` (by itself)	Use one time only	`<element (child)>`
`element-name?`	Use either once or not at all	`<element (child1, child2?, child3?)>`
`element-name+`	Use either once or many times	`<element (child1+, child2?, child3)>`
`element-name*`	Use once, many times, or not at all	`<element (child1*, child2+, child3)>`
`( )`	Indicates groups; may be nested	`<element (#PCDATA | child)*>` or `<element ((child1*, child2+, child3)* | child4)>`

For Dummies: Bestselling Book Series for Beginners

XML For Dummies, 4th Edition

Cheat Sheet

Basic Schema Declarations

An XML Schema document is built of a series of declarations that provides very detailed information about your data structure.

Declaration Name	Purpose	Syntax
Schema	Identifies the language the schema uses	`<xsd:schema xmlns:xsd="http://www.w3.org/2001/XMLSchema">`
Element	Defines an element	`<xsd:element name="name">`
Attribute	Defines an attribute	`<xsd:attribute name="name" type="type">`
Complex type	Defines an element that contains other elements, contains attributes, or contains mixed content (elements and text)	`<xsd:complexType>`
Simple type	Creates a constrained datatype for an element or attribute value	`<xsd:simpleType>`
Sequence compositor	Specifies that attributes or elements within a complex type must be listed in order	`<xsd:sequence>`
Choice compositor	Specifies that any one of the attributes or elements within a complex type can be used	`<xsd:choice>`
All compositor	Specifies that any or all attributes or elements within a complex type can be used	`<xsd:all>`
Annotation	Contains `documentation` and/or `appInfo` elements that provide additional information and comments about the schema document	`<xsd:annotation>`
Documentation	Provides human-readable information within an annotation	`<xsd:documentation>`
Application information	Provides computer-readable information within an annotation	`<xsd:appInfo>`

Browser Support for XML and Style Sheets

The support across Web browsers for XML and style sheets — CSS and XSLT — is varied and less-than dependable. Knowing which browsers support which specifications can help you decide how to use XML and Web browsers in your XML solution.

Browser	XML?	CSS1?	CSS2?	XSLT 1.0?
Amaya 9.0	Yes	Yes	No	No
Internet Explorer 6.0	Yes	Yes	Yes	Yes
Mozilla 1.7.5	Yes	Yes	Yes	Yes
Mozilla Firefox 1.0	Yes	Yes	Yes	Yes
Netscape Navigator 7	Yes	Yes	Yes	Yes
Opera 7	Yes	Yes	Yes	No

Common Reserved Characters

There are reserved characters that can't appear in an XML document unless they're part of a `CDATA` section. Replace them with the character references in your content.

Character	Reference
<	`&lt;`
>	`&gt;`
&	`&amp;`
'	`&apos;`
"	`&quot;`

XML

FOR

DUMMIES®

4TH EDITION

XML FOR DUMMIES®
4TH EDITION

by Lucinda Dykes and Ed Tittel

WILEY

Wiley Publishing, Inc.

XML For Dummies,® 4th Edition

Published by
Wiley Publishing, Inc.
111 River Street
Hoboken, NJ 07030-5774

www.wiley.com

For general information on our other products and services, please contact our Customer Care Department within the U.S. at 800-762-2974, outside the U.S. at 317-572-3993, or fax 317-572-4002.

For technical support, please visit www.wiley.com/techsupport.

Wiley also publishes its books in a variety of electronic formats. Some content that appears in print may not be available in electronic books.

Library of Congress Control Number: 2005923240

ISBN-13: 978-0-7645-8845-7

ISBN-10: 0-7645-8845-1

Manufactured in the United States of America

10 9 8 7 6 5 4 3 2 1

4O/QT/QV/QV/IN

WILEY

About the Author

Lucinda Dykes started her career in a high-tech area of medicine, but left medicine to pursue her interests in technology and the Web. She has been writing code and developing Web sites since 1994, and also teaches and develops online courses — including the JavaScript courses for the International Webmasters Association/HTML Writers' Guild at www. eclasses.org.

Lucinda has authored, co-authored, edited, and been a contributing author to numerous computer books; the most recent include *Dreamweaver MX 2004 Savvy* (Sybex), *XML for Dummies* (3rd Edition, Wiley), *Dreamweaver MX Fireworks MX Savvy* (Sybex), *XML Schemas* (Sybex), and *Mastering XHTML* (Sybex). When she can manage to move herself away from her keyboard, other interests include holographic technologies, science fiction, and Bollywood movies.

Ed Tittel is a 23-year veteran of the computing industry. After spending his first seven years in harness writing code, Ed switched to the softer side of the business as a trainer and talking head. A freelance writer since 1986, Ed has written hundreds of magazine and Web articles — and worked on over 100 computer books, including numerous *For Dummies* titles on topics that include several Windows versions, NetWare, HTML, XHTML, and XML.

Ed is also Technology Editor for *Certification Magazine*, writes for numerous TechTarget Web sites, and writes a twice-monthly newsletter, "Must Know News," for CramSession.com. In his spare time, Ed likes to shoot pool, cook, and spend time with his wife Dina and his son Gregory. He also likes to explore the world away from the keyboard with his trusty Labrador retriever, Blackie. Ed can be contacted at etittel@yahoo.com.

Dedication

To the heroes at the W3C and OASIS, sung and unsung, especially members of the many XML working groups who have made the world (or the Web, at least) a better place through their tireless efforts, and to all those Web pioneers who generously offered help and support to those of us trying to figure out how to make our contribution to the Web in the early '90s.

Author's Acknowledgments

Lucinda Dykes: Thanks to everyone on the scene and behind the scenes who has contributed to making this project possible.

First, I'd like to thank Ed Tittel for giving me not only the opportunity to be involved in this book, but who also played a major role in my entry into the world of technical writing. Ed and I share a long-term interest in language, computers, and markup languages. I'd also like to thank everyone involved in any edition of this book for the excellent foundation they made for this edition to build on.

Next, thanks to the team at Wiley, especially Katie Feltman for her vision and support of this project, Paul Levesque for quiet and steady guidance in addition to excellent editing, Allen Wyatt for insight and outstanding technical editing, and Barry Childs-Helton for superb copy-editing as well as a delightful sense of humor. And thanks to Carole McClendon, my agent at Waterside Productions, who made it possible for me to lead this project.

On a personal note, special thanks to my mother, Doris Dykes, who instilled and supported a lifelong interest in learning and in books. She claims that I'm the first child she lost to the Internet — but that makes me easy to find. Mom: I'll be in front of the nearest computer screen. Thanks and love always to Wali for making it possible for me to spend all these late nights tapping away at the keyboard, and for always making me remember the things that are really important. Thanks to our dear friends, Rose Rowe and Karmin Perless, who walked softly and made room for having a writer around. And finally, thanks to Wendy Fries and Cheryl Kline for great conversation, good advice, and lots of laughter at our monthly writers' session at the Coffee Grove.

Publisher's Acknowledgments

We're proud of this book; please send us your comments through our online registration form located at www.dummies.com/register/.

Some of the people who helped bring this book to market include the following:

Acquisitions, Editorial, and Media Development

Project Editor: Paul Levesque

Acquisitions Editor: Katie Feltman

Copy Editor: Barry Childs-Helton

Technical Editor: Allen Wyatt, Sr.

Editorial Manager: Leah Cameron

Permissions Editor: Laura Moss

Media Development Specialist: Kit Malone

Media Development Manager:
Laura VanWinkle

Media Development Supervisor:
Richard Graves

Editorial Assistant: Amanda Foxworth

Cartoons: Rich Tennant
(www.the5thwave.com)

Composition Services

Project Coordinator: Maridee Ennis

Layout and Graphics: Andrea Dahl,
Stephanie D. Jumper, Julie Trippetti

Proofreaders: Leeann Harney, Joe Niesen,
Carl William Pierce, TECHBOOKS
Production Services

Indexer: TECHBOOKS Production Services

Publishing and Editorial for Technology Dummies

Richard Swadley, Vice President and Executive Group Publisher

Andy Cummings, Vice President and Publisher

Mary Bednarek, Executive Acquisitions Director

Mary C. Corder, Editorial Director

Publishing for Consumer Dummies

Diane Graves Steele, Vice President and Publisher

Joyce Pepple, Acquisitions Director

Composition Services

Gerry Fahey, Vice President of Production Services

Debbie Stailey, Director of Composition Services

Contents at a Glance

Table of Contents

Introduction

*W*elcome to the latest frontier of Web technology. In *XML For Dummies,* 4th Edition, we introduce you to the mysteries of eXtensible Markup Language *(XML)*. XML is helping developers capture, manipulate, and exchange all kinds of documents and data, ranging from news feeds to financial transactions. In fact, many experts believe XML represents a kind of "lingua franca" that can represent information in just about any imaginable form, more accessibly than ever before — not only to human readers, but also to all kinds of computer applications and services.

We take a practical and straightforward approach to telling you about XML and what it can do for your data and document capture, management, and exchange efforts. We try to keep the amount of technobabble to a minimum and stick to plain English as much as possible. We also try to keep the focus on practical applications of XML technology, including desktop applications such as Office 2003. We have carefully chosen what we feel are the most relevant XML technologies for developers today. Besides plain talk about XML — and the many special-purpose applications that XML supports for document designers and authors, graphics developers, and many other communities of technical and business interests — we include lots of sample markup to help you put XML to work in your organization, business, or personal life. (No personal life is quite complete without a little XML.)

 The Web page for this book is available at `www.dummies.com/go/xmlfd4e`. This Web page includes all the XML example files from this book, as well as numerous XML authoring tools, parsers, development kits, and other goodies for you to download. We hope you'll find it helpful for your own projects!

About This Book

Think of this book as your friendly, approachable guide to using XML for all kinds of interesting purposes. Using XML is a bit trickier than using HTML, so this book is organized to make it easier to grapple with XML's fundamentals, wrestle them to the ground, and use them well. We also document voluminous additional sources of information, both online and offline. Here are some of the topics we include:

- ✔ An overview of XML's capabilities, terminology, and technologies
- ✔ Tips for styling XML with CSS and XSLT

✔ Hands-on practice in developing DTDs and XML Schema for validating XML documents

✔ A beginner's guide to XPath

✔ An introduction to XForms and InfoPath

✔ A guide to XML application development, including Web services, databases, and news feeds

Because XML is essentially a markup language used to create other XML-based markup languages — or what we also call XML applications — it's not exactly accurate to call a document based on one particular XML application or another an "XML document." It really makes more sense to call it an "XML-based document" because the document itself contains markup defined using XML. But for brevity's sake, we call such documents *XML documents* in this book. After all, such documents must adhere to the rules of XML syntax and structure if they are to work properly. We could get all fussy and always refer to them (more correctly) as "XML-based documents" or "documents based on such-and-such an XML application." But that makes us squirm too.

Although you might think that using XML requires years of training and advanced technical wizardry, we don't think that's true. If you can tell someone how to drive across town, you can certainly use XML to build documents that do what you want them to. The purpose of this book isn't to turn you into a true-blue geek, complete with pocket protector. Rather, *XML For Dummies, 4th Edition* shows you which design and technical elements you need so you can get a practical handle on what XML is and how it works. We also provide numerous examples and case studies to illustrate how XML behaves, so you can gain the know-how and confidence to use XML to good effect!

Conventions Used in This Book

Throughout this book, you see lots and lots of markup. All XML markup appears in monospace type, like this:

```
<Greeting>Hello, world!</Greeting>. ..
```

When you type XML tags or other related information, be sure to copy the information exactly as you see it between the angle brackets (< and >), because that's part of the magic that makes XML work. Other than that, we tell you how to marshal and manage the content that makes your pages special, and we tell you exactly what you need to do to mix the elements of XML with your own work.

Because the margins in this book can't accommodate some long lines of XML markup and still stay legible, sometimes we have to break lines of code. That tends to happen in designations for Web sites (called *URLs,* for *U*niform *R*esource *L*ocators) or special XML identifiers for namespaces and other information objects (called *URIs,* or *U*niform *R*esource *I*dentifiers) and also in the odd monstrously long line of markup that wraps to the next line. On your computer, these wrapped lines would appear on-screen as a single line of XML or as a single URL or URI — so don't insert a hard return when you see any such lines wrap in the book. Here are some examples of wrapped lines:

```
www.infomagic.austin.com/nexus/plexus/lexus/praxis/
   this_is_deliberately_long.html
```

and

```
<Item>Scientists have developed a robot that "learns" to walk like a toddler,
             improving its step and balance with every stride.</Item>
```

XML is sensitive to how element text is entered. If you're following our examples from the comfort of your living room, keep in mind that you have to use uppercase, lowercase, or other characters exactly as they appear in the book (or, more important, as they're defined in the document description that governs any well-formed, valid XML document — be it an XML Schema or a Document Type Definition, or *DTD*). To make your work look like ours as much as possible, enter all element text exactly as it appears in this book. Better yet, download the file from the Web page for the book (www.dummies. com/go/xmlfd4e)!

Foolish Assumptions

Someone once said that making assumptions makes a fool out of the person who makes them and the person who is their subject. Even so, we're going to make a few assumptions about you, our gentle reader:

- ✔ You're already familiar with text files and know how to use a text editor.
- ✔ You have a working connection to the Internet.
- ✔ You're hip to the difference between a Web browser and a Web server.
- ✔ You want to build your own XML documents for fun, for profit, or because it's part of your job.

Also, we assume that you have a modern Web browser — one that can support XML directly. As we write this, that elite includes Internet Explorer 5.5 (and higher), Netscape Navigator 6 (and later), Opera, Firefox, Mozilla, and

Amaya — all have decent XML parsing and rendering capabilities. Don't worry, though, if you don't have such a browser. Part of what you find in these pages and on the Web page for the book is a collection of pointers to help you obtain the tools you need to work directly with XML on your own computer. You don't need to be a master logician or a programming whiz to work with XML; all you need are the time required to discover its ins and outs and the determination to understand its intricacies and capabilities.

Even if you were one of those who fled English Composition in school and hid out in the computer lab, take heart: If you can write a sentence and you know the difference between a heading and a paragraph, you can build and publish your own XML documents. If you have an imagination and the ability to communicate what's important to you in an organized manner, you've already mastered the ingredients necessary to build useful, information-rich XML documents and data collections. The rest is details — and we help you with those!

How This Book Is Organized

This book contains six major parts; each part contains three or more chapters; each chapter has (in all modesty) lots of good stuff. Any time you need help or information, pick up the book and start anywhere you like, or use the table of contents and index to locate specific topics or keywords. This section of your friendly intro offers a preview of the six parts and what you find in each one.

Part I: XML Basics

Part I sets the stage. It begins with an overview of XML's special capabilities and discusses what XML is and what XML is not. We tempt you toward the XML side of the Force (hopefully) by exploring the many uses for XML — and checking out the applications to which it's so well suited. We also briefly discuss the relationships between and among the many XML languages and let you know which ones we think are particularly useful for today's developer. We conclude Part I with a look at techniques for analyzing and classifying your data so that you can make XML documents meet your data requirements. You also get to see how XML documents gain their structure and content — from a thorough analysis of requirements and examples.

Part II: XML and the Web

In Part II, you find out all about displaying XML content on Web pages. First, we cover what's involved in converting HTML to its XML-based equivalent, XHTML, as a way of introducing XML's syntax and structure.

Chapter 5 picks up that thread, and you find out how to construct an XML document piece by piece while playing by the rules of XML. We show you how to create well-formed documents and discuss how XML documents and data can be made subject to formal descriptions (a great way to define a set of rules that humans and computers can follow with equal ease). You find out why you might (or might not) want to validate your XML documents with a DTD or XML Schema.

In Chapter 6 we explore character sets and related entities that XML depends on to represent content and explain how to use them in your documents.

We conclude Part II with an explanation of what's involved in bringing XML documents to the Web and talk about the best ways to use styles to make their contents more presentable. To that end, we explore ways to use Cascading Style Sheets (CSS) to make native XML documents (or XML content transformed into HTML) easier to read and appreciate online.

Part III: Building in Validation with DTDs and Schemas

In Part III, we explain the purpose and functions that Document Type Definitions (DTDs) can play in describing XML documents. We use a DTD to teach you about the XML markup that it enables. We explain how to read a DTD to recognize the elements, attributes, and content models it contains.

After that, we look at an "all-XML, all the time" alternative to DTDs called XML Schema — an application that provides even more capabilities to describe, use, and control XML documents. One part of XML Schema's appeal derives from its basis in XML itself. Because XML Schema is just another XML application (albeit one that allows you to describe other XML applications), you've got a leg up if you already have a working knowledge of XML: You can apply that knowledge to describing XML applications without having to learn yet another markup language. DTDs (on the other hand) are based on SGML, not XML; you have to have XML under your belt before you can use, customize, or create DTDs that describe XML applications. Another major part of XML Schema's appeal derives from its broad selection of built-in datatypes and support for user-derived datatypes; you can be as specific as you want (or need) to be in describing your data.

We explain how to create elements, attributes, datatypes, and content models to work in XML Schemas. We provide details on how to construct a valid XML Schema document and show you how to use this document to create new XML documents in Word 2003.

We conclude Part III by explaining how to combine XML Schemas and how to mix and match XML Schema contents or components to maximize this technology. We also introduce XML namespaces and take a look at converting DTDs to XML Schemas.

The four chapters in this part represent some of the most important nuts and bolts in the entire book.

Part IV: Transforming and Processing XML

In Part IV, we jump into the ins and outs of the eXtensible Stylesheet Language *(XSL)* that can be used to turn XML-based data or documents into just about any form or format imaginable. After that, we explore the details of transforming an XML document into different formats — and dispel the mysteries involved in putting XSL to work for you when you change things around.

Next, we show you how to use XPath to describe the precise location of elements, attributes, and their values in an XML document.

To conclude Part IV, our final stop is inside the machinery that makes XML usable, as we explore what's involved when a computer reads and absorbs an XML document and list what kinds of capabilities the necessary software (usually called an XML processor) can deliver.

Part V: XML Application Development

In Part V, we explore what you can do with XML when you've got some ready to work with — and show you many possible ways to get things done with a little help from XML.

First, we take a look at an exciting set of XML-based applications designed to advertise, locate, and use so-called "Web services" — a software and messaging architecture that enables service providers to advertise their services on the Web and users to locate and use such services. Web services can involve anything from access to proprietary databases, remote storage or processing, or even access to basic productivity applications (word processing, spreadsheets, e-mail, and so forth) that users normally see on their own desktops but often show up running elsewhere on the Internet. There's plenty of hype and hope for the future of Web services, and you explore the reasons why this is the case.

Next, you find out all about using forms to collect XML data and take a close look at two very different ways to use forms with XML: XForms, the W3C's "next generation" of Web forms, and InfoPath, Microsoft's visual XML forms editor.

In Chapter 17, you explore using XML with databases and how to import and export XML data using Word, InfoPath, XMLSpy, and Access.

To conclude Part V, we explain how to use XML on the Web for syndicating content with RSS news feeds. You get the word on how to create an RSS file, as well as how to validate your file and submit it for syndication.

Part VI: The Part of Tens

Part VI introduces our picks of the best XML tools, applications and resources. We begin this part with a brief survey of popular, widely used XML tools and technologies. These include special-purpose XML editors and authoring tools, XML-based management tools, XML-capable browsers, parsers and engines, and conversion tools.

In Chapter 20, you have a chance to observe some of the best and brightest uses of XML and to understand why a certain set of XML applications is of such great interest to so many content designers and developers. Finally, in Chapter 21, you can read about some of the most appealing and useful sources of information about XML and related applications known to man and woman.

Glossary

In the glossary, you can find definitions for all terms that make you go "Huh?" We did our best to choose the ones that really need an explanation and to define them in a way that's easy to understand.

The materials on the *XML For Dummies,* 4th Edition Web site (`www.dummies.com/go/xmlfd4e/`) are designed to help you match up the markup and examples that appear within the pages of the book to their electronic counterparts on the Web site. In addition, we've provided links to as comprehensive a collection of tools and programs for XML as we could gather here for your delectation and use.

Icons Used in This Book

This icon signals technical details that are informative and interesting but not critical to writing XML. Skip these if you want (but please, for the sake of your inner geek, come back and read them later).

This icon flags useful information that demystifies (and helps uncomplicate) XML markup, Web-page design, or other important stuff.

 This icon points out information that you shouldn't pass by — don't overlook these gentle reminders (the life you save could be your own).

 Be cautious when you see this icon. It warns you of things you shouldn't do; the bomb emphasizes that the consequences of ignoring these bits of wisdom can be severe.

Where to Go from Here

To keep up with the latest version of these references, please visit the related *XML For Dummies* site at www.dummies.com/go/xmlfd4e/. Here, you find the results of our best efforts to keep the information in the book current and a list of errata to straighten out any mistakes, boo-boos, or gotchas that we weren't able to root out before the book went to publication. We hope you find this a convincing demonstration that our hearts are in the right place (we already know we're not perfect).

Please share your feedback with us about the book. We can't claim that we'll follow every suggestion or react to every comment, but you can be pretty certain that suggestions that occur repeatedly — or that add demonstrable value to the book — will find a place in the next edition!

Good luck on your journey, and don't forget to keep your eyes on the road and your hands on the wheel as you cruise the information highway.

Enjoy!

Part I
XML Basics

The 5th Wave   By Rich Tennant

SOFTWARE
DOCUMENT
PUBLISHERS

"They're moving on to the XML APIs section.
That should daze and confuse them enough
for us to finish changing the tire."

In this part . . .

Here you get a gentle-but-formal introduction to the eXtensible Markup Language, also known as XML. Starting in Chapter 1, you get a look at XML's capabilities, strengths, and versatility. You get tips on the best uses of XML, and draw a bead on the other pieces that may be necessary for an XML solution. In Chapter 2, we introduce you to the options for XML output — including Web pages, print documents, forms, spreadsheets, and databases. Then the wide variety of XML languages comes to light. Finally, Chapter 3 rounds out your basic toolkit with a close look at how to develop and test a classification scheme for your data.

Chapter 1

Getting to Know XML

*H*ave you ever needed a document format that you could use to exchange data — either across the Internet or across an intranet? Well, eXtensible Markup Language (XML) may be just the solution. In fact, many different industries have discovered the wonders of XML — and use it extensively to help organize and classify their data.

XML is a *markup language* — it uses tags to label, categorize, and organize information in a specific way. *Markup* describes document or data structure and organization. *Content,* such as text, images, and data, is that part of the code that the markup tags contain; it's also what's of greatest interest to most everyday humans who read or interact with data or documents. XML isn't limited to a particular set of markup — you create your own markup to suit your data and document needs. The flexibility of XML has led to its widespread use for exchanging data in a multitude of forms.

And that's not all! With XML, you can send the same information to various locations — say, to a person using a mobile phone and a person using a Web browser — at the same time. In addition, you can customize the information sent out so it's displayed appropriately on the various devices.

Getting started with XML isn't difficult. Just check out this chapter, and you'll get the skinny on what markup languages are, what XML is, and what you can use XML to do.

XML (eXtreMely cooL)

If you take a close look at the use of XML in today's business world, you soon recognize that pinning down a single, definitive use for XML is nearly impossible. In fact, it is precisely the open-ended nature of XML that makes it so useful for many different things — and so difficult to put into a single, small box. Read on to see what we mean.

Mocking up your own markup

You may be familiar with *Hypertext Markup Language* (HTML), the markup language used to display information on Web pages. Both XML and HTML are derived from the "mother of all markup languages," Standard Generalized Markup Language (SGML) — but any similarity ends there.

HTML includes a set of predefined tags that format information for display on the Web. XML has no predefined tags — instead, you can create your own XML tags to structure your XML document so its content is in a form that meets your needs. Basically, you design your own custom markup language (actually an XML application) to do data exchange in a way that works for you.

Although XML doesn't include predefined tags, it does include very specific rules about the syntax of an XML document. You'll get a chance to explore those rules (and use said rules to create your own XML document) in Chapter 5.

X*HT*ML is yet another markup language — designed as a transition language between HTML and XML. In a nutshell, XHTML is a version of HTML that follows the strict syntax rules of XML. After you've used it for a while, you're well prepared to use XML. (We uncover the mysteries of XHTML in Chapter 4 — where you also get a chance to create an XHTML file to view on the Web.)

Separating data and context

Among the many benefits of using XML is that it automatically separates data from *context* (presentation). An XML document by itself includes no instructions about how to display the content contained in the document — it only defines the structure of the document. You can then add *styles* — formatting instructions for displaying the content — in a separate document called a *stylesheet.* This separation is actually pretty handy; you can change the display instructions without having to make any changes to your XML document. If the same style sheet is used with more than one document, you can make uniform style changes in all those documents simply by making changes in the stylesheet. All the associated XML documents follow the stylesheet's orders.

XML can be combined with both two different types of stylesheets — Cascading Style Sheets (CSS) and/or Extensible Stylesheet Language Transformations (XSLT) — for extra versatility. This makes it possible to view XML documents on the Web as more than just raw document markup — and you can change this display easily to accommodate different output devices. For example, you can use one stylesheet for display on a PDA and a separate one for printout.

We'll have more to tell about the world of CSS formatting in Chapter 7, where (lucky you) we even show you how to create and link a CSS stylesheet to an XML document. XSLT gets the same treatment in Chapter 12, where you get a chance to explore the power of XSLT stylesheets for formatting the display of an XML document.

Making information portable

XML is all about managing your data — using the best possible format available to you. To talk about how XML can handle your data as discrete bits of information, what better format is there to use than a bulleted list? Check out the following items:

- ✔ XML enables you to collect information once and reuse it in a variety of ways.

- ✔ XML data is not limited to one application format. You can design an XML document that allows you to collect data online for use in other documents, databases, and spreadsheets.

  For example, suppose your business collects sales information on a group of products by using an XML document to contain the data. The same XML data could be used to create customer purchase records, commission reports, and product-sales graphs.

- ✔ Making information portable does require planning and design before the information is collected. (You get a chance to explore the art of developing strategies for data collection in Chapter 3.)

XML means business

XML provides an easy way for businesses to manage and share information. Although XML was originally created by the World Wide Web Consortium (W3C) as a way to disseminate complex, structured data and documents over the Web, its use has expanded. Now no longer a Web-only format, XML is right at home on the business desktop.

Microsoft Office 2003 is one notable application package that includes XML tools for office applications. Using Office 2003, office documents can be created in XML format and information tagged and collected for re-use in other office applications as well as on the Web. We highlight some uses of XML in Office 2003 throughout this book.

Figuring Out What XML Is Good For

Case studies of XML never fail to mention new and exciting possibilities where XML adds value to existing environments — or solves previously intractable problems. That's probably why XML applications are widely used for everything from displaying chemical formulas to setting up a family tree. So how can *you* use the power of XML?

Classifying information

One of the most useful functions of XML involves classifying information. To see how this would work, imagine yourself in the business of selling books.

Books can be classified in many ways, but we kind of like the following classification scheme:

- Title
- Author
- Publisher
- Price
- Content Type (Fiction, Nonfiction)
- Format (Paperback, Hardback)
- ISBN

Using XML, you can create tags to classify this information. The following code shows a possible XML format for one book:

```
<book>
 <title>Night Fall</title>
 <author>Demille, Nelson</author>
 <publisher>Warner</publisher>
 <price>$26.95</price>
 <contentType>Fiction</contentType>
 <format>Hardback</format>
 <isbn>0446576638</isbn>
</book>
```

Giving your tags meaningful names that actually reflect the content makes it easier to work with the information.

Classifying the information as shown here makes it possible for you to search for — and retrieve — any item with ease. For example, after the information on all the books for your imaginary book business is collected and tucked away in XML format, you can create a list of all the authors — or authors and titles, or titles and ISBNs, whatever information you want to access. (Talk about power at your fingertips!)

We go over all the gory details of classifying information in Chapter 3, but do keep this imaginary book business in mind as you make your way through the other chapters of this book: For the sake of illustration, you get to become the next giant (imaginary) bookstore chain. We expand the book-business example in later chapters to demonstrate how you can use XML to collect and use information about inventory, customers, stores, and sales, however massive a success you become.

Enforcing rules on your data

XML excels at allowing you to create rules for the format of your data. Using either Document Type Definitions (DTDs) or XML Schemas to validate your data gives you two immediate advantages:

- ✔ It helps ensure the accuracy of the information you collect.
- ✔ It helps ensure that the information gathered is in the most usable format for your business needs.

Not sure what a DTD is? Check out the "Getting to know markup-language lingo" sidebar, later in this chapter.

Taking another look at the XML we came up with in the previous section for your imaginary book business, you can see several items for which you might want to include rules to govern how the data is formatted, such as

- ✔ A currency format for the price
- ✔ A number format for the ISBN
- ✔ A restricted selection for content type (Fiction or Nonfiction)
- ✔ A restricted selection for format (Paperback or Hardback)

You get a detailed look at creating and using DTDs and XML Schemas in Part III of this book.

Getting to know markup-language lingo

You don't have to be a markup pro to read this book or to use XML. If you're new to the markup world (or if you need to brush up on your vocabulary), the following list should help you out.

These terms are the most common ones you run into in the XML world. As you get to know them, you also get a handle on markup languages in general (including XML):

- **Attribute:** In XML, a property associated with an XML element that's also a named characteristic of the element. An attribute also provides additional data about an element, independent of element content. For example:

  ```
  <book location="GatewayMall">Whiteout
  </book>
  ```

  In this case, the element (book) content is Whiteout, but the attribute (location) provides additional data (GatewayMall).

- **Document Type Definition (DTD):** This is a statement of rules for an XML document — based on SGML (the ancestor of XML) — that specifies which *elements* (markup tags) and *attributes* (names and values associated with specific elements) are allowed in your documents. A DTD also governs the order in which the elements and attributes may appear — or (if you want to get strict) must appear.

- **Element:** A section of a document defined by start and end tags (or an empty tag), including any associated content.

- **Metalanguage:** A language used to communicate information about a language itself; many experts consider both SGML and XML to be metalanguages because they can be used to define other markup languages.

- **Nesting:** An ordering of elements that opens and closes a child element before its parent element is closed. (*Child elements* nest within *parent elements*.)

- **Schema:** An XML-based statement of rules that represents how an XML document models its data and defines its elements (or objects), their attributes (or properties), and relationships between elements.

- **Syntax:** The rules that govern the correct construction of intelligible statements in a markup language.

- **Tag; empty tag:** The markup used to enclose an element's content. An *empty element* employs a single tag; a *regular element* (which isn't empty) has an opening and a closing tag.

- **Valid:** Said of a document if it adheres to the rules outlined in an associated DTD or schema document.

- **Well formed:** Said of a markup-language document that adheres to the syntax rules for XML — which are explicitly designed to make documents easy for a computer to interpret.

Outputting information in a variety of ways

Outputting your data means releasing it from its storage locker — presumably somewhere inside the guts of your computer — and getting it to some other place where it can be a bit more useful. The great thing about XML documents is that they're not limited to any particular form of output; they can end up in a variety of different places, in whatever form is appropriate — for example, in a database, a computer monitor, a printer, or a PDA.

XML documents are at home in a wide range of processes. The phrase *post-processing* was practically tailor-made for XML; it means taking information from a document and using it in some other process or program. For example, suppose you receive a purchase order in the form of an XML document. An application that understands XML purchase orders can use that data to determine which items (and in what quantities) have been ordered — and can even send instructions to another piece of software to generate a pick list so the order can be picked, packed, and shipped from the warehouse. (Now, *that's* our kind of post-processing!)

In many cases, XML documents are used with stylesheets to provide high-quality output on-screen. You can use the same data, however, to send information to a speech-synthesis program that reads the text to a person who is vision impaired. Alternatively, that same data might also create output on a Braille reader. The same document with a layout program and a stylesheet also might be used for high-quality printouts. (Figure 1-1 gives you an idea of the infinite variety of output choices that XML makes available to you.)

The beauty of this concept is that you never need to fuss and fidget with the XML data to create output for different devices. You need only use different pieces of software that can read XML and can provide the output for a particular format or output device.

Using the same data across platforms

The good news looks, at first, like no news: XML documents are not specific to any particular platform or programming language. Okay, why is that something to e-mail home about? Think versatility. Suppose you want to exchange database information across the Web — say, use a Web browser to send information from a user questionnaire back to a Web server. To accomplish this task (and many others), you need a document format that is

- ✔ **Extensible:** An *extensible* format is one that can be tailored or customized for specific applications.
- ✔ **Open:** It's well documented and widely available.
- ✔ **Nonproprietary:** It's expressed in an accepted or standard form of notation that isn't the exclusive property of some individual, company, or organization.

These characteristics enable the document to adapt to changing conditions, to take best advantage of the work of others, and to avoid incurring extra expense or legal liability.

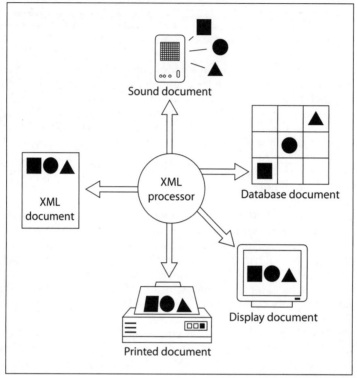

Figure 1-1:
Use XML for
different
outputs.

Guess what? XML meets all three requirements for a document format for exchanging data — it's open, extensible, and nonproprietary. No surprise, then, that XML is the best choice for data exchange; those three magic characteristics make it a handy, consistent way to hand data around among multiple applications and multiple platforms with the most efficiency and least hassle.

Check out Chapter 2 for additional information and examples of the many uses of XML, as well as an introduction to the world of XML technologies.

Beyond the Hype: What XML Isn't

The previous section spells out what XML is — an extensible markup language that allows you to create your own tags to develop XML applications. Now it's time to clarify what XML is *not*.

It's not just for Web pages anymore

Although the World Wide Web Consortium (W3C) developed XML, it's not specifically designed only for Web pages. In fact, if you display an XML document on the Web in its raw form (without adding styles to format the display), all you'll see is the XML markup itself. Figure 1-2 shows an XML file in Internet Explorer — not much to look at! And there's even less to see when this same file is displayed in Netscape Navigator, as shown in Figure 1-3.

So banish this Web-only idea from your thoughts. XML is a markup language that allows you to organize information by creating tags to construct a specific document structure. XML documents can be viewed on the Web, but unlike HTML documents, they're not limited to the Web.

Figure 1-2:
An XML file
as it looks
in Internet
Explorer.

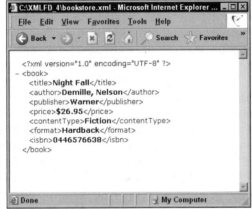

Figure 1-3:
An XML file
as it looks in
Netscape
Navigator.

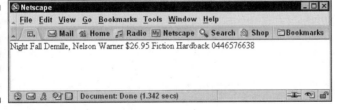

Browser support for XML is limited and variable. Hopefully this will change in the next generation of browsers, but for now XML works well in Web pages only when combined with another language (CSS) or XML technology (XSLT) to format the display of the XML information. Figure 1-4 shows our XML file when it's combined with simple CSS style instructions — now, that's more like it!

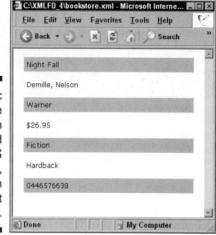

Figure 1-4:
An XML file
with an
attached
CSS
stylesheet,
shown in
Internet
Explorer.

It's not a database

Whether XML "is" a database depends on your definition of *database*. If you're defining a database as a collection of data, then yes, XML qualifies as a database. If you're defining a database as a Database Management System (DBMS) program, such as Microsoft Access, XML has some DBMS features (storage, queries, programming interfaces) but doesn't have others (queries across multiple documents, security, indexes). So, okay, you *could* use XML as a database for a small amount of data — but it wouldn't be efficient to use XML as a database for large amounts of data. (Why would you want to, when DBMS programs are designed to do exactly that?)

That's not to say XML is in any way database unfriendly. XML documents work well for both input and output, going to and from a database — and you can also use them to display database information in print or on the Web. (You get a closer look at how to use XML effectively with databases in Chapter 17.)

It's not a programming language

One of the most common misconceptions about XML is that it's a programming language. Although XML can be used with programming languages for certain types of application development, it's a markup language, not a programming language. A markup language is essentially descriptive; a programming language is for issuing logical commands. Programming languages include (for example) variables, datatypes, operators, loops, functions, and conditional statements. XML doesn't include any of these features, so it's no programming language.

Part of the confusion here is that some XML document types do include some features *found* in programming languages. For example, XML Schemas (which are themselves XML documents) include several built-in datatypes and also allow user-defined datatypes. But wait a minute: Although XML Schema documents can include datatypes — one feature of programming languages — that doesn't make them full-fledged programming languages with all the features just listed here. They remain XML documents — with an XML document structure, created with a markup language (XML). You can get XML to describe how a document will look; you can't get it to dim your house lights or start your car — at least, not without some help from an actual programming language.

Building XML Documents

When it comes to actually getting your XML tags in a row, regular old-fashioned text editors (such as Notepad) can do the job if you're just getting your feet wet with XML. If you're using Windows, you can access Notepad by choosing Start➪Programs➪Accessories➪Notepad. A new Notepad window opens. You can save the files just as you would in a word processor — and do simple functions such as copy and paste. Aside from that, though, Notepad is a pretty bare-bones program — you must insert all the markup yourself when you use a text editor such as Notepad.

Avoid using the WordPad text editor to create an XML document; it won't let you save a file with the .xml extension.

If the bare-bones approach just isn't good enough, you may want to check out text editors that are built specifically for XML. (We think they are definitely the way to go if you plan on using XML regularly.) These editors often look like a blend of traditional word processors and HTML editors. In fact, most XML editors work so much like word processors that you could easily forget you're working with XML.

XML editors can make your job easier and help keep those creative juices flowing! (Tracking tags and cleaning up structures can interrupt — even completely destroy — the creative train of thought.) XML editors have two distinct features that are essential for creating good XML documents:

  ✔ **Ease of markup:** XML editors, such as XMLSpy, Turbo XML, and XML Pro, can add markup to text as simply as you can turn text **bold** in today's word processors. All XML editors provide the capability to select text with a cursor and choose which markup you want to apply from a menu of selections. (See Chapter 19 for more on XMLSpy, Turbo XML, XML Pro, and other XML-authoring tools.)

✓ **Automatic enforcement of XML document rules:** For many applications, XML editors can determine which element types can appear in certain contexts. In this way, the editor helps you avoid making syntax or structure mistakes. For example, if you specify that the `ChapterTitle` element is valid only at the beginning of a chapter and never within an ordinary paragraph, the editor can make sure that your rule is enforced if you accidentally break it.

XML is a subset of SGML, so many authoring tools and editors previously used for SGML have been recast and are now ready to take on XML.

Chapter 2

Using XML for Many Purposes

*B*usinesses generate, store, and share information in a variety of ways, including text-based reports, forms, spreadsheets, and databases. Often, this important data is not collected and saved in a format that makes it possible for anyone to reuse, index, or search this information. For example, business data in a text document may be available only in that document; a spreadsheet program that could create a graph from this same information may not be able to get at it — and that means typing in the data all over again. Duplicate entry of the same data is not only inefficient, but also creates more opportunities for errors.

XML makes it possible to collect information once — and then access and use that data in as many different formats as you need. Although it requires some planning up front (and a close look at the kinds of data you actually collect), XML is not difficult to implement as a solution for data collection, storage, and exchange,

You don't have to be a technical whiz to start using XML. XML is accessible to users at all levels, from beginners creating their first XML documents in Word 2003 to the more technically savvy users out there entrusted with the task of constructing XML schemas to validate those documents.

Moving Legacy Data to XML

Using XML for your data doesn't necessarily land you back on Square One; you don't have to start collecting and processing your data all over again. You may be able to import, export, and otherwise shape-shift your current data into an XML format. Here's a glimpse of what's possible:

✔ **Is your data in spreadsheets?** You can transform this data into XML format by creating an XML schema for the data and then using that schema in Excel 2003 to create a map that connects the spreadsheet cell data and the schema. You can then export the spreadsheet file as an XML document. (See the "Getting started in Excel" section later in this chapter for more details on using XML with Excel 2003.)

✔ **Is your data in database tables?** In Access 2003, you can export data in XML format from one or more tables. Access can create and export an XML document — along with an XML schema and an XSLT stylesheet that creates an HTML document to display the data on the Web — automatically. You can also use XMLSpy (an XML editor) to import and convert database information from various databases — including Microsoft SQL Server, Oracle, MySQL, IBM DB2, Sybase, Access, or any ADO (*ActiveX Data Objects*) or ODBC (*Open DataBase Connectivity*) source — into XML format. See Chapter 17 for more information on using XML with databases.

✔ **Is your data in CSV (comma-separated values) text files?** You can use XMLSpy to import and convert these text files into XML format.

Even if your current data isn't in any of these formats, you can take stock of your data and organize it for efficient use in XML — if you follow the advice we offer in Chapter 3, that is.

The Many Faces of XML

After your data is in XML format, you have many ways you can present and share it. The same data can be accessed through Web pages, print documents, forms, spreadsheets, and databases.

Creating XML-enabled Web pages

All this XML versatility does require just a little extra tweaking: Your content (that is, the data) is separate from its context (the way you present it) in XML documents. That means you have to add some formatting information if you want to display more than just "raw" XML markup on a Web page.

When it comes to actually adding formatting information, you have a couple of options. You can link an XML document to a CSS (Cascading Style Sheets) stylesheet — which would (hopefully) make the information easier to read as well as visually interesting. Figure 2-1 shows (on the left) an unformatted XML file in a Web browser.

Figure 2-1:
An XML file
in Internet
Explorer.

If you use an XSLT (eXtensible Stylesheet Language Transformations) stylesheet with your XML document, voilà! You can generate an HTML page with a formatted display — with almost no effort. As you can see at right in Figure 2-1, the information is now in a much more usable form for the Web. And by the way — this XML file and XSLT stylesheet were both generated from a database table in Access 2003!

We show you all the details about how to create a CSS stylesheet and link it to an XML document in Chapter 7 — and do the same for XSLT in Chapter 12.

Print publishing with XML

Okay, suppose you want a hard copy of your XML data. No problem: SGML, the parent language of HTML and XML, was developed to meet the publishing industry's need for a language that could mark up electronic documents so they could be edited, reused, and shared. XML documents are well suited for creating printed documents — especially technical manuals and other large, organized collections of information in text form.

Microsoft Office 2003 includes features that take full advantage of XML and give it an expanded role on the desktop. All versions of Word 2003 and Excel 2003 can save documents in XML format. The professional version of Office 2003 takes this a step further, offering a way to add customized XML schemas to your documents. Result: XML is now even easier to use with print documents.

At heart, XML files are text files — you can open, modify, or create them in any text editor. If you prefer to use a word processor, Word 2003 includes features designed to make XML documents easy to create and use in Word.

Word 2003 uses a built-in schema document called WordML for XML documents. If you're using the professional version, you can also add any schema to any XML document in Word.

When you open an XML document in Word, you can display the document in one of two ways:

✔ As XML markup with visible XML tags, as shown in Figure 2-2.

✔ As content without tags, as shown in Figure 2-3.

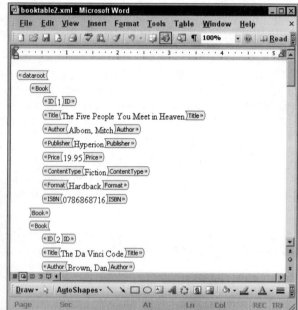

Figure 2-2:
An XML file displayed with markup tags in Word 2003.

You can toggle back and forth between these views by using the Show XML Tags in the Document check box in the XML Structure task pane (located to the left of the main window). To open the task pane, select View➪Task Pane, and then select XML Structure from the drop-down menu at the top of the task pane.

If you have an XSLT stylesheet for your XML document, you can open the "transformed" XML document in Word by using the drop-down menu from the Open button (File➪Open, as shown in Figure 2-4), selecting Open with Transform, and then browsing to the location of your XSLT file. XML files used to print documents are similar to the XML files used with Web pages — they aren't formatted until you add display information (in this case, with an XSLT stylesheet).

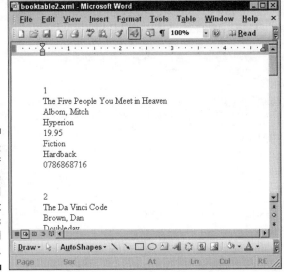

Figure 2-3:
Content of
an XML file
displayed
without
markup tags
in Word
2003.

Figure 2-4:
Options for
opening an
XML file in
Word 2003.

You can also save an XML file as a Word template and use it to create new XML files in the same format:

1. **Save the XML file in Word, using the** .dot **extension.**

   The .dot extension identifies the saved file as a template.

2. **Attach a schema to the template you just saved (Tools⇨Templates and Add-Ins⇨XML Schema).**

   This step formats the XML document; any documents you base on it will have the same format.

When Word isn't what you want

If you create an XML document in Word that you want to use outside of Word, you're going to need to do some fiddling. More specifically, you're going to need to delete the following from your document:

```
<?mso-application progid="Word.
   Document"?>
```

This little snippet is a processing instruction that indicates that the document is to open in Word. If you're *not* going to open it in Word, then leaving this snippet in is going to cause problems.

As to how you actually get rid of the little snippet, there hangs a tale. Word documents hang on to their processing instructions; you can't use Word to get rid of something Word wants to keep, so you have to open your XML document in a plain-text editor (such as Notepad) to do the job. There, you can view the code. delete this particular line, and save the document.

If you open an XML file in Word that was created in another program, the file won't contain this processing instruction, so you won't have to worry about it — unless, of course, you save the XML file as a Word document.

Using XML for business forms

Forms are a very useful way to collect data and can be used in text documents or on a Web page. You can create XML documents that include HTML forms by adding an XSLT stylesheet to generate the HTML form markup. You can also use XForms, an XML technology, to create forms that submit the form data as XML. (For more on XForms, see Chapter 16.) Or, for an easy way to create XML forms that you can use online or even send by e-mail, check out InfoPath. (Not sure what InfoPath is? Read on and find out!)

InfoPath — part of Office 2003 — is an XML forms editor that conforms to the principle of WYSIWYG (*What You See Is What You Get*): It shows you what your finished form will actually look like, whether on-screen or printed out. In InfoPath, you can create a form based on an XML document or XML schema, use one of InfoPath's 25 sample forms, or design your own form. (If you design your own, InfoPath will create a schema for you.)

InfoPath forms can be used in a Web page or sent in e-mail. Users can complete the forms online or download them and make entries offline. InfoPath can even create form-validation code automatically, so the information you gather is formatted to meet your needs — no extra tweaking required.

Figure 2-5 shows a preview of an InfoPath form that was automatically created from an XML schema and then populated with data from an XML file.

You can create a form template in InfoPath that can then be used to collect new data or be filled with data from a pre-existing XML file. The form can be published online directly from InfoPath or sent in e-mail. You can even export the form data to Excel 2003, if you want.

Okay, all this convenience is just a *little* proprietary — users must have InfoPath installed on their computers in order to fill out InfoPath forms.

You'll have the opportunity for a closer look at creating forms with InfoPath in Chapter 16.

Figure 2-5: An InfoPath form, populated with book data.

Incorporating XML into business processes

XML makes it possible for businesses to bring together information from diverse sources, such as text documents, forms, and spreadsheets, and then reuse, search, store, and aggregate that information. A crucial piece of collecting this information is for a business to decide what data they want to collect and then design XML Schemas or DTDs (short for *Document Type Definitions*) to define the structure of their documents so that they're able to capture this data through the course of everyday business procedures. (You can find more about using data categories in Chapter 3 — and unearth a plethora of info on creating DTDs and schemas throughout Part III.)

Multiple uses of the same set of data

We've said it before, and we'll say it again: Being able to reuse data is a vastly important feature of XML! This capability is what makes it economical to integrate XML into your business flow. Gather information once and using it over and over in multiple applications — without ever having to collect and process the data all over again — you can almost hear the efficiency experts cheering.

To drive this point home, picture in your mind's eye that ubiquitous business tool — the spreadsheet. Spreadsheets have traditionally been used in most businesses as a way to collect and present information. They come in a familiar format, and their features are generally well known to anyone in a business setting. With Excel 2003, you can now import and export XML data into and out of the familiar spreadsheet form — while at the same time still being able to use all of Excel's traditional data-analysis features (such as charts, graphs, and reports).

Excel creates an XML schema — Excel calls this an XML map — that connects items of XML data and the worksheet cells in which the data appears. You can use more than one map with a worksheet, in case you have different data sources using different schemas. (If you don't have a schema associated with your XML file, Excel creates one for you automatically.)

Getting started in Excel

When you open an XML file in Excel, an Open XML dialog box displays, and you can choose among the following three options for opening the XML file:

- ✔ **As an XML list:** XML tag names are displayed as data headings at the top of worksheet columns; any content in the XML file is displayed in worksheet cells. New data can be imported and added to the XML file — and it gets the same treatment automatically.

- ✔ **As a read-only workbook:** XML tag names and content are displayed, but no changes can be made, and no new data can be incorporated.

- ✔ **As a display in the XML Source task pane:** XML tag names are shown in Excel's XML Source task pane. From there, you can drag and drop elements onto the any worksheet, right where you want your data headings to appear. You can then Import (Data⇨XML⇨Import) or Refresh (Data⇨ XML⇨Refresh XML Data) the XML data to populate the worksheet cells.

The drag-and-drop task-pane method is easy to use and offers a distinct advantage: You can add only those elements that you want to view on a particular worksheet. Figure 2-6, for example, shows an Excel worksheet with only three columns of our book data: Title, Author, and ISBN.

Figure 2-6: Excel 2003 worksheet with XML data.

	A	B	C	D
1	Title	Author	ISBN	
2	The Five People You Meet in Heaven	Albom, Mitch	0786868716	
3	The Da Vinci Code	Brown, Dan	0385504209	
4	State of Fear	Crichton, Micheal	0066214130	
5	A Salty Piece of Land	Buffett, Jimmy	0316908452	
6	Black Wind	Cussler, Clive	0399152598	
7	London Bridges	Patterson, James	0316710598	
8	Night Fall	DeMille, Nelson	0446576638	
9	Life Expectancy	Koontz, Dean	0553804146	
10	Whiteout	Follett, Ken	0525948430	
11	I Am Charlotte Simmons	Wolfe, Tom	0374281580	
12				
13				

Serving up XML from a database

It should come as no surprise to you (given our touting of XML's flexibility) that you can import or export database information in XML format to create XML files from database tables or database tables from XML files. We'll get to all the messy details in Chapter 17, but write this down on your cuff — XML + databases = great idea.

If you are new to databases, we recommend Access 2003 for importing and exporting XML data. It's easy to use, it's part of the Office 2003 Professional Edition package, and it's a great place to start your work with XML and databases. If your business already uses another database technology, you can import and export information from your existing database by using a program such as XMLSpy.

Alphabet Soup: Even More XML

Although the term *XML* refers to the W3C *standard* for XML (www.w3.org/TR/REC-xml/), the same term (XML) is also commonly used for the entire family of W3C XML-based language formats. Although an exhaustive discussion of the whole XML family won't fit into this book, the following list introduces the major members of the XML group:

- **XLink and XPointer:** XLink and XPointer are XML languages for hyperlinks (XLink) and for document components with ID attributes (XPointer). XLink allows you to incorporate sophisticated linking mechanisms in XML documents. This capability goes far beyond simple HTML hyperlinks. XPointer enables you to travel to a specific item in a document by specifying element types, attribute values, character content, and position. If these technologies seem a little unfamiliar, there's a reason: They have been in development for years, but neither one is supported by today's browsers (yet).

- **XSLT, XPath, and XSL-FO:** All three of these XML technologies are parts of XSL (*Extensible Style Language*). XSLT (the *T* stands for *Transformations*) is designed to transform raw XML into complex display formats such as tables and indexes. XSLT is also widely used to generate HTML pages from XML documents. XPath is an XML language used to navigate an XML document. It's based on viewing an XML document as a tree of nodes and using this node structure to navigate the document. XPath is used with both XSLT and XPointer. XSL-FO (XSL-*Formatting Objects*) is used for completely formatting the layout, style, and *pagination* (dividing a document into pages) of documents that are rendered in print format. XSL-FO can be used with electronic documents such as PDFs, as well as traditional print documents. You'll find out more about these three languages in Chapters 12 and 13.

- **XForms:** XForms is an XML language created to collect and submit form information as XML data. XForms uses both XPath and XML schemas. You'll hear all about XForms in Chapter 16.

- **XML Encryption and XML Signature:** XML Encryption is an XML language developed for secure exchange of XML data. XML Signature is also used for secure data exchange. It provides syntax and processing rules for digital signatures.

- **XML Query:** XML Query is an XML language designed to *query* — request information from — any collection of XML data, whether that data is contained in an XML file or a database.

- **SOAP:** SOAP (*S*imple *O*bject *A*ccess *P*rotocol) is an XML language used for communication between a Web page requesting a Web service and the Web service application. You'll find out more about SOAP and Web services in Chapter 15.

- **SVG and SMIL:** SVG (*S*calable *V*ector *G*raphics) and SMIL (*S*ynchronized *M*ultimedia *I*ntegration *L*anguage) are XML languages for multimedia. SVG enables you to display 2-dimensional vector graphic images and animations from XML code. (*Vector graphics* use mathematical formulas to create images on-screen.) SMIL is used for integrating text, images, audio, and video content for multimedia presentations.

If you didn't know it before, you know it now: XML is for data, and data is for XML. Now it's time to take a closer look at organizing and collecting that data — which is precisely what you do in Chapter 3.

Chapter 3

Slicing and Dicing Data Categories: The Art of Taxonomy

*I*t's important to make sure that your markup fits your content the way (a) puzzle pieces fit together, (b) peas and carrots go together, or (c) a hand fits in a glove. (Choose your metaphor.)

You can create perfectly written XML, but if your perfect XML doesn't fit your content, all that work isn't going to do diddly for you. This chapter is devoted to helping you get a handle on the content that you're creating so you can use XML to describe it well. Content analysis isn't nearly as scary as it sounds; a little analysis early on (tell us what you see in these ink blots) can save you from going loco later.

After you assess your content, you can create a *taxonomy* — no, not the part where you mount deer heads on the wall, but rather a naming scheme: You break your content down into categories and subcategories according to a well-thought-out plan.

Taking Stock of Your Data

The process of becoming best friends with your content is often called *content analysis* or *information analysis*. Whatever name it goes by, analysis requires breaking down content into bite-size chunks to see exactly what pieces are going to become key components when you describe the data with a markup language (in this case, XML).

When we use the term *components,* we're referring to types of data that run throughout a document. (Titles and authors are two key components of a book description, for example.) Until you have a good handle on the components of your content, you can't create markup that fits it — or even use an existing markup language to describe it.

Looking at business practices and partners

Taking a close look at the flow of information in your business will help you identify the components of your content. For example, what data is collected when a customer places an order? What kind of inventory information do you maintain? Do you use a catalog of your products? Do you use a database? What happens to all this information you are amassing? Each different process is a specialized use of information.

If you're already familiar with the information that qualifies as content, then you've already got a leg up on the process. If you're unfamiliar with the content, however, take some time to talk to those people who create or frequently process the data. Find out

- ✔ What users do with individual pieces of information.
- ✔ What data users think is impossible to live without (and why).
- ✔ What data is unnecessary or optional (and why).

Gather enough information to sufficiently understand what the key components of the content are, why the content was created, and what's needed to make the content useful to the people who created it.

Gathering some content

To get started analyzing data, you need to gather up several samples of the data content to work with so that you can create as complete a *composite* (a collection made up of distinct parts) of the key data components as possible.

The more complete your collection of samples is, the better chance you have of creating markup that fits all your content. Here are some ideas:

- ✔ **Get data from multiple sources:** If you're working with data for a business, be sure to gather invoices, receipts, and other data from multiple vendors or customers. One vendor may exclude vital info that another vendor includes.
- ✔ **Get a lot of data:** If you need to describe data that will eventually go into an existing database, see whether you can get sample data that's already

in the database so that you can be sure that your markup and the database's requirements match.

You may have to make modifications to the database to make sure that all the available information is gathered and used to its fullest extent.

✔ **Get a lot of data from multiple sources:** If you need to describe complex reports, lay your hands on several different reports, written by different people if possible.

You're getting the drift, aren't you?

To create a complete picture, try to find five or six samples, at least, to work with.

Because your content is ultimately destined for a processing system of some kind, you should talk with the people building that system to see what their data requirements are for it (assuming there's no predefined DTD or schema already in place). You want your markup to work with their system; a little communication up front about their needs and expectations goes a long way toward avoiding a complete rework of your DTD or schema.

For more information on DTDs and schemas, see Part III (Chapters 8 – 11) of this book.

Checking whether a DTD or schema already exists

It's important that you look around for predefined schemas and DTDs before you try to create your own. If you find one that meets your needs, you can save yourself a lot of time by building on existing markup that at least one other person or group is using — and you know that much of your new markup already works. (If you're trying to work with an established system such as ASP.NET, for example, you won't have a choice; you have to use that particular DTD to make your instructions work with that system.)

ASP.NET is the next generation of ASP (Active Server Pages) and is part of Microsoft's .NET framework (a programming model for developing and using XML Web services). For more details on XML and Web services, see Chapter 15. For more information on the .NET framework, see

```
http://msdn.microsoft.com/netframework/programming/fundamentals/default.aspx
```

Lots and lots of DTDs and schemas are already available for your use. For example, the DTD used by the Open Financial Exchange (OFX) is freely available online. OFX enables online exchange of financial information between banks, businesses, and consumers. OFX accomplishes this goal by using XML to describe bank data and then transfer that data electronically via the Internet. OFX came about through an alliance among CheckFree, Inuit, and Microsoft. Because these three major players — and the banking organizations — can agree on a single format to describe banking data, information exchange is as easy as pie. They chose XML because it's a standard and is becoming the *de facto* format for data exchange. To discover more juicy stuff about OFX, check out `www.ofx.net`.

When you create a document according to a DTD or schema, you use a predefined structure that specifies how the components of markup (elements, attributes, and such) should be used to describe a particular kind of content. Predefined DTDs and schemas usually come from a couple of different sources:

- **Industry groups or organizations** that want to establish a common format for standard data — OFX is a perfect example of this source. Another good example is the Chemical Markup Language (CML), created by chemists to describe chemical equations.

- **Application builders** who created their systems to run with content described by a particular set of markup. For example, the ColdFusion Markup Language (CFML), created by Allaire/Macromedia, defines a particular set of markup for describing applications written to run in the ColdFusion system. ASP.NET from Microsoft also uses a similar predefined flavor of XML for creating Active Server Pages (ASP).

Searching for a schema repository

In the "early days" — in terms of XML, that means a few years ago — several schema repositories were available online at sites such as `www.Biztalk.org` and `www.schema.net`. You could search for a schema or DTD, or add one of your own to the repository. Microsoft's BizTalk schema repository ended in 2002 and is no longer available — and at least for now, `schema.net` is no longer active.

That doesn't mean public schemas and DTDs aren't obtainable — it's just harder to find them. There is *one* still existing schema repository hosted by OASIS (the *O*rganization for the *A*dvancement of *S*tructured *I*nformation *S*tandards) at `www.xml.org/xml/registry.jsp`. In addition, OASIS provides a very comprehensive list of proposed XML applications and industry initiatives at `www.oasis-open.org/cover/xml.html#applications` — also a great resource for finding schemas.

Industry groups and associations are good sources of information about what schemas or DTDs are used in specific industries.

When you're trying to decide whether you need to build a new DTD or schema for your content or use an existing one, remember that the most important issue is the way that the markup fits your content. The whole point of using XML is to make your content as accessible to a system as possible. That goal is thwarted when you force your content into an existing markup scheme because the markup doesn't accurately reflect the content.

Content analysis with XML in mind is much easier when you have a handle on the ins and outs of XML Schemas and DTDs and how to put them together. Once again, keep what you read here in mind as you check out DTDs and schemas in Part III.

Breaking Down Data in Different Ways

When we developed our hypothetical book-selling business, we went through the same data-analysis process we're sharing with you. After we gathered our documents (invoices, inventory reports, mailing lists) and familiarized ourselves with them, we took a good hard look at what we learned about our content. Here's what we came up with:

- **Books can be categorized in a number of different ways, including:**
  - Author
  - Title
  - Publication date
  - Publisher
  - Edition
  - Language
  - Number of pages
  - Size
  - Type: Fiction, Nonfiction
  - Genre: Historical, Fantasy, Biography, Mystery . . . and so forth
  - Special features: illustrations, color plates, ornate end papers, leather binding . . . and so on
  - Format: Paperback, Hardback, Audio, Large Print, New, Used
  - Price: Retail, Wholesale
  - ISBN

✔ **The customer information we collect includes:**

- First Name
- Last Name
- Address
- City
- State
- Zip Code
- E-mail Address
- Phone Number

✔ **The sales information we gather in addition to customer information includes:**

- Date
- Item Number
- Price
- Total Cost

We also do (at least in our hypothetical world) both direct retail sales online (from our online catalog) and traditional wholesale to four brick-and-mortar department stores.

Winnowing out the wheat from the chaff

When we analyzed our content, we made some judgments about what information we needed to collect. Many possible categories — genre, number of pages, size — were not useful information for our specific book business, so we chose to exclude them from our taxonomy strategy.

In the end, we discovered that the book business can be very complex and have a variety of component types. Some components are consistent across all books (such as author, title, publisher), but others are found only in some (such as illustrations). We created our book business to help you understand XML — not to produce an overly elaborate markup language that covered all the bases. (We left special features out of the fray, for example.) That decision was as much of the content-analysis process as discovering that illustrations are a possible content element. Knowing the purpose of your markup can help you keep your goals in sight — and in check.

Types of data that can be stored in XML

XML content can be divided into two main groups: data-intensive and document- or text-intensive.

On the data end of the spectrum, you find collections of data like those that reside in a database. Each collection consists of a more or less arbitrary number of record *structures,* in which each record contains

- **A unique identifier or key:** This value, unique to each record, is to help locate individual records. For example, an ISBN could serve as a unique identifier for each book in a book collection.

- **A common collection of named, organized values:** Think of an address book, a card catalog in a library, or a set of medical records in your doctor's office. For example, each card in a card catalog contains the same categories of information: title, author, publisher, publication date, keywords, and description.

On the document or text end of that continuum, the content to be captured and represented fits typical notions of text or hypertext materials — that is, a collection of words, graphics, and other information meant to be read or viewed as a structured object. Examples on this end of the spectrum include books, articles, magazines, narratives, training materials, and so forth.

Then, too, XML can capture and represent data that describes other collections of data — for example, start and stop dates for time-sensitive files, status information, modification data, and so forth. That handy capability makes all kinds of helpful information easy to describe and use — whether stored in a document or data collection.

As you explore the kinds of data and documents that XML can capture and represent, remember that the term *XML document* embraces a whole lot more than text. XML can handle many kinds of data. In particular, it can accommodate (or point to) binary information — and that means it can supply data to other computer applications outside XML's control. Thus, an XML document can reference anything that a computer can represent — including video, graphics, multimedia, and other specialized kinds of data!

Developing Your Taxonomy

After you look at your content, you can start breaking it down into categories and subcategories. (If you haven't already made decisions about what content to include, this process will also help you make those judgments.)

Here's how we broke it down for our hypothetical book business:

✔ Book
- Item Number
- Title
- Author
- Publisher
- Price
- Content Type
- Format
- ISBN

✔ Sales
- Item Number
- Price
- Shipping
- Total Cost
- Date
- Source

✔ Customer
- Customer Number
- First Name
- Last Name
- Address
- City
- State
- Zip Code
- E-mail Address
- Phone Number

As you can see, some subcategories show up under more than one major category. In particular, Item Number appears as a subcategory in both the Book and the Sales categories. The Item Number is unique to each copy of a book, which makes it easy to keep track of sales and inventory.

Testing Your Taxonomy

You might be surprised by this tidbit, but one of the best ways to start testing your taxonomy is to jump in and write some markup that describes how it should be used — after you have a good understanding of what it takes to create and use the content, of course. What you start with may only slightly resemble your finished markup language, but you do have to start somewhere.

During this process of writing markup, you're really doing a detailed analysis of the content, which means that at the end of the day you're going to have two (count 'em, two) results: a solid content analysis *and* a working draft of the markup that you need to describe it.

To create your markup, pick an invoice and start creating elements. Every XML document has one *root element* that contains all the other elements in the document. In our own initial round of markup, we used `book` as the root element because we thought that each book would have its own document. After giving it some thought, we realized that we might want to include several books in one document (such as an invoice for more than one book). Thus we made `books` the root element and set the `book` element to delineate each individual book in a document.

Using trial and error for the best fit

We're not going to lie to you: A lot of this stuff is plain old-fashioned trial and error. As you work with your markup, experiment with using combinations of elements and attributes until you get the best results. For example, initially, we used two *nested elements* to specify the content type for a book:

```
<book>
  <contentType>Fiction</contentType>
</book>
```

This option would work very well if we thought that a book could have more than one type of content to work with. The markup would use as many `contentType` elements within the `book` element as there were categories, with at least one required.

In the end, we decided to go with `contentType` as an *attribute* of the `book` element instead, as shown here:

```
<book contentType="Fiction"/>
```

We decided on this route because we thought that we'd want to predefine the category names and require that valid documents choose one of the names from the list in our DTD or schema. This choice narrows the category to one but allows us to enforce category names.

As you become more comfortable with content analysis, you'll know instinctively that some data components work best as attributes and other data components work better as elements. As you discover the details of the XML syntax for elements and attributes — and how they work together (see Part III) — you develop a firm basis for deciding what should be an element and what should be an attribute.

While creating your initial markup, you may find that you have new questions about the content that you need to answer before going on. That's okay. (We might even say that's a *good* thing, but that's because we're perfectionists.) Just keep in mind that analysis is part science and part intuition.

Testing your content analysis

The best way to test your final (or final draft) markup is to apply it to as many content samples as you can lay your hands on. With each test, you may find something that you need to tweak or change outright. However, after much testing, you'll end up with a final product that serves you well.

In a perfect world, you would have talked with the system's developer early in the process to find out what content the system needs to work with, using that knowledge while conducting data analysis. (We'll pretend that's exactly what you did.) Show your markup to the system developers and make sure it has the information they were expecting; expect more tweaks and changes. Feed sample documents into the system and see what happens. Tweak and change some more. Listing 3-1 shows the final draft of our bookstore markup.

Listing 3-1:   bookstore.xml

```xml
<?xml version="1.0" standalone="yes"?>
<books>
 <book contentType="Fiction" format="Hardback">
  <bookInfo>
   <title>The Da Vinci Code</title>
   <author>Brown, Dan</author>
   <publisher>Doubleday</publisher>
   <isbn>0385504209</isbn>
  </bookInfo>
  <salesInfo>
   <price priceType="Retail">$24.95</price>
   <itemNumber>0385504209-1</itemNumber>
```

```
  <date>January 12, 2005</date>
  <source sourceType="Retail" />
  <shipping>$5.00</shipping>
  <cost>$29.95</cost>
 </salesInfo>
</book>
<totalCost>$29.95</totalCost>
<customer custType="newRetail">
 <custNumber>5594</custNumber>
 <lastName>Blow</lastName>
 <firstName>Joe</firstName>
 <address>52 Joetta Lane</address>
 <city>Cottage Grove</city>
 <state>OR</state>
 <zip>97424</zip>
 <phone>767-3333</phone>
 <email>jblow@pacinfo.com</email>
</customer>
</books>
```

The first line in our code `<?xml version="1.0" standalone="yes"?>` is an XML declaration. You'll learn all about XML declarations and all the other details of XML syntax in Chapter 5.

Our document went through lots of changes from our initial look at categories to our final-draft version of the markup. We deleted some subcategories and added some new ones. And you can expect even more changes as you test out your markup and design a DTD or schema for validating it.

Looking Ahead to Validation

If you want to play the eXtensible Markup Language (XML) game, you have to know the rules. But the *X* in XML means *eXtensible*; the element names you can use and define are unlimited. That is, you get to make up as many (or as few) rules as you want or need to make the markup do what you want it to. For example, you can create a document definition for a bookstore to define precisely what kind of data can go into any future XML documents that adhere to your definition.

The rules that you create with XML can dictate which elements make up an XML document, which kinds of content these elements can contain, and how such elements may be ordered. Document descriptions even support rules about which elements are optional, which ones are required, and how many times that certain elements can (or must) appear.

Creating XML document descriptions enables you to state the rules that a whole class of documents must follow.

The two main forms of XML document descriptions in use today are DTDs and XML schemas — and there's more about both in Part III.

DTDs work well for validating XML with text-intensive content, while XML schemas work well for validating XML with data-intensive content.

Before you can actually validate your XML document, you need to make sure it's *well formed* — in other words, does it follow the rules of XML syntax? You'll learn these rules in Chapter 4 and 5. After your XML document is well formed, you can then validate it against your XML document description (i.e., your DTD or schema) to make sure that your document follows the rules in your document description. There are pros and cons to validating your documents, and you'll find out about all the angles to consider in Part III.

When you've got a pretty firm handle on all the ins and outs of content analysis, it's time to tackle the rules for creating XML markup. Chapter 4 makes that transition into XML syntax via another markup language, XHTML.

Part II
XML and the Web

"Great goulash, Stan. That reminds me, are you still scripting your own Web page in XHTML?"

In this part. . .

First up in this part is the super-competent hybrid language XHTML — a reformulation of HTML that uses the stricter syntax of XML. You examine the structure and rules of XML documents, and delve into converting an HTML document into XHTML. In Chapter 5, you get a thorough grounding in the pieces and parts that make up any XML document, and get a crack at marking up your content using elements and attributes. You master the making of a well-formed XML document, and launch into the mysteries of the markup descriptions known as a Document Type Definition (DTD) and XML Schema, which govern most XML documents. Chapter 6 explains how to use alternate alphabets, special symbols, and all kinds of character sets in your XML documents. Chapter 7 covers viewing XML content on the Web; it's a must if you're looking to marry modern XML content with those creaky old Web browsers (they're *soooo* 20th-century . . .). We also reveal how to use XML with CSS to make your XML documents on the Web easier to view.

Chapter 4

Adding XHTML for the Web

In This Chapter

▶ Understanding the limitations of HTML

▶ Comparing HTML with XML

▶ Getting the best of both worlds: XHTML

▶ Converting HTML to XHTML

*H*TML (*H*ypertext *M*arkup *L*anguage) and XML (e*X*tensible *M*arkup *L*anguage) are two very different markup languages. They appear similar because, like all markup languages, they both use tags to mark up document content, but the similarity ends there. XHTML combines features of both HTML and XML — this chapter highlights those features as well as the benefits of using XHTML.

Your choice of markup language depends on your content and information handling needs. You can easily convert HTML to XHTML — and we'll show you how in an upcoming section, "Converting a document from HTML to XHTML."

HTML, XML, and XHTML

HTML, XHTML, and XML represent stages in the development of markup languages. Of these three, HTML, designed to display content in Web browsers, came first. HTML uses *markup tags,* but these specialized bits of markup are limited to a predefined set created by the W3C (Worldwide Web Consortium). XML, intended for data exchange, came next. Although the rules of XML syntax are also defined by the W3C, the tags are defined by each creator of a specific XML document. XML markup can be viewed in some Web browsers (such as Internet Explorer 6), but unlike HTML, it's not limited to the Web. Then came XHTML — which uses the markup tags of HTML and the strict syntax of XML, and is considered a transition language between HTML and XML.

What HTML does best

Although you purchased this book to find out about XML, you wouldn't get your money's worth if we didn't take some time to talk about HTML. As a Web designer/developer, you're forced to work in an imperfect world. For example, new markup language capabilities take center stage every few months, but new browser versions don't always follow suit. Therefore, a user's browser doesn't always support every bit of standard or nonstandard markup. The two main groups of browsers — Microsoft Internet Explorer (IE) and the Gecko-based browsers (such as Firefox and Netscape Navigator, versions 6 and later) — still don't fully support Cascading Style Sheets (CSS) Level 2 . . . so don't expect their next versions to support XML completely, either. If your target audience is the world at large, you may have to use HTML or XHTML on the Web for some time to come; a complete switch over to XML markup may not be practical yet.

Gecko-based browsers include Mozilla, Firefox, Safari, and newer versions of Netscape Navigator (versions 6 and later). Gecko is the open-source Web browser layout engine developed by Mozilla.

For more information on using XML in Gecko-based browsers, see "Loading XML into Gecko-based browsers" at `http://builder.com.com/5100-6371-5195655.html`.

HTML makes our Web world look pretty. In some instances, *pretty* is all that's needed for a Web page, such as a personal site that you create for your family. You want an easy, cheap way to let others know what you've been doing and to post a few pictures of your new baby, kitten, Chia Pet, or electronic gadget.

Most Web sites use straight HTML to display data — say, a portfolio (as shown in Figure 4-1.) The site would have little need for flexibility and wouldn't need a database.

If you want to sell the infamous widget from your Web site, however, you have to jump through additional hoops. You may want to create a database with product codes, styles, and colors, and you also may want your customers to be able to select any combination of this data. In this case, HTML isn't the best tool to represent widget data in text form: You want something that can do a better job of representing (and presenting) database fields and values as such. That's where XML comes in.

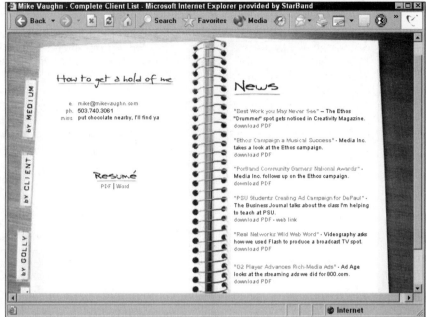

Figure 4-1:
A basic
HTML page,
displayed
with a
browser's
default
settings.

The limits of HTML

The idea behind HTML is modest: HTML is meant to describe only basic page content, providing rudimentary control over how that content should appear in your browser. Since its public introduction, however, HTML has been forced to provide solutions for problems it was never meant to solve. HTML was enlisted to perform some pretty specific tasks:

- ✔ **Allow tight control** over document display.
- ✔ **Provide the flexibility** to describe different, specific types of information and data.
- ✔ **Convey information** from a variety of media and in various formats.
- ✔ **Define complex linking relationships** between documents.
- ✔ **Publish a single set of information** across a variety of media.

And that was about it. Web designers, however, quickly got finicky. Sometimes they caught themselves thinking, "But my heading has to be in 45.5-point Arial type, centered in the second two-thirds of the page." Although this sentiment is a bit overstated, many Web designers *do* expect that much fine-tuned control from HTML; then they're left wondering why HTML can't live up to those expectations.

Web designers sometimes try to achieve the same formatting control over Web documents that they have over, say, printed documents. They want what they see on their screens with their browsers to be exactly what any visitor to their sites may also see. (Even if they can't pronounce WYSIWYG, they want "what you see" to be "what you get.") Two overarching problems prevent Web designers from achieving this control with HTML:

- ✔ **HTML lacks fine controls.** First and foremost, HTML by itself doesn't include mechanisms for fine control. You can't specify a document's display size or control the size of a browser window. A user's monitor size and display settings can dramatically affect how a browser displays HTML documents. Although HTML 4.01 does include a `font` element to help you manipulate font style, size, and color, users can override your settings with their own.

- ✔ **Displays vary.** Along with the different versions of the two most common browsers (IE and Navigator), users view Web pages on different platforms, such as Windows XP, Unix, or Mac OS X. And you can't realistically test every Web page on every available browser on every platform just to see what your users see.

Although adding CSS (*Cascading Style Sheets*) to your arsenal gives you more flexibility than HTML alone, it doesn't solve every Web design problem.

Stylesheets have become an integral part of the XML discussion. For an in-depth look at the use of stylesheets with XML, please visit Chapter 7 (CSS) and Chapter 12 (XSLT).

Comparing XML and HTML

Right off the bat, we want to tell you in no uncertain terms that XML won't — and can't — replace HTML. XML and HTML are not the same kind of markup language. But XML and HTML both derive from the same parent, SGML, so they must be similar, right? The answer is: "Yes, they're similar, but not identical, and they can't pinch-hit for each other."

HTML and XML both use tags and attributes. Indeed, XML and HTML look similar. But whereas HTML defines basic text elements and includes defaults (and more explicit controls) for how text may be displayed in a browser window, XML tells us only what each element means. XML says nothing about how elements should or must be displayed — XML separates content and the presentation of that content.

Using XML to describe data

Unlike HTML, XML is not limited to any fixed set of *tags* or *element types* (which is the proper name for the whatchamathingies that show up between the opening ⟨ and closing ⟩ characters in XML markup). By using XML, you can define your own sets of elements and even your own attributes that you may then use within your documents. On the other hand, XML has already been used to define lots of specific markup languages (called *XML applications*) that you can use within your documents as well.

Although it might seem that the terms *tag* and *element* are interchangeable, they're not. One example of a tag is the opening ⟨p⟩ tag; an example of an element is ⟨p⟩text⟨/p⟩. An *element* includes the opening and closing tags for a tag pair — *and* everything in between. A *tag* is just a tag, all by itself.

With this power, XML enables you to give meaningful names to your markup. In HTML, the paragraph element (p) is one of the most frequently used elements. In XML, you can replace the paragraph element with something more descriptive.

For example, suppose you have HTML text that looks like this:

```
<html>
<p>
This book is about the foundations of the Extensible Markup Language (XML)
 and how to use it for your own applications.
</p>
<p>
The authors are Lucinda Dykes and Ed Tittel.
</p>
</html>
```

Looks like a plain old HTML document; you know nothing about the meaning of the data. In other words, the first sentence could be a very long title, a description in a catalog, the first line of a book, the chorus of a new song, or something else entirely.

HTML is used to describe the display of data as seen through a Web browser. We could have just as easily written

```
<html>
<p>
Blah blah blah blah blah blah blah blah blah blah blah blah blah blah blah (XML)
 blobbity blobbity blobitty blah blah blah blah.
</p>
<p>
Blah blah blah Lucinda Dykes blah Ed Tittel.
</p>
</html>
```

and you would have gained just as much (or as little, depending on your point of view) insight as to the function of this data. But you *would* know that the data is displayed in two distinct paragraphs, because the paragraph tags <p> and </p> define the appearance of the data.

Consider this alternate form of expression, in which cover copy (the information found on the cover of a book) is provided and divided into specific, named elements:

```
<Cover>
<Abstract>
 This book is about the foundations of the Extensible Markup Language (XML)
 and how to use it for your own applications.
</Abstract>
<AuthorInfo>
The authors are <Author>Lucinda Dykes</Author> and
 <Author>Ed Tittel</Author>.
</AuthorInfo>
</Cover>
```

The Cover, Abstract, and AuthorInfo elements identify the previous markup as XML based. By using the elements in this markup language, you can now identify cover copy and specify further what that cover copy includes (say, an abstract plus a section for author information). In addition, this markup identifies each of the book's authors individually.

Never fear, XML also provides numerous ways to translate this information so it looks the way you want it to on-screen. These ways include CSS and XSL. (See Chapter 7 of this book for more about CSS and Chapter 12 for more about XSL.)

XML enables you to define and use your own elements and attributes. This is what XML is all about and explains why XML is called the *extensible* markup language.

After you get your head wrapped around the differences between XML and HTML, it's a lot easier to think of ways to increase the information associated with particular elements. For example, perhaps the Author element should include not only an author's name, but also a brief biography.

In "The limits of HTML," earlier in this chapter, we outline the shortcomings of HTML. Perhaps you're wondering why you would want to use it at all. HTML does have some advantages (see the following section); and in the short term, you have no real choice in the matter. Besides, HTML can create a reasonably consistent Web-page presentation for users. As the expectations of businesses and end-users increase, however, so does the need for more flexible markup languages. XML rises to meet that challenge.

The benefits of using HTML

Why use HTML? Because it's quick, easy, and cheap. In addition, HTML is way easier than the alternative — which is to use an XML-based source document along with a document created with XSLT (or something similar) to define the display attributes for your document's contents.

Anyone can create an HTML document by using a text editor and a little knowledge. Even if you don't know HTML, you can use an HTML editor — a What You See Is What You Get-style (that is, WYSIWYG-style) editor such as FrontPage or Dreamweaver — to produce readable Web pages in minutes.

The most important reason not to write off HTML just yet lies in where it's headed: XHTML. HTML isn't out of the game. (See "XHTML Makes the Move to XML Syntax," later in this chapter, for more information.)

The benefits of using XML

XML seems to be brimming with benefits. Here's a list that puts these benefits in a nutshell:

- **Unlimited elements:** You get to create your own elements and attributes instead of working with a restricted, predefined set.
- **Structured data:** Applications can extract information that they need from XML documents.
- **Data exchange:** Using XML enables you to exchange database contents or other structured information across the Internet or between dissimilar applications.
- **XML complements HTML:** XML data can be used in HTML pages.
- **XML documents are well formed:** XML documents must follow certain rules. This consistency makes such documents easier to read and create.
- **Self-describing:** No prior knowledge of an XML application is needed. Of course, knowing HTML can really help you understand more about XML (but software thrives on self-describing documents and data).
- **Search engines:** XML delivers a noticeable increase in search relevance because it provides ample contextual information and explicit labels for document elements.
- **Updates:** No need to update an entire site page by page; the Document Object Model (DOM) built into XML documents permits individual elements to be accessed (and updated).
- **User-selected view of data:** Different users can access different information or can present the same information in various ways.

Intelligent XML-based pages that contain human-readable data offer exciting potential for users. For example, they can go beyond HTML-based search tools that use keywords and text strings; XML-based search tools can also use metadata and data structures. XML-powered searches produce more relevant results — and quicker.

A Web designer/developer reaps several benefits from XML as well. For example, if you maintain a site that sells widgets, and inflation kicks in, raising prices by $1.50 per widget is easy to implement across an entire site. No late nights spent changing each page — you're working with intelligent data now.

The benefits of XML are endless. Trust us, large corporations have good reasons for using XML-based markup languages to maintain their intranets.

XHTML Makes the Move to XML Syntax

XHTML is the successor to HTML 4.01; in effect, it's the final version of HTML. This progress was needed; HTML has some limitations (spelled out, appropriately enough, in "The limits of HTML," earlier in the chapter). XHTML is a clever reformulation of HTML 4 *as an application of XML 1.0.* By definition, this arrangement offers you the benefits of XML in any XHTML documents. If you're familiar with HTML 4.01, XHTML 1.0 won't seem all that revolutionary as long as you don't let the new acronym scare you. (If it helps, think of XHTML as HTML 4.01 with a facelift.)

We're focusing on XHTML version 1.0 in this section. XHTML 1.0 documents are compatible with current browsers and closely resemble HTML documents. Other forms of XHTML have already been developed, though. XHTML modules have been created to allow you to create documents with subsets of XHTML. These modules are described in the document "Modularization of XHTML", available at `www.w3.org/TR/2004/WD-xhtml-modularization-20040218/`. XHTML Basic, XHTML 1.1, and XHTML 2.0 (currently a W3C Working Draft specification) are all built from these modules. These versions of XHTML offer expanded XML features and aren't as similar to HTML as XHTML 1.0. Details on the newer versions of XHTML would take up too much space in this book about XML, but you can get more information about them in *Beginning Web Programming with HTML, XHTML, and CSS,* by Jon Duckett (also published by Wiley).

Why do we like XHTML? Let us count the ways:

✔ XHTML documents can be viewed, edited, and validated using XML tools.

✔ Well-formed XHTML documents mean better-structured documents. This improvement and uniformity in structure makes it easier to interface XHTML documents with databases and with other highly structured documents.

✔ XHTML documents can be delivered using different Internet media types and output devices, such as handheld computers, Internet-enabled cell phones, and specialized browsers such as speech-enabled browsers.

✔ Using valid XHTML gives you the best chance of having your document displayed the way you intend, especially if you're using a browser that's compliant with Web standards, such as Internet Explorer 6 or Netscape Navigator (versions 6 and later).

Web standards are the specifications created by the W3C and other standards organizations for Web content. The XML and XHTML specifications are part of these standards. For more information, see `www.webstandards.org`.

Making the switch

Making the switch from HTML to XHTML means mastering the rules of XHTML — in particular, XML syntax and structure. Mastering XHTML is a jump-start to finding out how to create XML documents (as described in Chapter 5).

You have only a few major rules to get under your belt, but you have to follow them if you want to create a valid XHTML document. Here they are in a nutshell:

✔ Every tag in an XHTML document must be closed.

✔ Empty elements (elements without content, such as a `br` tag) must be correctly formatted with a closing slash. For example, a break tag is formatted `<br />`.

✔ All tags must be *nested* correctly — the tag you open last must be the tag you close first.

✔ All XHTML tags must be written using only lowercase.

✔ All attribute values must be put in quotation marks.

These requirements are pretty straightforward, even though they aren't strictly necessary in HTML. If you want to transform an HTML document into an acceptable XHTML document, you have to keep in mind that the document has to work with an XML-based application (namely XHTML).

An acceptable XML document must be *well formed* (which means it follows the rules of XML syntax). XML won't let you use HTML shortcuts and is unforgiving of syntax errors. Although they impose a bit more fuss and bother, these requirements make XML and XHTML documents easy for computers to read and digest. For these reasons, each requirement is worth a closer look — coming right up in the next several sections.

Every element must be closed

The first XHTML requirement is that all nonempty elements (that is, those that contain actual text) must have a start tag and an end tag. Several HTML elements, such as p and li, act as text containers but don't explicitly require end tags. Those tags work in nonpair containers because a special SGML shortcut allows the HTML parser to assume an end tag must occur before another start tag for the same element. So in effect

```
<p>text text text
```

is the same as

```
<p>text text text</p>
```

. . . at least, that's the case in HTML. Doing without an end tag just doesn't fly in XHTML. You have to add closing paragraph tags where they belong if you want the resulting lines to work right.

You also need to add ending list item tags (</li>) if you have list items, whether those lists are numbered or bulleted.

Empty elements must be formatted correctly

The XML way to format empty elements may seem a bit strange, but remember that all nonempty XML elements must use both a start tag and an end tag to be correct.

An *empty element* is a singleton tag (also called an *empty tag*) that hangs around by itself. (A *nonempty* element sandwiches some text between a pair of tags.) Empty tags in HTML include the <br>, <hr>, and <img> tags.

The `hr` element looks like this in HTML:

```
<hr>
```

In XHTML, it looks like this:

```
<hr />
```

For backward compatibility with older browsers, you have to put a space in front of the closing slash that occurs near the end of each XHTML empty element (like this: `<br />`). Doing so permits older, XML-ignorant Web browsers to recognize empty elements. When native XML markup is used (or, more to the point, interpreted properly), that extra space isn't necessary.

If you validate your XHTML document, you'll find that you can either include the space before the closing slash or not — your document will validate in either case. The extra space is a browser issue, not a validation issue.

Tags must be properly nested

The rules of XHTML syntax say that tags must be nested in the correct order.

The rule is always to close first what you opened last, working your way from the inside to the outside tags. So even though this HTML markup

```
<p>This book was written by <i><b>Dan Brown</i></b>.
```

looks fine in a browser, the line is technically ill formed. To make it a well-formed line, you must make these changes:

```
<p>This book was written by <i><b>Dan Brown</b></i>.</p>
```

You probably noticed that we also added a closing paragraph tag (`</p>`) to follow the previous rule about closing all elements.

Case makes a difference

HTML is not case sensitive; XHTML is. When you use HTML, it doesn't matter what case you use for elements and attributes. For example, for the opening body tag, you can use `<BODY>`, `<body>`, or even `<Body>` — they all work fine. In fact, you can even mix case between opening and closing tags (for example, `<BODY>` and `</body>`, respectively), and it won't make a difference in a browser.

XHTML, on the other hand, is a bit more finicky about case. All XHTML elements and attribute names must be in lowercase or your page won't validate. You can, however, use any case for the *value* of an attribute — for example, `<h3 align= "CENTER">` will work just as well as `<h3 align= "center">`.

Attribute values are in quotation marks

HTML requires that only some attribute values, such as text strings and URLs, be in quotation marks. Other values, such as image dimensions and font sizes, produce the desired results whether quoted or not. In XHTML, all attribute values must be in quotation marks.

The following markup works just fine on an HTML page:

```
<tr align=right>
```

If you want to create valid XHTML, however, you have to add quotation marks around the attribute value, like this:

```
<tr align="right">
```

Both single quotation marks (') and double quotation marks (") are legal in XML and XHTML. You see double quotation marks used more, mostly because they're easier to see.

Table 4-1 highlights the major rules for XHTML syntax and shows how markup looks in HTML and XHTML. Some additional rules are highlighted in Chapter 5 when you create an XML document. If you'd like to see the full set of rules, check out the "HTML Compatibility Guidelines" document in the XHTML 1.0 specification at

```
www.w3.org/TR/xhtml1/#guidelines
```

Table 4-1	Correct Formats for XHTML versus HTML	
Rule	*Looks Like This in XHTML*	*Looks Like This in HTML*
XHTML tags must be written using only lowercase.	`<b>This text is bold</b>`	`<B>This text is bold</B>`
Empty tags in XHTML must include a trailing `/ >` or `/>` in all empty elements.	`<img src="goblin.gif" alt="goblin" />` ` `	`<img src="goblin. gif" alt="goblin">` ` `

Rule	Looks Like This in XHTML	Looks Like This in HTML
All nonempty elements in XHTML must have closing tags.	`<p>Closing tags mean no errors</p>`	`<p>Closing tags mean no errors`
All elements in XHTML must be nested properly; elements can't overlap.	`<b>this text is in <em>bold</em></b>`	`<b>this text is in <em>bold</b></em>`
In XHTML, attribute values must always be in quotes.	`<col width="20" />`	`<col width=20>`

Converting a document from HTML to XHTML

You'll find that it's very easy to convert an HTML document to XHTML. Our sample HTML page — which we also convert to XHTML — is a document that contains an HTML table with listings for two of the books in our hypothetical bookstore. You can see the page itself in Figure 4-2; it uses the HTML markup you see in Listing 4-1.

Listing 4-1: The HTML Document to Convert to XHTML

```
<HTML>
<HEAD>
 <TITLE>Book</TITLE>
</HEAD>
<BODY>
<H3 ALIGN=CENTER>Bestselling Books</H3>
<BR>
<TABLE BORDER=1 BGCOLOR=tan CELLSPACING=0 CELLPADDING=2>
 <TR ALIGN=LEFT>
  <TH>ID
  <TH>Title
  <TH>Author
  <TH>Publisher
  <TH>Price
  <TH>ContentType
  <TH>Format
  <TH>ISBN
 <TR>
```

(continued)

Listing 4-1 *(continued)*

```
   <TD>1
   <TD>The Five People You Meet in Heaven
   <TD>Albom, Mitch
   <TD>Hyperion
   <TD>$19.95
   <TD>Fiction
   <TD>Hardback
   <TD>0786868716
  <TR>
   <TD>2
   <TD>The Da Vinci Code
   <TD>Brown, Dan
   <TD>Doubleday
   <TD>$24.95
   <TD>Fiction
   <TD>Hardback
   <TD>0385504209
 </TABLE>
 </BODY>
 </HTML>
```

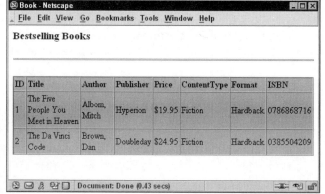

Figure 4-2:
Start out
with some
HTML.

Okay, we admit it — we broke all the XML rules here so we could review the important syntax rules one more time. So what would it take to convert this breezy HTML document to valid XHTML? Four changes:

- ✔ Convert all the uppercase HTML tags to lowercase.

- ✔ Add closing tags to all elements.

- ✔ Change the formatting for empty tags.

- ✔ Add quotes to attribute values.

So even in this worst-case scenario, it's really not difficult to convert an HTML document to valid XHTML. If you changed our original HTML markup as indicated here, the result would be a proper XHTML document that looks like Listing 4-2. We're not even going to show you the figure for this, because what shows up on-screen looks the same as Figure 4-2!

An XHTML file has a `.htm` or `.html` file extension.

Listing 4-2 The HTML Document After Conversion to XHTML

```
<html>
 <head>
 <title>Book</title>
 </head>
 <body>
 <h3 align="center">Bestselling Books</h3>
 <br />
 <table border="1" bgcolor="tan" cellspacing="0" cellpadding="2">
  <tr align="left">
   <th>ID</th>
   <th>Title</th>
   <th>Author</th>
   <th>Publisher</th>
   <th>Price</th>
   <th>ContentType</th>
   <th>Format</th>
   <th>ISBN</th>
  </tr>
  <tr>
   <td>1</td>
   <td>The Five People You Meet in Heaven</td>
   <td>Albom, Mitch</td>
   <td>Hyperion</td>
   <td>$19.95</td>
   <td>Fiction</td>
   <td>Hardback</td>
   <td>0786868716</td>
  </tr>
  <tr>
   <td>2</td>
   <td>The Da Vinci Code</td>
   <td>Brown, Dan</td>
   <td>Doubleday</td>
   <td>$24.95</td>
   <td>Fiction</td>
   <td>Hardback</td>
   <td>0385504209</td>
  </tr>
 </table>
 </body>
</html>
```

You can convert your HTML to XHTML with ease by using Dave Raggett's free open-source program, HTML Tidy. The maintenance of HTML Tidy is now provided by Source Forge. Check it out at http://tidy.sourceforge.net/. For a version that's even easier to use than the original, see the HTML-Kit at www.chami.com/html-kit/.

The Role of DOCTYPE Declarations

Actually, there's one further requirement for a valid XHTML document: A valid XHTML document needs a valid XHTML DOCTYPE declaration.

The DOCTYPE declaration serves several purposes:

- ✔ It allows your page to be validated as XHTML.
- ✔ It tells the browser which version of which markup language you used to create the page and references the specific DTD for that language.
- ✔ It enables your page to be displayed properly in Web-standards-compliant browsers (Internet Explorer 6, Netscape Navigator 6 and later, Mozilla, Firefox, and Opera 7 and later).

The newer versions of Internet Explorer and Gecko-based browsers use two different modes to display HTML and XHTML pages: *standards-mode* and *quirks-mode* (yes, really). If you don't include a DOCTYPE declaration, then your page — regardless of whether it's HTML or XHTML — is rendered in quirks-mode. This means the browser will attempt to parse your page in so-called "backward-compatible" mode using proprietary DOMs (not the W3C DOM) and other old rules.

You have three different DOCTYPES to choose among for an XHTML 1.0 document: strict, transitional, and frames.

- ✔ Use the strict DOCTYPE declaration if you're using CSS for styles and there's no presentational markup in your document (for example, if there's not even one font tag or align attribute):

```
<!DOCTYPE html PUBLIC "-//W3C//DTD XHTML 1.0 Strict//EN"
"http://www.w3.org/TR/xhtml1/DTD/xhtml1-strict.dtd">
```

- ✔ Use the transitional DOCTYPE declaration if your document includes any presentational markup:

```
<!DOCTYPE html PUBLIC "-//W3C//DTD XHTML 1.0 Transitional//EN"
"http://www.w3.org/TR/xhtml1/DTD/xhtml1-transitional.dtd">
```

✔ Use the frames DOCTYPE declaration, of course, if your document is in frames, like this:

```
<!DOCTYPE html PUBLIC "-//W3C//DTD XHTML 1.0 Frameset//EN"
"http://www.w3.org/TR/xhtml1/DTD/xhtml1-frameset.dtd">
```

Frankly, we find the transitional DOCTYPE declaration to be the easiest to use. It allows us to write valid XHTML — and to convert older HTML documents to XHTML without scouring the documents for any vestiges of presentational markup.

The XHTML DOCTYPE declaration must be followed by an additional line of markup:

```
<html xmlns="http://www.w3.org/1999/xhtml" xml:lang="en" lang="en">
```

This line replaces the opening <html> tag and adds information about the XHTML namespace. (A *namespace* is basically a vocabulary of elements and attributes. You find out more about namespaces in Chapter 11.)

An XHTML document is technically an XML document. As detailed in Chapter 5, XML documents can include an *XML declaration* as the first line in the document, something like this: <?xml version="1.0" encoding="UTF-8"?>. This line tells the XML processor that this is an XML document, it's created in version 1.0 of XML, and the character encoding is UTF-8. That's all fine and good for XML documents, but it can cause problems with XHTML documents in many browsers. If that happens, the browser may not display your page.

So for XHTML documents — at least for now — we recommend that you leave out the XML declaration. Start your XHTML document with a DOCTYPE declaration. If you need to add encoding information to your XHTML document, you can always include that information in a meta tag. (You find out more about character sets and encodings in Chapter 6.)

Are you ready to actually start creating some XML documents? We thought so! In Chapter 5, you'll find out how to create well-formed XML documents, as well as how to validate your XML files with DTDs and schemas.

Chapter 5

Putting Together an XML File

In This Chapter

▶ Creating well-formed XML documents

▶ Adding style to XML

▶ Upgrading to valid documents

XML was created to help people *do* things — why make an XML document if the document doesn't have a function . . . or (even worse) won't function at all? This chapter gives you a brief overview of the different components that you should include in every XML document so that it's well formed. To add to the fun, we show you how to be sure your documents are also valid. (If you haven't figured it out already, as soon as you start creating your own XML documents, you'll understand the importance of terms like *valid* and *invalid*.)

Validation — the capability to check individual documents against a governing collection of rules — is what gives XML so much power. Validation also enables you to use a general-purpose approach (XML itself) to create all kinds of document types or XML applications. In turn, this kind of open-ended extensibility — there's that "X" word again — puts few limits on the imagination and ingenuity of individuals who design document descriptions (DTDs and XML schemas).

Anatomy of an XML File

Obviously, a document that describes the elements in a complex chemical formula is a bit more intricate than one that describes the different pieces and parts of an address book, recipe, or novel.

No matter. XML documents are exactly as simple or as complex as they need to be to do the job that you have in mind for them. They don't need any extra fluff added along the way just for good measure. And whether an XML document is extremely complex or very simple, it must — we repeat, *must* — follow a basic set of rules.

XML documents that play by all the official rules are *well formed*. Figure 5-1 shows an XML document with some pointers to the parts that make it well formed.

A document that isn't well formed doesn't go far in the XML world, because it doesn't qualify technically as an XML document. Heed and beware: You'll be sorry if you don't take the time to make sure that every document you create plays by these very basic rules. (Fortunately, they aren't that hard to follow.)

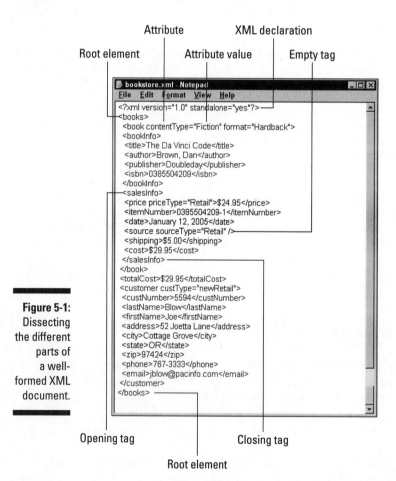

Attribute

XML declaration

Root element   Attribute value   Empty tag

```
bookstore.xml - Notepad
File   Edit   Format   View   Help
<?xml version="1.0" standalone="yes"?>
<books>
 <book contentType="Fiction" format="Hardback">
  <bookInfo>
  <title>The Da Vinci Code</title>
  <author>Brown, Dan</author>
  <publisher>Doubleday</publisher>
  <isbn>0385504209</isbn>
  </bookInfo>
 <salesInfo>
  <price priceType="Retail">$24.95</price>
  <itemNumber>0385504209-1</itemNumber>
  <date>January 12, 2005</date>
  <source sourceType="Retail" />
  <shipping>$5.00</shipping>
  <cost>$29.95</cost>
 </salesInfo>
 </book>
 <totalCost>$29.95</totalCost>
 <customer custType="newRetail">
  <custNumber>5594</custNumber>
  <lastName>Blow</lastName>
  <firstName>Joe</firstName>
  <address>52 Joetta Lane</address>
  <city>Cottage Grove</city>
  <state>OR</state>
  <zip>97424</zip>
  <phone>767-3333</phone>
  <email>jblow@pacinfo.com</email>
 </customer>
</books>
```

Figure 5-1:
Dissecting the different parts of a well-formed XML document.

Opening tag   Closing tag

Root element

The XML declaration

The first thing to include in every XML document is an *XML declaration*. This statement specifies that the document is XML compliant. The declaration is always the first line and looks something like this:

```
<?xml version="1.0"?>
```

This particular line of code makes two things clear to the processor:

✔ This is an XML document.
✔ This document is based on XML version 1.0.

XML 1.0 is the most commonly used version of XML. The W3C XML 1.1 specification was released in February 2004, but the W3C recommends that you continue to create documents in XML 1.0 unless you need the new features of XML 1.1 (changes in the use of character encoding). You'll find out more about character encoding in Chapter 6. For more details on XML 1.1, see `www.w3.org/TR/2004/REC-xml11-20040204/`.

You can also add two other attributes to your XML declaration:

```
<?xml version="1.0" standalone="yes" encoding="UTF-8"?>
```

The attribute `standalone` with a value of `yes` means that the document isn't dependent on any other document to be complete. You can still reference stylesheets, Document Type Documents (DTDs), schemas, and other such documents, but what you're saying with this attribute is that you don't have to; the application that processes the document won't have to look for any other documents to get a complete set of content. Most XML documents are standalone. Look for more information on this topic in Chapter 8.

The `encoding` attribute specifies the character encoding used in the document. UTF 8 corresponds to what most of us know as 8-bit ASCII characters.

You'll find out about other encoding options in Chapter 6.

The XML declaration is part of the *XML prolog*. The prolog can include additional items, as we'll detail in Chapter 8.

Marking up your content

After you've started your XML document creation with an XML declaration, it's time to get down to the details of the markup. If you've already done your *content analysis* — the stuff we discuss in Chapter 3 — it's easy to start marking up your content. (If you haven't yet ventured into Chapter 3, now may be the time to do so.)

XML elements are the basic building blocks of XML document structure. XML elements can contain other elements and/or text content. XML attributes are used to provide additional information about an element or its content. Attributes are contained within an element tag. For example, in the following markup

```
<source sourceType="Retail"/>
```

an empty element (`source`) contains an attribute (`sourceType`) that adds information about a subcategory (`Retail`).

You could use two elements to provide the same content:

```
<source>
  <sourceType>Retail</sourceType>
</source>
```

You find out more using attributes in the section "Adding attributes," later in this chapter.

Choosing a root element

The XML declaration (in a well-formed document, anyway) is followed by the opening tag of the root element. The *root element* is the most important element in any XML document. The root element contains all other elements — in effect, everything else in the XML document. All the markup is contained between the opening and closing tags of the root element. In any well-formed HTML document, `html` is always the root element. In XML, however, the root element can be just about anything you want it to be. In XML, you create a root element and then put all the related XML elements inside it.

For our bookstore example, it makes sense for us to designate `books` as the root element. Because our document contains one or more books, our root element's name sets the stage for our document, which can contain a single book or many books.

At this point in the process, our markup looks like this:

```
<?xml version="1.0" standalone="yes" encoding="UTF-8"?>
<books>
</books>
```

When you think about your root element, keep in mind that every other element has to fit neatly inside it. Don't be surprised if a couple of candidates for your root element appear. With a little trial and error, you can find the one that works right for you.

Defining elements

The categories and subcategories that you extracted during your content analysis — all that Chapter 3 stuff — are a good place to start when you're defining elements. These should include all the important content areas for your data.

For our bookstore, we chose to include these categories (and subcategories):

- **Book :** Title, Author, Publisher, ISBN, Content Type, Format
- **Sales:** Item Number, Date of Sale, Source, Price, Shipping, Cost per Item (Price + Shipping), Total Cost
- **Customer:** Customer Number, First Name, Last Name, Street Address, City, State, Zip Code, Phone, E-mail Address

For the first draft of our markup, we include all these categories and subcategories as elements — and add opening and closing tags for each element, like this:

```
<books>
   <book>
      <title></title>
      <author></author>
      <publisher></publisher>
      <isbn></isbn>
      <contentType></contentType>
      <format></format>
   </book>
   <sales>
      <itemNumber></itemNumber>
      <date></date>
      <source></source>
      <shipping></shipping>
      <cost></cost>
      <totalCost></totalCost>
   </sales>
```

```
<customer>
    <customerNumber></customerNumber>
    <firstName></firstName>
    <lastName></lastName>
    <address></address>
    <city></city>
    <state></state>
    <zipcode></zipcode>
    <phone></phone>
    <email></email>
</customer>
</books>
```

Looking at the family tree

The elements in an XML document are like one big happy family that comes together to describe your content. Imagine a family tree with a single trunk that splits into branches — which in turn split into branches with leaves at the end. An XML document has the same structure: The root element is the trunk that forms the foundation for the tree; the branches and their branches are the elements and (ultimately) content in your document.

- ✓ **Parent elements:** An element becomes a parent element when it contains other elements.

- ✓ **Child element:** A child element is — yep, you guessed it — an element that sits inside of a parent element.

- ✓ **Sibling element:** When a parent has more than one child element, those elements are *siblings* of one another. Sibling elements occupy the same level in the document hierarchy.

But what about grandparents, aunts, uncles, and cousins? Well, no. XML doesn't take the family-tree metaphor to such an extreme.

The categories and subcategories we list here are all child elements of the root element `books` — and all the categories are sibling elements to one another. The subcategories are child elements of category elements, and — no surprise here — are all sibling elements to one another.

Mapping relationships

Using the family-tree structure is a convenient way to map our document hierarchy and look at relationships between elements.

As you glanced over the first draft of our markup, you may have noticed a problem with our family structure: The `totalCost` is a child of the `sales` element. Because we want to be able to include more than one book in our documents, and because each book has a cost (price plus shipping), `totalCost` won't work well as a child of the `sales` element. We need to take `totalCost` out of the `sales` element and make it a separate element, like so:

```
<sales>
 <itemNumber></itemNumber>
 <date></date>
 <source></source>
 <shipping></shipping>
 <cost></cost>
</sales>
<totalCost></totalCost>
```

Because each book includes information about the book itself, such as the title, and sales information for that book, we added a new category (bookInfo) that wasn't included in our original content analysis. We also changed the name of the sales element to salesInfo just to keep things consistent. The new draft of our markup looks like this:

```
<books>
   <book>
      <bookInfo>
         <title></title>
         <author></author>
         <publisher></publisher>
         <isbn></isbn>
         <contentType></contentType>
         <format></format>
      </bookInfo>
      <salesInfo>
         <itemNumber></itemNumber>
         <date></date>
         <source></source>
         <shipping></shipping>
         <cost></cost>
      </salesInfo>
   </book>
   <totalCost></totalCost>
   <customer>
      <customerNumber></customerNumber>
      <firstName></firstName>
      <lastName></lastName>
      <address></address>
      <city></city>
      <state></state>
      <zipcode></zipcode>
      <phone></phone>
      <email></email>
   </customer>
</books>
```

So, Notes to Self: Change the hierarchy of the document so that totalCost is now a child of the root element, books. Also add a bookInfo element and change sales-element name to salesInfo.

Adding attributes

With a little savvy about elements in hand, you can turn your attention to the *attributes* that modify or manage the content that those elements may contain. Not only can attributes help clarify what content elements may contain, but they can also help define what an element does and how it relates to other elements.

To help you decide when to use an attribute with an element, here's a quick quiz:

- ✔ Are you defining a particular aspect of an element, such as size, height, or color?
- ✔ Do you need a way to provide more information about individual instances of an element?
- ✔ Do you want to be sure that every time an element is used, certain information is included with it?

Keeping these guidelines in mind while you're looking at the first draft of our document markup, behold! Two elements appear to be good candidates for attribute status: contentType and format, both child elements of the book element. With a little ingenuity, we can add attributes to these elements so they end up bearing a bit more of the informational burden. Our ingenuity is on display in the final draft of the markup:

```
<book contentType="Fiction" format="Hardback">
```

We also added other attributes that weren't included in our initial content analysis. Because our bookstore does both retail and wholesale sales, we realized we needed to add categories for the aspects of price, source, and customer. So our final markup also includes three additional attributes, priceType, sourceType, and custType, like so:

```
<price priceType="Retail">$24.95</price>
...
<source sourceType="Retail"/>
...
<customer custType="newRetail">
```

The custType attribute also allows us to include information about whether a customer is a new or repeat customer.

As you can see from the process we went through to create our final markup document, using content analysis, creating markup, and testing the markup allow you to create the XML document that best meets your needs for data storage and exchange.

The final form of our markup is shown in Listing 5-1. You'll notice another change — the line after the XML declaration is a processing instruction for adding a CSS stylesheet. (You get a look at adding a stylesheet in the section called "Adding Style for the Web," later in this chapter.)

Listing 5-1:   bookstore.xml

```
<?xml version="1.0" encoding="UTF-8"?>
<?xml-stylesheet type="text/css" href="bookstore.css"?>
<books>
   <book contentType="" format="">
      <bookInfo>
         <title></title>
         <author></author>
         <publisher></publisher>
         <isbn></isbn>
      </bookInfo>
      <salesInfo>
         <price priceType=""></price>
         <itemNumber></itemNumber>
         <date></date>
         <source sourceType=""/>
         <shipping></shipping>
         <cost></cost>
      </salesInfo>
   </book>
   <totalCost></totalCost>
   <customer custType="">
      <custNumber></custNumber>
      <lastName></lastName>
      <firstName></firstName>
      <address></address>
      <city></city>
      <state></state>
      <zip></zip>
      <phone></phone>
      <email></email>
   </customer>
</books>
```

Our document at this point doesn't include any information about what order elements should appear in, and it also doesn't indicate whether elements are required or optional, or whether they can occur more than once in the document. To add these kind of rules, you need to add validation for your document with a DTD or XML schema. Before you can validate an XML document, though, you need to ensure that it's well formed, as outlined in the following section.

Playing by the Rules: Well-Formed Documents

A well-formed XML document follows all the rules of XML syntax. XML is very flexible; its syntax is rigid. This is a good thing, because it guarantees that all XML documents adhere to the same basic rules (and computers *like* data that follows the rules).

If you think some of these rules are a bit nitpicky, you're right. Remember, the intended audience for your XML isn't a human being who can intuit what you "meant to mark," but a computer that can only work with what you give it.

We introduce the rules of XML syntax in our discussion of XHTML in Chapter 4; this chapter throws in a couple more rules for good measure. The following list includes all the rules introduced so far and adds one more rule so that you have everything you need to create well-formed XML documents:

- **You need an XML declaration.** The first line in every XML document is a simple declaration that specifies that the document is an XML document. In its simplest form, it looks like this:

  ```
  <?xml?>
  ```

- **You need a root element to contain all the other elements.** All elements and content within an XML document must live within a single top-level element, appropriately called the *document element* or *root element*.

- **Every nonempty element must have a start tag and an end tag.** If you open an element with a tag, make sure that you close it with a tag.

- **Empty elements have to end with a slash (/).** Elements that consist of only a start tag — such as the source element in our example — are called *empty elements* because they don't hold content between opening and closing tags (they don't even *have* closing tags). To avoid confusion and to prevent your XML tools from searching endlessly for closing tags that don't exist, identify all empty elements with a slash (/) before the closing greater-than sign (>), like this:

  ```
  <source sourceType="Retail"/>
  ```

In XHTML documents, you add a space before the closing slash in empty elements so that older browsers can recognize them as empty elements. You don't need to include a space before the ending slash in an XML document — the XML processor will recognize an empty element without that extra space.

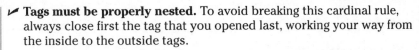

✔ **Tags must be properly nested.** To avoid breaking this cardinal rule, always close first the tag that you opened last, working your way from the inside to the outside tags.

A good way to remember to nest your elements correctly is to think of nested suitcases. Before you can close and zip the outer suitcase, you have to close and zip the inner suitcase. Think of tags as suitcase tops: You can't close the one on the outside until you close the one on the inside.

✔ **All attribute values must be in quotation marks.** You *must* enclose every attribute value in quotation marks (either single or double quotes — double quotes are used most often). If you forget even one set of quotation marks, you can count on the markup to break somewhere along the line.

✔ **Tags have to be built the right way.** Every XML tag must begin with a less-than sign (<),. XML tools don't know what to do with tags that don't play by this rule and usually treat them as plain ol' content. Not a total disaster (if you fix the error) — but certainly not a boon to the document if you leave it alone.

A corollary to this rule is that every XML entity must begin with an ampersand (&). *Fine,* you say, *but what's an entity?* We're glad you asked. An *entity* is a virtual storage unit that can contain text, binary files such as graphics or sound clips, or non-ASCII characters such as the copyright symbol. You reference an entity in an XML document by using a string of characters that begins with an ampersand (&) and ends with a semicolon (;).

XML supports non-ASCII characters. In Chapter 6, we discuss the XML use of characters and entities in depth.

If you're worried that building well-formed documents by hand will be tedious and not worth the effort, don't abandon us (and XML) here. Take a look at the sidebar "Staying well formed with good tools" elsewhere in this chapter to find out how a good XML tool picks the nits for you.

We've found that people with HTML experience have a harder time learning to adhere to the rules of well-formedness simply because Web browsers seem to encourage breaking rules instead of following them. Although this shift in thinking happens gradually (some may say *painfully*), with a little practice, you'll be over the HTML hump. (We made it without too much discomfort.)

TIP

Staying well formed with good tools

You're probably wondering how you can possibly remember all the rules that we describe in this chapter when you develop XML documents. Even veteran document designers forget a quotation mark or two here and there — not to mention occasionally forgetting a closing tag or a slash at the end of an empty tag. If you try to send such a malformed XML document to the application that is going to work with it, the application will spit it right back out at you or spit out error messages (and that's just as bad). Before you get your document to your application, it pays to ensure that it's well formed and valid (if necessary).

The best way to make sure your documents are well formed is to build your XML document with a text editor designed specifically for XML documents. XML editors can check documents as

you build them so that easy-to-make mistakes don't fester long enough to grow into ugly, malformed documents. Believe us, you'll be a happier and less-stressed camper if you go out and find yourself a good editor — we promise! XML editors are available for a variety of platforms and range in price from free to fairly expensive. Every editor has extra gimmicks and functions, but no XML editor is worth its salt if it can't check documents to make sure they're well formed.

In Chapter 19, we focus entirely on XML-related tools, including a section on XML editors. Read more about the editors available for your platforms of choice and then download a few and try them out. The best online resource that we've found for XML software is `www.xml software.com`.

Adding Style for the Web

Although XML is a great tool for storing data for all kinds of stuff, it's not completely Web compatible yet. But because the Web is hot, hot, hot, it's no surprise that content developers — like you — want to deliver their data through the Web. So if you want to transmit XML through the Web, Cascading Style Sheets (CSS) provide a mechanism to display XML documents directly.

A CSS stylesheet is a plain-text file that lists style properties. It's saved with a `.css` file extension. CSS is so important that we've devoted a whole chapter to it (Chapter 7), but for now, you only need to know a bit of CSS syntax to add a stylesheet to your XML markup for an enhanced Web view of your content.

We like CSS because it's human-readable and uses a simple-but-flexible syntax. To understand CSS, you only need to remember this magic formula:

```
selector {property: value}
```

The *selector* identifies the XML element to which a particular style rule applies. The *property* indicates the name of the CSS property, and the *value* specifies the value of the CSS property. For example, the following code shows the style information for the `title` element as included in the stylesheet we attached to `bookstore.xml`:

```
title {
  display: block;
  margin-bottom: 10pt;
  margin-left: 10pt;
  font-family: Verdana, Arial, Helvetica, sans-serif;
  font-size: x-small;
  background-color: #7fff00;
  padding: 5px;
}
```

In this code, the `title` element is the selector, and the CSS properties we applied to this element are `display`, `margin-bottom`, `margin-left`, `font-family`, `font-size`, `background-color`, and `padding`.

The stylesheet is attached to `bookstore.xml` to make our XML document more readable on the Web, as displayed in Figure 5-2. To attach a stylesheet, just add an additional processing instruction to your XML file:

```
<?xml version="1.0"?>
<?xml-stylesheet type="text/css" href="bookstore.css"?>
```

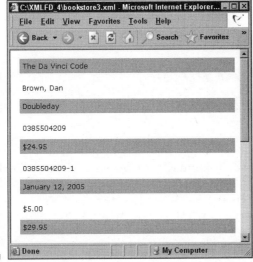

Figure 5-2:
An XML page (bookstore.xml), viewed in Internet Explorer with an attached CSS stylesheet.

Listing 5-2 shows the stylesheet (`bookstore.css`) for the XML file (`bookstore.xml`).

Listing 5-2:   bookstore.css

```
books {
        display: block;
        margin-bottom:30pt;
        margin-left: 0;
}

title, publisher, price, date, cost, custNumber, firstName, city, zip, email {
        display: block;
        margin-bottom: 10pt;
        margin-left: 5pt;
        font-family: Verdana, Arial, Helvetica, sans-serif;
        font-size: x-small;
        background-color: #7fff00;
        padding: 5px;
}
author, itemNumber, isbn, shipping, totalCost, lastName, address, state, phone
        {
        display: block;
        margin-bottom: 5pt;
        margin-left: 5pt;
        font-family: Verdana, Arial, Helvetica, sans-serif;
        font-size: x-small;
        background-color: #ffffff;
        padding: 5px;
}
```

The entire CSS file, `bookstore.css`, along with all the other listings for this book, is included on the Web site for this book at `www.dummies.com/go/xmlfd4e`.

Seeking Validation with DTD and XML Schema

In order to validate your well-formed XML document, you need to add a *document description* — either a Document Type Definition (DTD) or a schema. An XML document description is nothing more than a formal statement of the rules that govern how content can (or must) appear in any XML document that claims to follow those rules. Software grabs and digests the document descriptions, and then checks the structure and content of individual documents against the descriptions' rules. Whether a document adheres to or breaks those rules becomes easy to determine.

Computer scientists in general — and XML document wizards in particular — recognize document descriptions as a form of *metadata* (data that describes other data). Document descriptions are considered metadata because they incorporate lots of crucial information, including:

✔ A description of the various elements within the document.

✔ An explanation of what kinds of content the various elements can contain.

✔ The order in which elements can or must appear.

✔ The ranges of values from which element attribute values or actual element content must be chosen.

✔ Rules governing the occurrence of specific elements. (They may be optional or required, and if required, they may be constrained to occur some specific number of times.)

✔ The relationships between and among elements in a document.

The metadata definitions *don't* contain the actual data that you care about; they just contain rules for *describing* the data.

Why describe XML documents?

At this point, you may be asking yourself why you need to bother creating a formal XML document description. Before those sinister visions of essay questions start dancing before your eyes, consider: Creating a document description may be just the thing for your situation — or not. Situations vary; so do arguments for and against document descriptions. That's why Table 5-1 describes both the pros and cons of creating your own XML document description.

Table 5-1	XML Document Descriptions: Pros and Cons
Pros	*Cons*
When you need to accommodate or incorporate specific types of content or document structures not readily available elsewhere, creating a document description helps meet those needs.	When an existing document description can accommodate your data or documents, you don't need to create a document description. Why bother if the work's already done for you?
When you want to check documents automatically against a set of formal rules (be it for quality control or other purposes), using a document description and a validator makes such checks easy to automate and apply.	Well-formed XML documents that don't refer to a DTD or an XML schema needn't conform to a document description; they need only to conform to XML syntax rules. For single-use or trivial applications, invoking a formal document description may be overkill.

(continued)

Table 5-1 *(continued)*

Pros	Cons
When you have a great deal of specific data to collect, store, and maintain, a detailed and formal document description for such data helps organize and control that process.	When data or document collections are small (or very simple in structure and/or content), creating a document description may be overkill. On the other hand, when numerous instances abound, see the column to the left!

In general, it's not worth creating your own formal XML document descriptions unless one or more of the following conditions is true:

✔ You've got sizable collections of documents or data to manage.

✔ Your data collection (whether large or small) is pretty complex; you could benefit from the analysis and documentation that a document description represents.

✔ You want to promote a new industry standard.

Even if creating document descriptions seems desirable, it's only worthwhile when what you've got doesn't fit nicely into some existing, predefined XML markup language. This is when you create what is known as an *XML application*. XML applications invariably include one or more document descriptions at the core of their formal specifications, so feel free to lean on them if they meet your needs.

The *extensible* part of XML (*X* marks that spot) also means that you can extend not only existing XML documents, but also XML document descriptions. Before creating document descriptions from scratch, survey the landscape of existing XML applications and see whether you can recycle one or more of 'em. Don't be afraid to reuse pieces and parts of existing document descriptions. You, too, can stand on the shoulders of the XML giants who've gone before you!

Choosing between DTD and XML Schema

If you're on the horns of the document-description dilemma, here are a few simple guidelines for deciding between the use of a DTD and an XML Schema:

✔ **Examine the data to be described.** One of the two approaches will suggest itself as more workable. In general, DTDs work better for document- or text-intensive collections; an XML Schema works better for data-intensive collections.

✔ **Go with what you know.** If you're already familiar with DTDs and understand how they work, the learning curve is behind you. Ditto for XML Schema. If you work with a description language that you already know, you can concentrate on describing XML documents, rather than learning a description language.

✔ **Consider whether you're going to have to master XML structure and syntax anyway.** That's the favorite argument of XML Schema proponents. (Gee. Ya think?) They figure it this way: If you want to build XML documents, why not also use a document-description language based on XML?

Office 2003 supports XML Schema as its preferred document-description language. If you're going to be creating and using XML documents in Office 2003, cut to the chase and use XML Schema.

Of course, there are pros and cons for both languages. We cover each of these major approaches in Part III of this book. You can pick whichever language you like best, try your luck at both of them, or flip a coin and go from there.

Now for something completely — well, almost! — different. Chapter 6 highlights the use of character sets in XML. The use of character sets is important if you plan to distribute your XML documents to a global audience. (Cyrillic or Mandarin, anyone?) See Chapter 6 for more information.

Chapter 6

Adding Character(s) to XML

· ·

· ·

*T*he topic of character sets might seem a little obscure at first glance. You may well ask, "Why do I need to know anything about character sets? Character encoding is one little attribute value, and I usually use UTF-8 — end of story." Well, not quite — if you deal with an international audience, then character encoding is an important issue. Have you checked statistics for your audience lately? You might be surprised at how international your audience actually is. The latest (February 2005) statistics from World Internet Usage (www.internetworldstats.com/stats.htm) show the following breakdown for world Internet users:

▶ Asia: **32.6%**

▶ Europe: **28.3%**

▶ North America: **26.7%**

▶ Latin America/Caribbean **6.8%**

These statistics also include a small percentage of users in Africa, the Middle East, and Australia. The point is — if your audience isn't international now, chances are very good that it will include international visitors in the future.

Although the majority of Web content is in English — 56 percent, according to a 2002 survey — that doesn't mean English is the only language that the Web supports. As Web technology becomes increasingly global in scope, the ability to use character sets beyond the traditional Roman alphabet will help you reach a truly global audience in their native languages.

As you've probably noticed by now, all the markup and syntax related to XML 1.0 uses Roman characters — ASCII text, to be specific. Although that's all well and good for those of us in the Western world, it doesn't get you very far when you want to create localized sites or application for deployment in Asia with content available in both Mandarin and Cantonese. To expand the scope of your content to encompass the whole world and all of its character sets, you need a good understanding of how XML works with characters (letters) — and of how you can use XML's character conventions (called *encoding*) to make your XML content available in any language. Armed with knowledge about character encoding, you can take further advantage of XML's extensibility — making content available to multiple applications and in multiple spoken languages.

When you get right down to it, computers think in *binary* — 1s and 0s. Those 1s and 0s are called *bits,* and they're the most basic unit of storage in a computer. To give you some perspective, a byte is always made up of 8 bits — even if you're only using 4 of them. When you put 1,000 bytes together, you have a kilobyte (the *k* in 64K). Early computers used 7-bit strings to represent simple alphabetical characters; modern computers use a mix of 8- and 16-bit strings to represent a broad range of characters, depending on the application and the location. The more bits you have in your string, the more characters you can use (more about this in a minute). Normally, you don't use 16-bit character strings unless you want to work with non-Roman alphabets, such as those for Hebrew or Japanese.

In keeping with its intent to be friendly to all Web users, XML is designed to support 16-bit character encoding. *Encoding* is the technical term for specifying how many bits describe your characters. 16-bit character encoding uses 16-bit strings to represent characters in XML documents. This encoding already includes character strings for most of the world's known alphabets, plus all kinds of symbols for disciplines from genetics to mathematics. It even has room left over to accommodate more character sets and symbols as the need for them arises.

This chapter is full of a bunch of technical stuff. We apologize in advance for the pounding "huh?" headache that may accompany this chapter. But if you've always wanted to know more about Unicode — or if your work in XML involves an international audience and languages other than English — this chapter is definitely for you. Otherwise, feel free to move on to Chapter 7.

About Character Encodings

Clearly, the trend is toward longer bit strings to encode character data, so size does matter when representing character data. Here's why:

✔ A 7-bit string can represent a maximum of 2^7, or 128, different characters. This is enough for the 26-character basic Roman alphabet in uppercase and lowercase *(A–Z* and *a–z)*, plus a modicum of symbols, punctuation characters, and so on. In short, a 7-bit string works fine for simple Roman alphabets and related characters — but just barely.

✔ An 8-bit string can represent a maximum of 2^8, or 256, different characters, including everything a 7-bit encoding can handle, and leaves room for what some experts call higher-order characters (accented letters, trademark symbols, and so forth). An 8-bit string permits computer character sets to add all kinds of control characters and a modest set of diacritical marks not frequently used in English but frequently used in German (with its umlauts), French (with its accent marks), and other European languages.

✔ A 16-bit string can represent a maximum of 2^{16}, or 65,536, different characters. This captures everything an 8-bit encoding can handle — *and* allows for another 65,280 character codes (more than 99.6 percent of the available character space). This leaves room for most of the major human alphabets, from ancient Aramaic and Greek to modern Hangul (Korean), plus all kinds of symbols and other special characters — but it doesn't allow for all the characters of (for example) some Asian languages, such as Mandarin. In the following section, you find out how Unicode found a way to go beyond the 16-bit ceiling.

Some modern computers still use 8-bit encodings to represent most character data, especially in English — the bottom line is that it's faster to process 8-bit characters than it is 16-bit characters. Windows NT, Windows 2000, and Windows XP, however, use 16-bit encoding for internal representations of text, and most global solutions use 16-bit encoding to support all possible languages and characters. The encoding you use will depend entirely on what characters you need to represent.

Introducing Unicode

An industry group called the Unicode Consortium was formed in January 1991 to promote an open, standard, fully international, 16-bit character encoding technology. Not surprisingly, this encoding is also known as Unicode. Today, Unicode 4.0 (the current, standard version of Unicode) represents the fourth generation of the consortium's work in defining a single character-encoding technology to accommodate nearly every known human character set under a single representational scheme. Pretty amazing stuff!

In addition, the Unicode Consortium has maintained an ongoing relationship with the International Organization for Standardization (ISO). This produced an organized, international ISO standard (how's that for redundant?), known as ISO 10646, that represents almost the same information as the Unicode standard. By 1993, the ISO working group responsible for incorporating Unicode as an official ISO standard had completed its initial work, and ISO 10646-1:1993 came into being. The *-1* after the number indicates that it is the first draft of the standard; *1993* indicates that it was approved in 1993. ISO has updated 10646 to stay synchronized with the most current Unicode standards. ISO 10646:2003 is synchronized with Unicode 4.0.

Today, Unicode defines just over 96,000 different character codes. Of this range, 70,000 characters are defined for the Han ideographs used for Mandarin and other Chinese languages; over 11,000 characters are defined for Hangul (Korean). The nearly 15,000 remaining characters represent most other written languages. For convenience, the Unicode character codes for 0 through 255 (8-bit character codes, in other words) match the character set defined for ISO-8859-1 — which is also known as *ISO-Latin-1,* the default character set used to encode all HTML documents on the Web.

So if a 16-bit string can represent a maximum of 65,536 character codes, how can Unicode 4.0 represent over 96,000 character codes? Through the use of encoding formats such as UTF (Unicode Transformation Format) and UCS (Universal Character Set) and the use of surrogate pairs of values to represent numbers greater than 65,536. You find out more about these encoding formats and surrogate pairs later in this chapter.

Many people — including numerous XML experts — refer to the XML character set as "Unicode" (and we think there's good reason to do so). However, if you ever spend any time perusing the W3C XML specifications, you'll notice that *they* refer to character sets by their ISO designations. You'll see plenty of references to ISO 10646 but only scant mention of Unicode. Go figure!

Note that XML 1.0, 2nd Edition (www.w3.org/TR/2000/REC-xml-20001006) references Unicode 2.0 and 3.0, and XML 1.1 references Unicode 4.0, whereas the 1st Edition of XML 1.0 references only Unicode 2.0. If your XML documents are used internationally, make sure that you are using a Unicode version (and an associated XML version) that contains representations for all the characters that may be used in your documents.

The terms *Unicode* and *ISO 10646* are often interchanged as if they were exactly the same thing. The Unicode standard, however, includes much more in-depth information on implementation issues such as character rendering.

For more information about Unicode characters, symbols, history, and the current standard, you can find a plethora of information at the Unicode consortium's Web site at www.unicode.org.

You can even join a Unicode-oriented mailing list that operates at unicode@ unicode.org by sending an add request in the Subject field of an e-mail message to unicode-request@unicode.org. If you're seeking a definitive reference to Unicode, the Unicode Consortium has authored a book entitled *The Unicode Standard, Version 4.0* (published by Addison-Wesley Developers Press). Although it lists for $60, it's a worthwhile reference if you want to be able to check that your browser is interpreting a character code correctly.

Character Sets, Fonts, Scripts, and Glyphs

Although XML can represent just about any kind of character data imaginable, that's just the beginning of what's involved to make exotic character data appear on a computer's display. The raw character data — which XML can handle just fine, thank you very much — represents a set of written characters, called a *script,* which may or may not use a conventional Roman alphabet.

To see what's in XML scripts that 7- or 8-bit character encodings can't cover — which means special symbols or non-Roman alphabets — you'll need a few extra local ingredients:

- ✔ **A character set that matches the script you're trying to read and display.** For the purposes of this discussion, a *character set* represents a collection of 16-bit values that maps to some specific symbol set or alphabet.

- ✔ **Software that understands the character set for the script (or at least the general encoding type).** Such software includes the underlying operating system on your computer. Fortunately, most modern operating systems — including various flavors of UNIX, Linux, and Windows 9*x*, NT, 2000, and XP — can handle 16-bit character codes. Mac OS X, depending on the particular configuration of the OS, can handle 16-bit character codes, and conversion tools are readily available for Mac OS 9*x*. Likewise, that character set must be interpreted by an application (such as your Web browser or a word processor; some browsers can handle 16-bit character codes, and others can't).

- ✔ **An electronic font that allows the character set to be displayed on screen (and in print, and so forth).** A *font* is a complete set of graphical bitmaps that correspond to character codes that appear in a character set, so that each character has its own unique bitmap — usually following a consistent design for the entire set. These bitmaps are scaled (to create font sizes) and styled (to create font appearances, such as bold and italic) to create bitmaps for display on-screen or in print image files. Each individual bitmap in a font is known as a *glyph.*

All these ingredients are necessary to work with alternate character sets because humans understand scripts, computers understand numbers (or bit patterns, if you prefer), and displays require images. Character sets represent a mapping from a script to a set of corresponding numeric character codes. Fonts represent a collection of glyphs for the numeric character codes in a character set. All three elements are necessary to represent and render characters on-screen.

Finally, to create text to match the alphabet used in a script, you need an input tool — such as a text or XML editor — that can work with the character set and its corresponding font. The goal is to create additional text that uses the same character set so you can use the alternate alphabet in your document — and (oh, yeah) to see what you're doing.

For Each Character, a Code

In the Unicode/ISO 10646 character set, individual characters correspond to specific 16-bit numbers. For convenience, most character sets occur in the form of sequential ranges of such numbers — where uppercase and lowercase characters, as well as characters for the digits 0 through 9, are in sequence. To determine the code that represents a character, you have to look it up in the Unicode or ISO 10646 specification. (Here's where the Unicode book we mentioned earlier in this chapter comes in handy.)

Even if you don't have access to an editor or text-entry tool that understands a particular character set, you can always use numeric entities to represent those characters. In general, *numeric entities* take one of two forms, decimal or hexadecimal (as indicated in the comments in the code that follows):

```
&#4096;
<!-- &# indicates a decimal number -->
&#x0F00;
<!-- &#x indicates a hexadecimal number-->
```

In this case, each of these two types of numeric entity represents the first character in Tibetan script — in decimal form, that's 4096, which is the same as 0F00 in hexadecimal (Base-16) notation.

Each *numeric entity* in XML has an associated text encoding. If some specific encoding is not defined in a numeric entity's definition, the default is an encoding called UTF-8, which stands for Unicode Transformation Format, 8-bit form.

UTF and UCS (Universal Character Set) are mechanisms for implementing Unicode. UTF versions include UTF-32, UTF-16, UTF-8, UTF-EBCDIC, and UTF-7; UCS versions include UCS-4 and UCS-2. The numbers represent the number of bits in 1 unit (UTF) or in 1 byte (UCS). In UTF-32 or UCS-4, 1 unit is enough for any character. In UTF-8, a single character code may require 3 units, but UTF-8 represents the Roman alphabet efficiently, requiring only a single byte for common characters.

UTF-16 is used mainly for internal processing — for example, for internal representations of text in Microsoft Windows. UTF-16 uses a distinct 16-bit string to represent each character whose character code value is less than or equal to 65,536. For those character code values greater than 65,536, Unicode uses surrogate pairs of values in the range D800 – DFFF. For example, 65,536 is represented in hexadecimal as FFFF. The next hex number after FFFF is 10000. This is represented in UTF-16 as D800 DC00. Bottom line? Unicode 4.0 currently defines around 90,000 different characters. With the use of surrogate pairs, there is room for 1,114,112 characters.

Key Character Sets

Around the world, computers use a variety of character sets, depending on the languages (or scripts, if you prefer) that their users employ to represent text. Most computers today use some variant of the *American Standard Code for Information Interchange (ASCII),* an 8-bit character set that handles the basic Roman alphabet used for English, along with punctuation, numbers, and simple symbols. To augment this meager character set, extensions to support additional characters or diacritical marks are added on a per-language basis. Most European languages match standard ASCII values from 0 to 127 and go on from there to define alternate mappings between character codes and local script characters for values from 128 to 255.

Non-Roman alphabets, such as Hebrew, Japanese, and Thai, depend on special character sets that include basic ASCII (0-127, or 0-255, depending on the implementation) plus the character sets for the script that corresponds to the "other alphabet" in use. The number of bits in such character encodings depends on the size of the other alphabet. It's not uncommon for such encodings to use 16-bit values to accommodate a second character and symbol set along with the ASCII set. (A listing of character sets built around the ASCII framework appears in Table 6-1.)

Table 6-1		ISO 8859 Character Sets
Character Set	*Script*	*Languages*
ISO-8859-1	Latin-1	ASCII plus most Western European languages, including Albanian, Afrikaans, Basque, Catalan, Danish, Dutch, English, Faroese, Finnish, Flemish, Galician, German, Icelandic, Irish, Italian, Norwegian, Portuguese, Scottish, Spanish, and Swedish. Omits certain Dutch, French, and German characters.
ISO-8859-2	Latin-2	ASCII plus most Central European languages, including Czech, English, German, Hungarian, Polish, Romanian, Croatian, Slovak, Slovene, and Serbian.
ISO-8859-3	Latin-3	ASCII plus characters required for English, Esperanto, German, Maltese, and Galician.
ISO-8859-4	Latin-4	ASCII plus Estonian, Greenlandic, Lappish, and most Baltic languages, including Latvian and Lithuanian; now superseded by ISO-Latin-6 (ISO-8859-10).
ISO-8859-5	Latin/Cyrillic	ASCII plus Cyrillic characters for Slavic languages, including Byelorussian, Bulgarian, Macedonian, Russian, Serbian, and Ukrainian.
ISO-8859-6	Latin/Arabic	ASCII plus Arabic characters.
ISO-8859-7	Latin/Greek	ASCII plus Greek characters.
ISO-8859-8	Latin/Hebrew	ASCII plus Hebrew.
ISO-8859-9	Latin-5	Latin-1, except that some Turkish symbols replace Icelandic ones.
ISO-8859-10	Latin-6	ASCII plus most Nordic languages. plus Inuit (Greenlandic Eskimo), non-Skolt Sami (Lappish), and Icelandic.
ISO-8859-11	Latin/Thai	ASCII plus Thai.
ISO-8859-12	Not currently in use	At one point, this was to be used for ASCII plus Celtic; now superseded by Latin-8 (ISO-8859-14).
ISO-8859-13	Latin-7	ASCII plus the Baltic Rim characters.
ISO-8859-14	Latin-8	ASCII plus Celtic.
ISO-8859-15	Latin-9	Variation on Latin-1, including Euro currency sign, plus extra accented Finnish and French characters.
ISO-8859-16	Latin-10	ASCII plus Romanian.

The use of Unicode characters in XML 1.1

XML 1.1, released as a W3C specification in February 2004, incorporates major changes in the use of Unicode characters. In fact, this is the biggest difference between XML 1.0 and XML 1.1.

The Unicode standard has been growing and evolving — no new tentacles or legs, but it has more capabilities these days. XML 1.0 was created back in the era of Unicode 2.0, with its cast of 40,000 Unicode characters. XML 1.1 is more up-to-date; it references Unicode 4.0, which has 96,000 characters.

Even beyond the increase in characters, though, XML 1.1 makes some major changes in how Unicode characters can be used. For example, the old XML 1.0 has specific lists of characters that can be used as newline characters or as valid characters in the names of elements or attributes — and only those characters are legit. XML 1.1, however, allows *any* Unicode character that's not expressly forbidden to be used as part of an element or attribute name and adds support for `NEL` (the new-line character in IBM mainframes).

The change in valid element and attribute names makes it possible for any document creator to use his/her native language for XML element and attribute names — and that's the good news about XML 1.1.

However, this change in the rules of XML syntax also changes the definition of a well-formed document. That wouldn't be a big deal if it didn't open the possibility that XML 1.1 documents won't be backward compatible with XML 1.0 applications and processors. But it does — and that's the bad news about XML 1.1.

We're hoping that XML 2.0 will incorporate some means of supporting internationalization while maintaining backward compatibility with earlier versions of XML — stay tuned!

A careful reading of Table 6-1 shows that most character sets can render English and German, plus a collection of other, sometimes-related languages. When choosing a variant of ISO-8859, remember that all the languages you want to include must be part of that variant; otherwise, you must use Unicode.

XML goes beyond such idiosyncratic or customized character sets and uses Unicode because it can house character codes for the vast majority of known human scripts in a single encoding. Even if an XML processor can't display certain character codes — because (for instance) necessary fonts are not present — such processors must be capable of handling any valid character code in the Unicode range.

Using Unicode Characters

Any software that supports XML files directly, including the XML tools and editors listed on the download page on the Web site for this book at www. dummies.com/go/xmlfd4e, supports Unicode or UTF-8 formats. So do many modern word processors — for instance, Word 97 and later versions support a format called *encoded text* that uses Unicode encoding.

If you don't have ready access to such tools and want to save XML files in Unicode format, you must use a conversion tool. Several different tools, both freeware and commercial products, are available, depending on your OS. Search "Unicode converters" in your favorite search engine for more details.

For an example of text conversion into Unicode, see the free Unicode Encoder/Converter page at www.pinnacledisplays.com/unicode-converter.htm. You enter a string of text, click a button, and immediately you see the Unicode equivalent. For example, if you enter

```
Bob's your uncle
```

the Unicode equivalent you get is

```
&#66;&#111;&#98;&#39;&#115;&#32;&#121;&#111;&#117;&#114;&#32;&#117;&#110;&#99;&#
108;&#101;
```

If you can't convert your XML text to UTF-8 or to straight Unicode encodings, you can tell the XML processor what kind of character encoding you're using. If you do so, however, you're taking a chance — not all XML processors can handle arbitrary encodings. Fortunately, however, widely used tools such as Netscape Navigator (Version 4.1 or newer) and Internet Explorer (Version 5.0 or newer) can handle most ISO-8859 variants. If you want to use an alternate character encoding, you must identify that encoding in your XML document's prolog as follows:

```
<?xml version="1.0" encoding="ISO-8859-9"?>
```

In addition to the encoding names that appear in Table 6-1, you can use other encoding names — within a certain approved range. For a range of other possible encodings, check the official Internet Assigned Numbers Authority (IANA) list at

```
www.iana.org/assignments/character-sets
```

Please note that XML parsers are required to support only UTF-8 and UTF-16 (native Unicode) encodings, so the `encoding` attribute in an XML document prolog might not work with all such tools. If you try using an ISO-8859 variant (or some other character set) and don't get the results you want, you might have to figure out how to translate the document into Unicode. Ouch!

Finding Character Entity Information

Elsewhere in this chapter, we mention one excellent source for obtaining information about character entity assignments for Unicode — namely, the Unicode Consortium's book titled *The Unicode Standard, Version 4.0.* If the book's price tag makes your wallet start to gibber in fear, you can also find plenty of encoding information online. For example, here's the site of the Unicode Character Database:

```
www.unicode.org/ucd/
```

Likewise, the W3C has information about Unicode character ranges and encodings in Appendix B, "Character Classes," for the XML 1.0 Recommended Specification at

```
www.w3.org/TR/REC-xml#CharClasses
```

You'll also find the XHTML entity lists useful in this context:

- ✔ **Latin-1:** www.w3.org/TR/xhtml1/DTD/xhtml-lat1.ent
- ✔ **Special:** www.w3.org/TR/xhtml1/DTD/xhtml-special.ent
- ✔ **Symbols:** www.w3.org/TR/xhtml1/DTD/xhtml-symbol.ent

Accessing any of the three URLs shown here will open the File Download box of your browser.

A bit of judicious poking around via your favorite search engine, using search strings such as "Unicode encodings" or "XML character encodings", can turn up other interesting sources of this information online. Happy hunting!

Okay, it might have been a bit of a hike to get through a chapter about character sets — but as the Web gets increasingly international, you may be glad you did. And now for something just as important for your (potential) global audience: Chapter 7 briefs you on using CSS to format your XML pages for display on the Web.

Chapter 7

Handling Formatting with CSS

●●

●●

Although most of the cool things you can do with XML don't involve the Web, many of you *do* want to use XML to contribute to (or to drive) a Web-based solution. You've got it: That's what this chapter is all about. Without the addition of formatting instructions, XML documents display as plain text on a Web page — not a particularly useful way to present your data on a Web site. Adding CSS (Cascading Style Sheets) to your XML pages is an easy way to create a specific appearance for your XML pages on the Web by defining display properties such as font family, text color, background images and colors, and position of elements. We think CSS is so important for displaying XML on the Web that we've devoted a whole chapter to it.

CSS is a topic too big to cover thoroughly in this book — we leave that to *Beginning CSS: Cascading Style Sheets for Web Design,* by Richard York, published by Wrox Press.

A newer specification for stylesheets — XSLT — is more powerful and more complex than CSS. XSLT stylesheets allow you to transform your document as well as add style information. You get the goods on XSLT in Chapter 12. For the purposes of this chapter, CSS is powerful (and complex) enough.

Viewing XML on the Web with CSS

If you want to see how a CSS document can affect the look and feel of a Web page, visit Dave Shea's CSS Zen Garden page, at www.csszengarden.com, also shown in Figure 7-1. The CSS Zen Garden beautifully demonstrates the power of CSS. The site applies different CSS stylesheets to the same HTML file to produce different displays of the same information. What you see are good stylesheets at work — not tricks made possible by convoluted HTML or XHTML. In the end, building a good stylesheet is a much easier approach (after you get the hang of the underlying markup conventions), because it's designed to drive complex displays. You will be using the right tool for the right job.

Figure 7-1:
The CSS
Zen Garden.

CSS is really, really easy to use with XML — even if you're building stylesheets from scratch. This is a huge plus when you're trying to get a solution of any kind up and running quickly. Okay, we don't dispute that XSLT is more powerful than CSS — and robust enough to support many uses for XML. But XSLT is also more work — and may be overkill in some simple situations.

Figure 7-2 shows how the bookstore XML file looks with the addition of a different CSS stylesheet to display our book information. This time, we included a graphic among our styles, though there's more here than meets the eye. (We take a closer look at this stylesheet later in this chapter.)

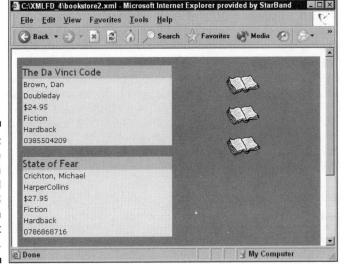

To use CSS with XML (or XHTML, for that matter), you need to know a bit about how to create CSS stylesheets. For openers, CSS is simply a set of rules that you use to create stylesheets — specifically, those that Web browsers recognize and can work with. CSS documents are just plain text, so you don't have to buy special software to use them — or do something awful to your browser to make it work with them. All you need to do to use CSS is to learn its syntax.

Basic CSS Formatting: CSS1

Cascading Style Sheets 1 (CSS1) was the first version of CSS developed for use with HTML. Partial support for CSS1 in Web browsers started with Internet Explorer 3.0 and Netscape Navigator 4.0.

Now, however, the newest versions of the big browsers (namely, Internet Explorer 6.0 and Netscape Navigator 6⁺) support all elements in CSS1. Can we hear a big *woo-hoo?* CSS1 deserves a cheer; it took a long time for this support to happen.

With CSS1, you can control the format and display of:

- Colors and backgrounds
- Fonts and text
- Lists
- Margins, padding, and borders

The Icing on the Cake: CSS2

Cascading Style Sheets 2 (CSS2) was published as a W3C recommendation in 1998. Unfortunately, developers and browser vendors have been slow to adopt CSS2, even though it provides more page-layout controls. Although it took a long time for browsers to support CSS2, the latest big browsers (Internet Explorer and Netscape Navigator, versions 6 and later) support almost all of the CSS2 specification. Even so, use CSS2 markup with care (and test your work carefully on your target browsers).

Additions to CSS1 in CSS2 include the following:

✔ Element positioning

✔ Element visibility

✔ Support for specifying page breaks

✔ Table styles

✔ Aural stylesheets (used for defining how your page sounds when read in a speech-enabled browser)

✔ Support for system colors and fonts

✔ Counters and automatic numbering

Building a CSS Stylesheet

In this section, you lift the hood on CSS and poke into some of the details involved in using CSS markup to create stylesheets. Here, the primary focus is understanding and using CSS markup, and understanding its capabilities and limitations.

Although a judicious mixture of XML and CSS creates a positive presentation, be aware that the combination may not always work the way you want or the way you think it should. You must also understand that not all Web browsers treat CSS definitions exactly the same, so experimentation and testing to achieve the right look may be required.

You're probably wondering what the *C* in CSS (Cascading) is about. Sorry, no waterfalls here. *Cascading* refers to the capability of applying multiple stylesheets to any document — in a hierarchy of importance — in a way that defines all styles and handles conflicting style definitions gracefully. Each CSS stylesheet attached to a document is either more or less important than those next to it in the overall scheme of style. If one stylesheet conflicts with another, the stylesheet with the heavier "weight" — that is, the one that's higher on the stylesheet food chain — takes precedence. Then the subordinate stylesheets fill in what's left — so smoothly that, okay, it might as well be a waterfall.

For example, if an individual Web page implements CSS, several stylesheets may apply to it: styles defined in the document itself (inline or embedded); the external CSS stylesheet that you created; the individual user's preference settings (if any), such as font sizes, styles, and colors; and the browser's default stylesheet. These three stylesheets *cascade* — are applied in order — to the Web page according to the following priority order:

1. User-defined stylesheets (a specific stylesheet created for the user)

2. Inline styles (created with HTML's `style` attribute)

3. Embedded styles (contained within the `head` section of an HTML/ XHTML document)

4. External stylesheets

5. The user's preferences

6. The browser's default stylesheet

We included all the options here for the sake of completeness, but some of them don't apply to XML documents: The second option applies only to HTML and the third option only to HTML and XHTML.

If your stylesheet indicates that the font size should be 10-point Times, but the user has set his or her user-defined stylesheet so that all text is always displayed in 12-point Garamond, the user's stylesheet wins.

User-defined stylesheets are uppermost in the hierarchy because they enable users with disabilities to be sure their preferred styles trump any and all other stylesheet settings and meet their specific needs.

Adding CSS to XML

Best to begin with basics — the XML to which we'll be adding a CSS stylesheet. Listing 7-1 shows our `books` XML file — which includes only book information (no sales or customer information).

Listing 7-1:   The Books XML Document (books.xml)

```xml
<?xml version="1.0" encoding="UTF-8"?>
<books>
 <book>
  <title>The Da Vinci Code</title>
  <author>Brown, Dan</author>
  <publisher>Doubleday</publisher>
  <price>$24.95</price>
  <contentType>Fiction</contentType>
  <format>Hardback</format>
  <isbn>0385504209</isbn>
 </book>
 <book>
  <title>State of Fear</title>
  <author>Crichton, Michael</author>
  <publisher>HarperCollins</publisher>
  <price>$27.95</price>
  <contentType>Fiction</contentType>
  <format>Hardback</format>
  <isbn>0786868716</isbn>
 </book>
 <book>
  <title>Night Fall</title>
  <author>Demille, Nelson</author>
  <publisher>Warner</publisher>
  <price>$26.95</price>
  <contentType>Fiction</contentType>
  <format>Hardback</format>
  <isbn>0446576638</isbn>
 </book>
</books>
```

This document includes the following elements (we've added display tips to each one — things such as "larger font" — so you know what we're planning when we build the stylesheet in the next section):

- `<books>` holds everything in the document (much like the `<html>` element in an HTML document). Its style rule should include margin information for the entire document, as well as specifications for background color and base font.

- `<book>` data should be separated for each book so it's easy to read on-screen.

- `<title>` should be emphasized with a larger font and a different color background so that each book is easy to locate on the page.

- `<author>`, `<publisher>`, `<price>`, `<contentType>`, `<format>`, and `<isbn>` work well together and should be displayed in a similar style on separate lines.

We could do quite a bit more with a stylesheet to create an impressive layout and design, but that only adds more lines of markup to our examples. For demonstration purposes, simple is beautiful. Feel free to enhance and build on this stylesheet, however, as you find out more about CSS.

A simple CSS stylesheet for XML

When you have a pretty good general sense of how you want the document to look on-screen, you have a guideline for creating the stylesheet to make it happen. Listing 7-2 shows a simple CSS stylesheet for our books XML file. We analyze this stylesheet in the following section of this chapter.

Listing 7-2:   books.css — CSS Stylesheet for books.xml

```
books {
 display: block;
 width: 100%;
 background-color: gray;
 background-image: url(officebooks.gif);
 background-repeat: no-repeat;
 background-position: 80% 10px;
 margin: 0;
 font-family: Verdana, Geneva, Arial, Helvetica, sans-serif;
}

book {
 display: block;
 background-color: Silver;
 width: 50%;
 margin-bottom: 20px;
 margin-top: 15px;
 margin-left: 10px;
}

author, publisher, price, contentType, format, isbn {
 display: block;
 background-color: #ffe4c4;
 font-size: x-small;
 padding: 2px;
}

title {
 display:block;
 color: Maroon;
 font-size: medium;
}
```

Dissecting a simple CSS stylesheet

A stylesheet is nothing more than a collection of style rules that tells the computer how to format of the various elements in an XML document when it puts them on-screen. All style rules use the same syntax, so even if you've never seen a CSS stylesheet, you can probably guess how to build a basic style rule.

The magic formula for building CSS style rules

CSS stylesheets consist of style rules called *statements*. A statement is made up of a *selector* that specifies which elements the statement applies to and a *declaration* that specifies which style properties to apply. The declaration includes a style property name and a value. The syntax looks like this:

```
selector {declaration}
```

Here's an example of a CSS statement from the `books.css` stylesheet:

```
books { background-color: gray;}
```

`books` is the selector, and the declaration includes `background-color`, a formatting property, and `gray`, the value of this formatting property.

Some of the declarations from our `books` stylesheet include these:

✔ `{background-repeat: no-repeat; background-position: 80% 10px;}`

This declaration displays the `books` element content on a page with a background image that appears only once — and shows up on-screen at a specific position: 80 percent of the page width from the left side of the page and 10 pixels down from the top of the page. This positions a graphic on our page — without using any HTML.

✔ `{font-family: Verdana, Geneva, Arial, Helvetica, sans-serif;}`

This instruction tells the computer to display the `books` element text content in a sans-serif font such as Verdana.

✔ `{margin-bottom: 20px; margin-top: 15px;}`

Here, the instruction says to display each `book` element with a 15-pixel margin at the top and a 20-pixel margin at the bottom.

✔ `{padding: 2px;}`

The specification creates 2 pixels of space in each direction around the content of the `author`, `publisher`, `price`, `contentType`, `format`, and `isbn` elements.

All specific CSS properties — and the values they can take — are predefined in the CSS1 and CSS2 specifications. The hardest part of learning CSS is remembering specific property names and their values.

A quick note about another important CSS term: *inheritance.* When you set style rules (as we did for the `books` and `book` elements) — and specify margins, background color, font, and text color — you don't have to set them again for every other element. When you create a style rule for an element, any other elements it contains are also subject to that style rule. Cool, eh? Just put together a whole bunch of selectors and declarations, and poof! — you have a stylesheet.

In our example, the `books` element is the root element that contains all other elements inside it — so the style rule is *inherited* by all other elements it contains.

Combining declarations

You can combine declarations in a style rule to include a collection of property-and-value combinations in a single selector. The syntax for this neat trick is to separate your *property: value* combinations with semicolons, as we did in most of our style rules, including this one:

```
title {
  display:block;
  color: Maroon;
  font-size: medium;
}
```

Efficiency is good: Combining selectors and declarations

What if you want to assign the same style rule to two different elements? Well, you *could* retype the declaration or cut and paste it. But then, if you change one instance of that declaration, you must make the same change in each and every selector where that declaration appears. It's much easier to simply apply one declaration to several selectors. To do so, simply list all your selectors separated by commas, as in

```
selector, selector . . . {declaration}
```

Our sample stylesheet combines selectors this way in a style rule:

```
author, publisher, price, contentType, format, isbn {
  display: block;
  background-color: #ffe4c4;
  font-size: x-small;
  padding: 2px;
}
```

Using a CSS editor

You can make it easy for yourself and learn CSS at the same time by using an excellent CSS editor such as Nick Bradury's TopStyle Pro, available for purchase at www.bradsoft. com/topstyle/. TopStyle Pro includes a split-screen view that allows you to create a stylesheet and immediately see the effects of your styles applied to the preview file that you selected. For example, you can choose an XML file for your preview file while you create a CSS stylesheet in TopStyle Pro. You know the results of your style rules instantaneously and without leaving TopStyle Pro. This sidebar includes a shot of the TopStyle Pro workspace for the books.xml file and the books.css stylesheet.

TopStyle Pro includes many additional features to make it as simple as possible to create valid CSS for your HTML, XHTML, and XML files. You can, for example,

✔ Check your CSS syntax in multiple browsers.

✔ Convert HTML to XHTML with TopStyle's integration with another software product, HTML Tidy.

✔ Upgrade any deprecated HTML presentation tags, such as font tags, to CSS specs.

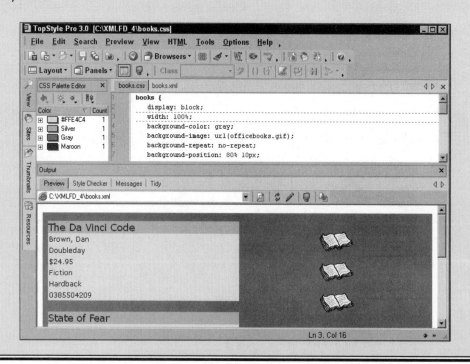

Note that this rule includes another `background-color` declaration — otherwise, these elements would inherit the background color of the `books` element.

Variations on the magic: Selector specifications

You can also apply specific styles when elements occur in a particular order. For example, you could create a style that applies to the `dog` element only when it follows the `cat` element. To do this just add a space between the element names and use them both as the selector, like so:

```
cat dog {color: teal}
```

That space between the element names tells the application processing the stylesheet to look for `cat` tags followed by `dog` tags. If those tags don't appear in that specific order, the style rule doesn't apply to the `dog` element.

The example in the previous paragraph is just one of the many variations on the selector portion of the magic formula. You can link selectors to different elements based on attribute values, context, type, parent–child relationships, and a variety of other options.

The specifics of selectors are too detailed to discuss here, but they are covered brilliantly in the CSS1 specification at

```
www.w3.org/TR/REC-CSS1
```

and the CSS2 specification at

```
www.w3.org/TR/REC-CSS2
```

Meanwhile, if you want a handy tool for creating and/or modifying a CSS stylesheet, check out the "Using a CSS editor" sidebar in this section.

Punctuating CSS rules

Punctuation plays a large role (one your grade-school grammar teacher probably never imagined) when you're creating CSS style rules. If you accidentally use a colon instead of a semicolon to separate *property: value* pairs in a declaration, your stylesheet will break. Table 7-1 provides a short-but-helpful guide to punctuating CSS properly.

Table 7-1		Punctuation in CSS
Character	*Name*	*What It Does*
	Space	Specifies that an element must appear after the other element for the rule to apply
,	Comma	Separates multiple selectors in a style rule
;	Semicolon	Separates multiple property/value combinations in a style rule
:	Colon	Separates a property from its value in a declaration

Linking CSS and XML

After you've built some stylesheets, the next step is to use them with XML. This process is pretty easy, but the method varies between XML and XHTML.

To reference a CSS stylesheet in an XML document, use a processing instruction that takes this format:

```
<?xml-stylesheet href="url" type="text/css"?>
```

For `books.xml`, we added this processing instruction as the line following the XML declaration:

```
<?xml-stylesheet type="text/css" href="books.css"?>
```

To reference a CSS stylesheet in an HTML or an XHTML document, use a *link element* that takes this format:

```
<link href="url" rel="stylesheet" type="text/css">
```

Listings 7-1 (the XML document) and 7-2 (the CSS document) are on the download page for this book at `www.dummies.com/go/xmlfd4e`. To see the CSS stylesheet from Listing 7-2 applied to the `books` XML document, save both listings in the same directory.

W3C devotes an entire recommendation to governing how stylesheets link to XML documents. Check it out at

```
www.w3.org/TR/xml-stylesheet
```

Adding CSS to XSLT

Just because CSS and XSL (including XSLT and XSL-FO) are competing technologies doesn't mean you have to choose one or the other to use forever-
more. CSS and XSL play well together — so well, in fact, that one of the most
powerful uses for *both* style mechanisms involves using them in tandem.

XSL (eXtensible Stylesheet Language) has two primary purposes: as XSL-FO,
to apply style to XML documents, and as XSLT, to convert documents written
according to one DTD or schema to documents that use another DTD or
schema. Many XML developers use the transformation side of XSL — XSLT —
to transform documents that were written using any XML vocabulary into
authentic XHTML documents.

If you take this approach, you can style your newly transformed XHTML documents with CSS for display on the Web. By using XSLT to convert XML documents to XHTML and then using CSS to control the display of the resulting
XHTML, you can use the power of XML for data storage, yet still deliver content to users through standard Web browsers. What's not to like?

As we've mentioned just a few times already — okay, maybe more than a
few — you can validate your XML documents with DTDs or schemas. In
Chapter 8, you'll learn all the details about creating and using DTDs for
validation.

Part III
Building in Validation with DTDs and Schemas

The 5th Wave   By Rich Tennant

"Can't I just give you riches or something?"

In this part. . .

Here's where you get a line on what formal descriptions for XML documents (known as DTDs and XML
Schemas) do, as well as why (and when) they can be
handy. Here's where the contents of Part II (all that good
stuff about XML document structures) can get down to
work. In Chapter 8, you find out how to read a DTD that
describes an XML document — as well as how to use that
information to build XML documents. Chapter 9 follows
up with a look at creating XML document descriptions by
using an "all-XML" approach: XML Schema — both the
application and the product of the application.

Chapter 10 explains how to build a custom XML Schema,
step by step. You get the goods on creating an XML
Schema in Word 2003 and using it to create new XML documents. In Chapter 11, you start modifying XML Schema
to meet your data and document needs — and you get a
handle on a crucial XML concept: namespaces.

Chapter 8

Understanding and Using DTDs

● ●

In This Chapter

▶ Defining DTDs

▶ Knowing when and why to use a DTD

▶ Using an XML prolog

▶ Exploring an XML DTD

▶ Declaring elements and their attributes

▶ Declaring an entity

▶ Noting notations

▶ Including internal and external DTDs

▶ Choosing between internal and external DTDs

● ●

*L*et's face it: What makes a document different from a useless pile of characters is consistency. To get that benefit, you declare a DOCTYPE (document type) in your XML document — in effect, telling it to invoke a Document Type Definition (DTD) you've prepared. The DTD defines the rules of the game for your document. In general, you use DTDs to add structure and logic, and to make it easier to ensure that all required elements and attributes are present — in the right order — in your XML document. Okay, DTDs aren't absolutely necessary when you're creating an XML document — but understanding what they are and how they work can reduce hassle by keeping the document consistent.

Using a DTD properly ensures that your document will be *valid* — that is, one that follows the rules set out in the DTD. Being valid isn't the same thing as being well formed (though a document that is both is a joy to behold). Chapter 5 outlines what it takes for an XML document to be well formed; this chapter covers creating an XML document that's valid when interpreted according to the rules defined in a specific DTD.

When you use DTDs, please understand that they define a set of rules for the documents that they govern — and rules are rules. If you break the rules in any DTDs that your XML documents invoke, those documents will fail to validate properly — and they may therefore be unusable. That's because some document processors quit processing when they find an error in syntax or structure. Okay, so. . . .

What's a DTD?

A *Document Type Definition* (DTD) is a set of rules that defines the elements and their attributes for an XML document. Any XML document that invokes that DTD gets the same treatment. You could say that a DTD defines the "grammar" for an XML document, because it tells applications — and the people using them — what each element means and how to use it. In essence, grammar is a set of rules that govern the way we speak and write a language. Well, when you use a DTD, you automatically become subject to a bunch of rules that tell you how to write — markup, that is.

DTDs consist of declarations for elements and their attributes. DTDs are really nothing new; in techno years, they're pretty darn old. Originally, DTDs were created as part of the Standard Generalized Markup Language (SGML) — XML's parent.

DTDs aren't actually required, because — unlike SGML — XML follows strict rules of construction. This enables XML processors to read a well-formed document and *infer* the rules that govern the document. The processors do this bit of magic by building a tree of all elements and their children and then drawing conclusions from the patterns in which elements occur. It's kind of like drawing your family tree by knowing who's related to whom and how.

Table 8-1 deciphers some of the terms you need as you get farther into DTDs in this chapter.

Table 8-1	DTD Lingo	
Term	*Example*	*What It Does*
XML declaration	`<?xml version="1.0" encoding="UTF-8" standalone="yes"?>`	Tells the processor which version of XML to use
Document type (DOCTYPE) declaration	`<!DOCTYPE Root-Element SYSTEM "filename.dtd">`	Tells the processor where a DTD is located
Element type declaration	`<!ELEMENT Name (#PCDATA)>`	Defines an element type
Attribute-list declaration	`<!ATTLIST Element-Name Name Datatype Default>`	Defines a name, datatype, and default value (if any) for each attribute associated with an element
Entity declaration	`<!ENTITY Entity-Name "text">`	Defines a set of information that can be referred to by name as an entity

Term	Example	What It Does
Notation declaration	`<!NOTATION NameSystem "externalID">`	Associates a notation name with information that can help find an external program to interpret that notation (used to accommodate data and executables within XML documents that XML processors themselves can't handle directly)

When to use a DTD

XML doesn't require you to use a DTD (though it's often a good idea to use one), so the first step in including DTDs in a document is to decide whether you want to jump off that particular bridge.

Why would you want to use a DTD? Well, here are several reasons:

- ✔ **To create and manage** large sets of documents for your company. DTDs allow you to create and maintain rules that all documents must follow.

- ✔ **To define clearly** what markup may be used in certain documents and how markup should be sequenced. DTDs make document rules explicit.

- ✔ **To provide a common frame of reference** for documents that many users can share. Big-name XML applications such as XPath have their own associated DTDs.

Therefore, when it comes to working with DTDs, standardization and control are what they're all about!

When NOT to use a DTD

Why might you want to scrap this chapter and create an XML document without a formal description? Well, sheer practicality. You may not need to use a DTD if:

- ✔ You're working with only one or a few small documents. Remember why you create DTDs: to make your life easier. If a DTD is bigger than the document that it describes, you may be wasting your time.

- ✔ You're using a nonvalidating processor to handle your XML documents. If the processor checks only for well-formedness, you don't need an external DTD.

In general, do what works. Let the XML documents or data that you work with drive you toward or away from creating formal document descriptions. Our experience has been that any application that involves more than a one-time or throwaway document or data collection is worthy of its own formal description (or at least, customization or outright use of an existing standard DTD). Because XML's rules let you skip the document description if you like, you may certainly decide otherwise.

Inspecting the XML Prolog

In order to use a DTD with your XML document, you need to add a DOCTYPE declaration to your document — and the XML prolog is where you put it.

The *XML prolog* is the first thing that a processor — or human eye, for that matter — sees in an XML document. You place it at the top of your XML document, and it describes the document's content and structure.

An XML prolog may include the following items:

- ✔ XML declaration
- ✔ DOCTYPE declaration
- ✔ Comments
- ✔ Processing instructions
- ✔ White space

Notice the phrase *may include.* An XML prolog doesn't have to include any of that information — but Listing 8-1 shows an XML prolog that does.

Listing 8-1:   An XML Prolog

```
<!-- Beginning of Prolog -->
<?xml version="1.0" encoding="UTF-8" standalone="no"?>
<!DOCTYPE books SYSTEM "bookstore.dtd">
<!-- End of Prolog -->
<!-- Beginning of Document Body -->
<books>
. ..
</books>
<!-- End of Document Body -->
```

Take a second to look at what we include in the prolog:

✔ The first line is the XML declaration.

✔ The second line invokes a specific `DOCTYPE` declaration named `books`.

✔ The next two lines are comments that denote the end of the prolog and the beginning of the document proper.

Examining the XML declaration

Generally speaking, a *declaration* is markup that tells an XML processor what to do. Declarations don't add structure or define document elements. Instead, they provide instructions for a processor, such as what type of document to process and what standards to use.

As you discover in Chapter 5, the XML declaration can include `version`, `encoding`, and/or `standalone` attributes:

```
<?xml version="1.0" encoding="UTF-8" standalone="no"?>
```

This statement tells the processor some essential stuff:

✔ This is an XML document.

✔ The version of XML is XML 1.0.

✔ The character encoding is UTF-8.

✔ An external document may be needed to complete the document content (`standalone="no"`).

DTDs can be internal (included within an XML document itself) or a separate external document. If we include a `standalone` attribute in our XML declaration, `standalone="yes"` implies that the document doesn't rely on markup declarations defined in an external document — such as an external DTD — but could include an internal DTD. If `standalone` is set to equal `"no"`, or if you don't include a `standalone` attribute, it leaves the issue unresolved — translation, it may or may not reference one or more external DTDs.

If you're not sure whether or not to include a `standalone` attribute, leave it out. The default value is `standalone="no"`, so the XML processor will load whatever documents it needs.

Discovering the DOCTYPE

The *document type (*DOCTYPE*) declaration* is markup that tells the processor where it can find a specific DTD. In other words, a DOCTYPE declaration links an XML document to a corresponding DTD. Please also note that the DOCTYPE declaration is an SGML construct and, therefore, follows SGML syntax and not XML syntax. This explains why only some values appear in quotes in this statement.

While you read this chapter, don't confuse document type (DOCTYPE) declarations with Document Type Definitions (DTDs). The DOCTYPE declaration is the *locator* — it simply tells the processor where to find the DTD.

Here's the basic markup of a DOCTYPE declaration:

```
<!DOCTYPE books SYSTEM "bookstore.dtd">
```

<!DOCTYPE marks the start of the DOCTYPE declaration. books is the name of the DTD used. SYSTEM "bookstore.dtd" tells the processor to fetch an external document — in this case, a file named bookstore.dtd.

In the preceding example, bookstore.dtd is a relative Uniform Resource Identifier (URI). URIs are basically filenames — in effect, locations. bookstore.dtd points to an external DTD that resides in the same folder as the XML document but not in the same document. We delve into how to reference external DTDs in the "Calling a DTD" section later in this chapter. (**Hint:** You might notice the resemblance between the terms *URL* and *URI*. No accident: A URL is a type of URI.)

Understanding comments

Comments — use them and read them! An author (yes, we mean you) can use comments to include text that explains a document better (humans love that sort of thing) without that text being displayed — or even processed. The syntax — the same as for HTML comments, because HTML is built on SGML — looks like this:

```
<!-- comment text -->
```

Comments are like an owner's manual; they can help you find your way through a document when something breaks down or when you need to make changes. Use them liberally, but know why and how to use them!

As long as you follow the correct format, comments remain visible only when you're viewing the markup itself. If you don't follow the correct format, though, parts of your comments may show up when users view your document ,or your document may not display correctly. The correct format is:

```
<!-- Include your comment here -->
```

You have two rules to live by when you're using comments:

- ✔ Never nest a comment inside another element.

- ✔ Never include - (hyphen) or – (double hyphen) *within* the comment text. Those characters might confuse processors into thinking that you're closing the comment — which means they'd end up treating the remaining comment content as a syntax error!

Processing instructions

Using comments enables you to leave human-style instructions (that is, comments) addressed to someone who reads the markup without disrupting the document's structure. *Processing instructions* are like comments addressed to machines; they provide a way to send instructions to computer programs or applications.

All processing instructions follow this format:

```
<?name data?>
```

A common example of a processing instruction in XML documents is a reference to stylesheets. For example, in the following processing instruction

```
<?xml:stylesheet type="text/css" href="bookstore.css"?>
```

the name is xml:stylesheet, and the data is type="text/css" and href="bookstore.css". If the processor recognizes the name, the data is used — otherwise, it's ignored.

All processing instructions must begin with <? and end with ?>.

How about that white space?

Any document has places where writing is and places where writing isn't — but in an XML document, many of the places that look blank are actually *white space* — nonprinting characters such as spaces, tabs, carriage returns, or line feeds. The XML specification allows you to add white space outside markup; it's ignored when the document is processed.

Think of it this way: If we wrote a book without paragraph breaks, readers would give up reading after a few pages. A line of white space between paragraphs (that is, a break) is easier on the eyes. The same logic applies to XML documents. When you write markup, consider adding a line of white space between sections. That way, when someone reads your XML document, he or she can read it without a hitch.

Some elements treat white space in a special way. Including white space *outside* XML elements is safe, but do your homework before you add extra white space *inside* an element. If you find yourself intrigued by the use of white space, read up on the `xml:space` attribute, which lets applications know when white space matters and when it doesn't. For more information on the `xml:space` attribute, check out the W3C site at `www.w3.org/TR/REC-xml#sec-white-space`.

The preceding section on the XML prolog refers to your XML document — not to a DTD. A DTD may include an XML declaration and comments, but those are optional — and a DTD is not required to have a prolog.

Reading a DTD

Even if you don't plan to create your own DTDs from scratch, knowing how to read them is helpful. In theory — and we hope in practice — XML (and DTDs) should be easy to read and understand. You should be able to look at a DTD, list all elements and their attributes, and understand how and when to use those elements and attributes.

Create a document tree to help you better understand the hierarchy of document elements. A document tree begins with one root element. All other elements are children of (in other words, nest within) that root element.

In the following sections, we dissect the bookstore DTD, shown in Listing 8-2. You need to get your mind around all the pieces and parts of a DTD before you try to create one yourself. (If you already recognize all the pieces of a DTD, feel free to move on over to Chapter 9 to find out more about XML schemas.)

DTDs aren't written in XML — they're written in SGML and follow SGML rules. The DTD terms must be used exactly as written below; in other words, `!ELEMENT`, `!ATTLIST`, `#REQUIRED`, `#PCDATA`, and `EMPTY` must all be capitalized. If you change the case, your DTD won't work.

Listing 8-2: The bookstore DTD, External Version

```
<?xml version="1.0" encoding="UTF-8"?>
<!ELEMENT books (book+, totalCost, customer)>
<!ELEMENT book (bookInfo, salesInfo)>
<!ATTLIST book contentType (Fiction | Nonfiction) #REQUIRED format (Hardback |
          Paperback) #REQUIRED>
```

```
<!ELEMENT bookInfo (title, author, publisher, isbn)>
<!ELEMENT title (#PCDATA)>
<!ELEMENT author (#PCDATA)>
<!ELEMENT publisher (#PCDATA)>
<!ELEMENT isbn (#PCDATA)>
<!ELEMENT salesInfo (price, itemNumber, date, source, shipping, cost)>
<!ELEMENT price (#PCDATA)>
<!ATTLIST price priceType (Retail | Wholesale) #REQUIRED>
<!ELEMENT itemNumber (#PCDATA)>
<!ELEMENT date (#PCDATA)>
<!ELEMENT source EMPTY>
<!ATTLIST source sourceType (Retail | Wholesale) #REQUIRED>
<!ELEMENT shipping (#PCDATA)>
<!ELEMENT cost (#PCDATA)>
<!ELEMENT totalCost (#PCDATA)>
<!ELEMENT customer (custNumber, lastName, firstName, address, city, state, zip,
          phone, email)>
<!ATTLIST customer custType (newRetail | prevRetail | newWholesale |
          prevWholesale) #REQUIRED>
<!ELEMENT custNumber (#PCDATA)>
<!ELEMENT lastName (#PCDATA)>
<!ELEMENT firstName (#PCDATA)>
<!ELEMENT address (#PCDATA)>
<!ELEMENT city (#PCDATA)>
<!ELEMENT state (#PCDATA)>
<!ELEMENT zip (#PCDATA)>
<!ELEMENT phone (#PCDATA)>
<!ELEMENT email (#PCDATA)>
```

Using Element Declarations

Because the heart of an XML document is made up of its elements, you must
define them in your DTD. To do so, you use *element type declarations*.
Element type declarations are important because they not only name your
elements, but also define any *children* (nested elements) that an element
might have.

We start with the root element for a document based on our example DTD:

```
<books>
. . .
</books>
```

All other elements occur inside the root (if they're not more deeply nested),
and all other elements relate back to the root somehow. Therefore, the root
element is topmost in a document's hierarchy of elements. Part of what
makes XML so great is that the element hierarchy is logical and easy to read
or understand.

In the world of DTDs, elements can be defined to contain four types of content, as listed in Table 8-2.

Table 8-2	Types of Content Found in Elements	
Content Type	*Example*	*What It Means*
ANY	`<!ELEMENT Name ANY>`	Allows any type of element content, either data or element markup information.
EMPTY	`<!ELEMENT Name EMPTY>`	Specifies that an element must not contain any content. (Not as silly as it sounds.)
Mixed content	`<!ELEMENT Name #PCDATA>`	
Or		
	`<!ELEMENT Name (#PCDATA | ChildName)*>`	Allows an element to contain character data or a combination of subelements and character data.
Element content	`<!ELEMENT Name (Child1, Child2)>`	Specifies that an element can contain only subelements, or children.

Perhaps you're wondering what the commas (,) and the pipe bars (|) in the table's examples mean. Stay tuned; we discuss them in an upcoming section ("Adding mixed content").

Using the EMPTY element type and the ANY element type

Sometimes, you may want an element type to remain empty with no content to call its own, so you use an empty element instead of an element with an opening tag and a closing tag. (Check out Chapter 4 to see the proper XML markup for empty elements.) Empty elements are like boxes you put in place but want left empty. To use them, first you have to point them out to the processor — by declaring them. Such a declaration looks like this:

```
<!ELEMENT Name EMPTY>
```

In our example DTD, the `source` element is an empty element:

```
<!ELEMENT source EMPTY>
```

The `source` element does include an attribute (`sourceType`), but it has no content.

If (on the other hand) you want your element to serve as a catch-all box that you can put anything in, you may want to use another type of content specification: `ANY`. If you declare an element to contain `ANY` content, you allow that element type to hold any element or character data. Using the `ANY` content specification creates no structure to speak of, however, so it's rarely used.

Adding mixed content

Mixed content allows elements to contain character data, or character data and child elements. In other words, it allows elements to contain a mixture of information types. Even if an element actually contains only character data, it's still said to contain mixed content.

Keep in mind that mixed content is one of four valid types of element content. (The other three are element content [children], `ANY`, and `EMPTY`.)

The basic structure for a mixed-content element declaration is as follows:

```
<!ELEMENT Name (#PCDATA | Child1 | Child2)*>
```

If the element contains only character data, then the structure looks like this:

```
<!ELEMENT Name #PCDATA>
```

White space is not recognized within parentheses in DTDs. For example, (`#PCDATA`) is the same as (`#PCDATA`).

In the following example, we take some liberties with our basic example DTD and fiddle with the declaration for the `author` element. The string `<!ELEMENT` begins the declaration; `author` is the element name.

```
<!ELEMENT author (#PCDATA | publisher )*>
```

Including `#PCDATA` means that the element may contain *parsed character data,* which is text that the document processor actually looks at and interprets to display both content and markup. (That's what the `PC` part is referring to — *parsed character.*) For example, entity references in the character data are replaced with their entity values. Whenever you want your element to contain parsed character data, use the `#PCDATA` keyword. If you simply want an element to contain character data with no markup, use (`#CDATA`) by itself for the content definition part.

What does | signify? In this example, | means that the author element may contain parsed character data *or* a publisher element. The purpose of mixed content is to enable the author to specify an element that may contain both text and other elements.

With mixed content, you can't control the order of the elements or how many times they appear. In effect, you give up control over some features of document structure when you use mixed-content models.

In the preceding example, you also find the element name publisher. This means that the element named publisher may nest within the parent element author. The * in the preceding markup is required in mixed-content element type declarations that contain both text and elements. It means that any number of the preceding group can appear — in other words, #PCDATA **and/or** any number of the nested elements listed. See the following section for more information on symbols in declarations.

You can work with mixed content in one of two ways:

- Use only parsed character data
- Allow an element to contain both text and other elements (In that case, don't forget the asterisk!)

Using element content models

An *element content model* describes the child elements that an element can contain. The basic structure is

```
<!ELEMENT Name (childName)>
```

which states that the element *Name* must contain the *childName* element.

In the following example, as with all element declarations, !ELEMENT begins the declaration. Then the element receives its name, books. Next comes the content specification, which states that books may have a child, book. The + is an occurrence indicator that states the book element must occur at least once — but also that it can be used as many times as needed. For clarity, the + is also called the *one or more times* occurrence indicator.

```
<!ELEMENT books (book+)>
```

The element content model uses occurrence indicators to control the order and number of times that elements can occur. Take a look at Table 8-3.

Table 8-3	Occurrence Indicators	
Symbol	*Example*	*What It Means*
, (comma)	`<!ELEMENT customer (custNumber, lastName, firstName, address, city, state, zip, phone, email)>`	All child elements listed must be used in the sequence shown.
| (pipe bar)	`<!ELEMENT books (book1 | book2)>`	Either the `book1` element or the `book2` element may occur inside `books`.
(No symbol)	`<!ELEMENT books (book)>`	Indicates that a single occurrence of `book` must occur inside `books`.
+ (plus sign)	`<!ELEMENT books (book+)>`	The `book` child element must be used one or more times inside `books`.
* (asterisk)	`<!ELEMENT books (book*)>`	The `book` element may be used zero or more times within `books`.
? (question mark)	`<!ELEMENT books (book?)>`	The `book` element may be used once or not at all within `books`.

Apply what you just read to our example. You use the , (comma) occurrence indicator to imply sequence when listing elements. The example DTD uses the following content model for the `customer` element:

```
<!ELEMENT customer (custNumber, lastName, firstName, address, city, state, zip,
          phone, email)>
```

The preceding declaration means that `custNumber` must precede `lastName`, which must precede the `firstName` element, and so on when nested within a parent `customer` element.

Declaring Attributes

In the "Using Element Declarations" section earlier in this chapter, you found out how to declare an element. In this section, you need to define an element's better half: its attributes. In techie terms, you need to include *attribute-list declarations* in your DTD whenever you want elements to use associated attributes. The attribute-list declaration lists all attributes that may be used within a given element and also defines each attribute's type and default value.

The basic format for an attribute-list declaration is:

```
<!ATTLIST element-name attribute-name datatype defaultvalue>
```

The attribute-list declaration begins with the !ATTLIST string, followed by white space. Remember, DTDs are case sensitive, so don't forget to use capital letters. Next come the element name, the associated attribute's name, its type, and a default value. Here's an example:

```
<!ATTLIST customer custType CDATA #REQUIRED>
```

The following list defines the terms that appear in attribute-list declarations:

- **Element name** is the name of the element to which the attribute belongs (customer, in this case).

- **Attribute name** is the name given to the attribute (custType, in this case).

- **Datatype** is one of the following nine kinds of datatype attributes:

  - CDATA, **or character data,** enables the author to include any string of characters that doesn't include the ampersand (&), less-than and greater-than signs (< or >), or quotation marks ("). These four characters may be represented using character entities (&, <, >, or ", respectively).

  - ID creates a unique ID for an attribute that identifies an element. This type is most often used by programs that process a document.

  - IDREF allows the value of an attribute to be the same as the ID of an element somewhere else in the document.

  - IDREFS is just like IDREF, but the value may be made up of multiple IDREFs.

  - ENTITY allows you to use external binary data or unparsed entities. You'll get the scoop on entities in the next section of this chapter.

  - ENTITIES allows you to link multiple entities.

  - NMTOKEN restricts the value of the attribute to any valid XML name.

  - NMTOKENS allows the value of the attribute to be composed of multiple XML names.

  - NOTATION allows you to use a value already specified with a notation declaration in the DTD. (Notations are covered later in this chapter.)

You can also use an enumerated list of values in place of a datatype. An *enumerated list* is an inclusive list of all possible value for an attribute, separated with vertical bars (|). The XML author has a choice! Here's an example:

```
<!ATTLIST price priceType (Retail | Wholesale) #REQUIRED>
```

✔ **Default value** consists of one of the following four options:

- #REQUIRED means you must always include the attribute when the element is used. No specific default value for the attribute can be included in this case, so you must include a value for it in your XML document, like this:

```
<!ATTLIST element-name attribute-name CDATA #REQUIRED>
```

- #IMPLIED means the attribute is optional. The attribute may be used in an element, but no default value is provided if the attribute isn't used. Here's what it looks like:

```
<!ATTLIST element-name attribute-name CDATA #IMPLIED>
```

- #FIXED means the attribute is optional, but if used, the attribute must always take on the default value assigned in the DTD. Thus:

```
<!ATTLIST element-name attribute-name #FIXED "value">
```

- value simply defines a specific value as the default value — end of story. You can use values other than the default value for this attribute — this option just provides a value to be used if none is included in your XML document. In other words, if your XML document includes the element but doesn't include the attribute, the processor assumes that the element has an attribute with the default value. Here's the code that does the job:

```
<!ATTLIST element-name attribute-name CDATA
"default-value">
```

Discovering Entities

Entity declarations are a little trickier than other declarations, but they sure save you time! An *entity declaration* defines an alias for a block of text. You can attach a name to a specific block of text and then insert the whole block by using just one name.

For example, think about how quickly you could include your company's address in different documents that all used the same DTD. Or what if the company moved? If your company address were defined as an entity, you wouldn't have to chase down every document to change the address — that address is centralized, so you can make the change en masse.

An entity declaration in a DTD looks like this:

```
<!ENTITY entityName "replacementText">
```

entityName is the name of the entity and is used to call up the *replacement Text* in your document. Nice, huh? This allows you to take those long footers — which you normally have to type again and again and again — and reference them with one word. No more extraneous typing — almost.

The two main classifications of entities are general entities and parameter entities. A *general entity* is an abbreviation for data that becomes part of the content of an XML document. A *parameter entity* is an abbreviation for data that becomes part of the content of a DTD.

General entities

The XML specification supports two types of general entities: internal and external. *Internal entities* hold their values in the entity declaration, whereas *external entities* point to an external file.

Internal entities

To declare a general internal entity, you must use the following syntax:

```
<!ENTITY entityName "replacementText">
```

or

```
<!ENTITY store1 "River Valley Center">
```

To reference an internal entity anywhere in the text of your XML document, you use an ampersand (&), followed by the entity's name, followed by a semicolon (;), as in &store1;.

Try turning common strings of text, like your company name or a standard copyright disclaimer, into entities.

Five commonly used internal entities are already defined as part of XML for your use and are listed in the following table. You don't have to define these entities in your DTD before you use them in your XML document; you can simply use them.

Entity	Refers To	Symbol
<	Less-than sign	<
>	Greater-than sign	>
&	Ampersand	&
'	Single quotation mark or apostrophe	'
"	Double quotation mark	"

External entities

External entities help you integrate external documents and files into your XML document. In general, you use them in one of two ways:

- **As a mechanism to divide your document into logical pieces.** Rather than creating a single, large, and unwieldy document, such as a book stored in a single document that holds all of the chapters, you can store each chapter in a separate file and use external entities to include those files in a book document whose only job is to bring the chapters together.

- **To reference images, multimedia clips, and other non-XML files.** Before you can include any non-XML file in your document, like a picture of a book cover, you first have to reference it as an external entity.

To declare an external entity, you use the following syntax:

```
<!ENTITY entityName SYSTEM "system-identifier">
```

The *system-identifier* is defined as a URI (or a URL). The most common URI is a filename. You may also use the following syntax to refer to a public identifier not stored on your system (for example, your local computer or the system running your XML application):

```
<!ENTITY entityName PUBLIC "system-identifier">
```

The benefit of using external entities is that they're *re*usable. If you want to use the same arrow image over and over again in a document, you have only to create the entity for it once — and you can reference the entity time and again. Or suppose you have a standard legal disclaimer — for example `"Warning, we can't promise you'll like our books"` — that you want to include at the end of every purchase order. You can save the disclaimer as a separate file, create an external entity that points to it, and then reference that entity at the end of every purchase order.

If you create a general external entity that references a non-XML file, like an image, Word document, or media clip, you can reference that entity only in an attribute value. See the "Understanding Notations" section, later in this chapter, for more information.

General entity references can be pretty handy, but they are subject to three important limitations:

- ✔ **You can't use an entity before you define it.** No general entity reference may occur in a document until it's been declared and defined in the document's DTD. To follow good DTD practices, always declare entities at the beginning of the DTD document.

- ✔ **Your entity references have to do something.** In other words, *circular entity references* — when an entity declaration mentions a second entity, and the second entity declaration mentions the first — just don't work. The following example is an example of a circular reference:

```
<!ENTITY loc "Library of Congress &US;">
<!ENTITY US "&loc; United States">
```

The problem with this pair of declarations is that neither one defines a plain, simple string by itself. Each declaration depends on the other, yet neither is completely defined — which makes both machines and people crazy. Avoid this error in your designs by all means possible!

- ✔ **The entity has to refer to data that's in the XML document.** In other words, you can't use entities as shortcuts to writing the DTD. General entity references can't handle text that is only part of a DTD (and not used as part of the XML document's content). The reason for this rule is that you might be tempted to abbreviate common DTD-reserved words, such as (#PCDATA), as in this example:

```
<!ENTITY PCD "(#PCDATA)">
<!ELEMENT Title &PCD;>
...
<!ELEMENT Item &PCD;>
```

DTDs do allow the use of another kind of entity — a parameter entity, which can define substitutable text usable inside DTDs themselves. More about this handy little item in the next section.

Parameter entities

A *parameter entity* is an entity that is created specifically for the purpose of helping you use shortcuts when you write a DTD. They don't refer to content in XML documents at all.

Similar to general entities, parameter entities may also be internal or external.

Internal entities

Internal parameter entities work well to eliminate the need to repeat commonly used element and attribute declarations. Like other kinds of entities, the parameter entity works like a gigantic = sign that says, "When I use this markup, **please replace it with** that markup."

In general, if you know that you need to repeat complex markup more than twice in a DTD, consider taking time out to create a parameter entity so you can use the entity reference instead of repeating the markup. This option ultimately simplifies document maintenance, not just for you, but also for anyone else who uses the DTD after you do.

As with general entities, parameter entities must be declared before they can be used. We hope that's intuitive: Without a definition, an XML parser can't know what to substitute for the *%name*; symbol when it appears in a DTD.

Here's the general syntax for an internal parameter entity declaration:

```
<!ENTITY % entityName "replacementText">
```

As with general entity references, *entityName* represents the name of the entity, and *replacementText* represents the text that replaces that name each time it appears as a parameter entity.

Unlike general entity references, parameter entities take the form *%name*; to reference the entity when you use it in the DTD.

External entities

External parameter entities work well for using parts of DTDs with more flexibility: You can use external parameter entities to carve DTDs into bite-size bits of declarations that are easy to read and manipulate. You can then save each bit in a separate file and create a single parameter entity in the master DTD that points to each individual file. Using parameter entities in this way lets you mix and match meaningful pieces of DTD markup in various XML projects. Just customize the DTDs, changing specific markup as needed.

These kinds of parameter entities are called *external parameter entity references* because they refer to information that's external to the DTD in which they appear. Thus, if you created three DTD files named book.dtd, sales.dtd, and customer.dtd, respectively, you could use the following markup to create a single DTD to combine their contents:

```
<-- Master DTD for book information, sales data,
    and customer information -->
<!ENTITY % Bks   SYSTEM "book.dtd">
<!ENTITY % Sls SYSTEM "sales.dtd">
<!ENTITY % Cust SYSTEM "customer.dtd">
%Bks;
%Sls;
%Cust;
```

Understanding Notations

General external entities can be one of two types: parsed entities or unparsed entities. If they contain text or XML, they are usually used as *parsed entities* — the XML parser analyzes them as it goes through an XML document. General external entities that are bypassed by the XML parser are called *unparsed entities*. The content of an unparsed entity can be anything — an image file, for example, or an audio clip, Flash animation, Microsoft Word 2003 file — anything the parser normally ignores.

When the XML parser identifies non-XML data, the parser returns control over that data back to whatever application called the parser. As with modern Web browsers, this standard operating procedure provides an opportunity to call a helper module or plug-in that knows how to handle this special non-XML data so that the special data can be rendered or displayed within the overall XML document.

All unparsed entities are general entities. Unparsed entities can only become part of an XML document, not part of a DTD. Parameter entities are always parsed entities. Parameter entities can only become part of a DTD.

To use unparsed entities you must use an entity declaration, a notation declaration, and an attribute declaration. The format for the unparsed entity declaration is:

```
<!ENTITY entityName SYSTEM "entity.url" NDATA id>
```

You declare an unparsed entity in a DTD, but it adds its content within an XML document.

The `entityName` is the abbreviation for the unparsed entity, `entity.url` gives the location of the file, and `id` is the notation type name that's used to specify the unparsed entity. For example, if you wanted to include a company logo in an XML document, you could use this entity declaration in your DTD:

```
<!ENTITY logo SYSTEM "logo.gif" NDATA gif>
```

The inclusion of the NDATA keyword in the declaration, followed by a notation type name, clues the parser into what's going on — and allows the application to invoke the right kind of help.

Then you must also create a <!NOTATION declaration to identify the NDATA type and provide the application with the necessary identification to call the correct helper or plug-in. A notation declaration represents a set of rules that describes how an identifiable class of non-XML data behaves, which is usually different from how XML data behaves.

The format for a notation declaration is:

```
<!NOTATION id SYSTEM contentType>
```

For example, a notation for your logo might look like this:

```
<!NOTATION gif SYSTEM "image/gif">
```

SYSTEM is an SGML and XML keyword that indicates an entity appears in a URL or URI. PUBLIC indicates that a standard name for an entity is used. You can use either SYSTEM or PUBLIC in an external entity declaration.

In order to use an unparsed entity in your XML document, you must use it as an attribute, so first add an element declaration to the DTD for the element that contains the attribute (in this case, the image element):

```
<!ELEMENT image EMPTY>
```

Then add an attribute declaration for the attribute, named source in this case:

```
<!ATTLIST image source ENTITY #REQUIRED>
```

At last you can use the unparsed entity in your XML document! (Whew! But it saves you work later. Honest.)

```
<book>
<image source="logo"/>
...
</book>
```

Calling a DTD

DTDs come in two flavors: internal and external. Internal DTDs are entirely contained in the XML prolog of an XML document. External DTDs are contained in an external file and are referenced in the DOCTYPE declaration of an XML document.

Internal DTDs

If your DTD is short and simple, and you don't need to include it in a large group of XML documents, you may want to use it as an internal DTD.

To add an internal DTD to your XML document, you include it within the DOCTYPE declaration, like this:

```
<!DOCTYPE rootElement [
... the entire DTD goes here ...
]
```

For the bookstore DTD, our root element is books, so our XML document with an internal DTD would have a format like this:

```
<?xml version="1.0" encoding="UTF-8"?>
<!DOCTYPE books [
<!ELEMENT books (book+, totalCost, customer)>
<!ELEMENT book (bookInfo, salesInfo)>
...
]
<books>
 <book contentType="Fiction" format="Hardback">
  <bookInfo>
...
```

Because we're planning to use the bookstore DTD for a large group of XML documents, we chose to use an external DTD instead, as discussed in the following section.

External DTDs

Using external DTDs is a great idea, because you can then share a single DTD among any group of XML documents. As long as all those documents use the markup described in the DTD, you can manage that markup by operating on a single, common DTD instead of having to slog through changing the same prolog information over and over across an entire set of XML documents.

To use an external DTD with an XML document, simply reference the external DTD in the DOCTYPE declaration in the XML prolog of your XML document.

As detailed earlier in this chapter, the format for a DOCTYPE declaration is:

```
<!DOCTYPE rootElement SYSTEM dtd.url>
```

The *rootElement* is the name of the root element in your XML document, and *dtd.url* is the location of the external DTD that you're using to validate the XML document.

To add bookstore.dtd as an external DTD in our bookstore.xml file, we do the following:

```
<?xml version="1.0" encoding="UTF-8" standalone="no"?>
<!DOCTYPE books SYSTEM "bookstore.dtd">
<books>
...
```

In this case, the URL is simply the file name, because the XML document and the DTD are in the same folder. If they aren't in the same folder, make sure the URL uses the correct file path to the location of the DTD.

When to use an internal or external DTD

Obviously, there are advantages and disadvantages to both internal and external DTDs. Your choice depends entirely on the form that works best for your XML document needs.

Formally, internal and external DTDs are called *internal* and *external subsets*. These two approaches follow the same markup structure but have some key differences, such as where they live. Sometimes, the best approach is to combine internal and external DTD subsets.

The inside view: Internal DTD subsets

The most important drawback to using internal DTDs is that only the document that contains them can use them. When you create an internal DTD, you're essentially keeping all the information in one single document. However, internal DTDs have a few benefits, as follows:

- ✔ A single file processes faster than multiple files.

- ✔ Validity and well-formedness are kept in the same place. Any processor can process your document without looking elsewhere.

- ✔ You can use internal DTDs on a local system without connecting to the Internet — you can take that file on the plane and run it on a laptop!

Calling for outside support: Referencing external DTDs

Although internal DTDs are quicker, easier, and more mobile, we don't necessarily recommend them over external DTDs. Compared with internal DTDs, external DTDs have many advantages:

- ✔ **They're recyclable.** You can use one DTD file for multiple documents. (For internal DTDs, there's one in every file.)

- ✔ **They're versatile.** Your external DTD can simply be a public one already created by someone else. (Internal DTDs are totally private and isolated.)

✔ **They're easy to change.** Editing an external DTD can be a breeze when you need to change one item found in multiple documents. (You can only edit internal DTDs one at a time.)

✔ **They're timesavers.** Because you can manage and maintain external DTDs in single, discrete documents (rather than multiple instances of the same in-line SGML markup in multiple XML documents), there's less work involved in keeping external DTDs up-to-date than internal ones.

Two are sometimes better than one

Sometimes, you need a large, complex external DTD; other times, you not only need a monster DTD, but you also want to define more information internally. We find that more often than not, authors combine internal and external DTDs to get the most from their XML document structure.

You already know how to read internal and external DTDs. Combining DTDs isn't much different. Live by these two major rules when mixing these two types of DTDs:

✔ An XML processor always reads the internal subset first. Therefore, the internal DTD takes precedence.

✔ Entities declared in the internal subset can be referenced in the external subset.

When you've had some practice at mastering all the ins and outs of using DTDs for validation, you can add some more tools to your kit. Thus, Chapter 9 introduces another approach to validation: using XML Schemas.

Chapter 9

Understanding and Using XML Schema

*A*lthough you can use any old markup to describe your XML documents, chances are any document you come up with will be more valuable if it includes a structure that the business solution can actually work with. For example, Office 2003 uses schemas for XML documents, so if your business uses Office 2003, XML Schemas are a good choice for validating your XML documents.

An XML Schema (created according to the XML Schema specification) defines rules for the structure and content of an XML document. Schemas specify the overall structure of an XML document and identify all of the components of the XML document. Like documents that adhere to Document Type Definitions (DTDs, covered in Chapter 8), documents that adhere to an XML schema are considered *valid documents*.

A valid document is not the same as a well-formed document. All XML documents must follow certain standards to be considered well formed — they must (for openers) contain a root element and follow proper syntax, and all additional elements must be nested. (We cover well-formed documents in Chapters 4 and 5).

A well-formed XML document is the first requirement for a valid XML document. On the other hand, not all XML documents have to be valid. A document is considered valid if it adheres to the rules of a schema — or to a DTD, for that matter. As long as you have a well-formed document, you don't have to worry about validity unless the application that is ultimately going to process your document requires that the document be valid. See Chapters 4 and 5 for more details on requirements for well-formed and valid XML documents.

If you're building an XML document according to a schema, you probably want it to be valid. When you follow the rules of a well-built schema, it can help you construct a document that's valid *and* well made.

What's an XML Schema?

You build an XML Schema document (just call it a *schema* for ease of both typing and reading) according to the rules of the XML Schema specification defined by the World Wide Web Consortium (W3C).

A schema lays down the rules a valid XML document should follow to ensure that the information contained in the XML document is in the right form. In effect, the schema acts like a template, specifying the form that the XML document must take. When a program processes an XML document written against a schema, it validates (compares and checks) the document against the schema.

You can, of course, build schema documents from scratch, but don't forget that you can also *reuse* schemas — either the ones you've created or third-party schemas that are available (for example) from industry groups. In Chapter 11, you look in on the process of modifying an existing schema.

As you see a bit later in the chapter, the XML Schema specification is nothing more than a guide to creating an XML document that defines the structure that other XML documents should follow. Despite their special purpose, schemas are just XML documents. You use XML markup to create them; the XML Schema specification tells you what markup to use and how.

If you've read up on DTDs, you know that a DTD can be partially or totally included in the XML document it governs. This means the DTD and XML document can be contained in one file. (Look back to Chapter 8 for all the details on the factors that govern where you put your DTD.) We bring this facet of DTDs up here because it's important for you to know that schemas don't work this way. Schemas are stored in a totally separate file from the XML documents they govern. In other words, all schemas are external to their documents; you can't combine a schema and its XML document into a single file.

As a separate document, a schema consists of declarations for elements and attributes, and specifies how those elements and attributes work together to define content and to establish a document structure. In addition, a schema allows you to restrict the content of these elements and attributes by using and defining very specific datatypes. (More on datatypes in the next section.)

XML Schema, though only one of many schema specifications, is the one recommended by the W3C. You can use one of the other schema options — such as REgular LAnguage for XML Next Generation (RELAX NG), Schematron, and Microsoft's XML-Data Reduced (XDR) schema language — but chances are you won't get a lot of support for these options beyond a few systems. We're a bit more mainstream in this book; when we talk about schemas, we're always referring to those written according to the XML Schema specification unless we say otherwise. For more information on the varieties of available schema mechanisms, see the XML Cover Pages at

```
www.oasis-open.org/cover/schemas.html
```

An XML Schema document includes many parts — conveniently listed in Table 9-1 — along with some examples from our favorite bookstore schema, bookstore.xsd.

Table 9-1		XML Schema Lingo	
Term	*Syntax*	*Example*	*What It Does*
XML declaration	`<xml version="version" encoding="encoding">`	`<xml version="1.0"encoding="UTF-8">`	Tells the processor which version of XML and which character encoding to use
Schema element	`<xsd:schema xmlns:xsd="namespace">`	`<xsd:schema xmlns:xsd="http://www.w3.org/2001/XMLSchema"`	Identifies the docu ment as XML Schema
Element declaration	`<xsd:element name="name">`	`<xsd:element name="books">`	Defines the element named books
Attribute declaration	`<xsd:attribute name="name" type="datatype">`	`<xsd:attribute name="sourceType" type="xsd:string">`	Defines the attribute named sourceType

Even if you don't plan on writing your own schemas from scratch, it's useful to know how to read and understand them. You should be able to look at a schema, list all the elements, attributes, and datatypes, and understand how and when to use those elements and attributes and how to format the data in your XML document.

Unlike a DTD, schemas are simply XML documents that use XML's standard markup syntax to define the structure for other documents. When you write a schema, you're simply writing XML. This means you don't have to learn a new language; you only have to learn how to use a particular set of XML elements and attributes.

Which is where this chapter comes in. Following a brief detour down the road to datatype land, you'll have a chance to look at each part of a schema so that you understand each piece of it before you read someone else's schema or create your own schema. (If you're already familiar with the components of an XML Schema document, go to Chapter 10 to find out how to build a custom XML Schema.)

So Many Datatypes, So Little Time

Unlike Document Type Definitions (DTDs), which are great for directing the development of documents that consist mainly of groups of text, schemas are great for directing documents that include lots of data, such as phone numbers, addresses, part numbers, or prices. Schemas work much better when you want to be sure a document not only follows a particular structure, but also uses particular kinds of data — numbers versus strings, for example — because it allows you to get very specific about the format of that data in the XML document.

Think about an invoice for a minute and the particular kinds of data it includes. It might include strings of text that describe services rendered or products sold, payment addresses, and terms of payment. It also includes a number of other things: the amount in dollars for a particular product or service, the quantity of something sold, or the number of hours spent delivering a particular service. A schema allows you not only to break down the invoice into a basic structure defined by elements and attributes, but also to define what kind of data each element and attribute can hold. For example, you can specify that any elements that describe amounts can hold only numbers with two digits after the decimal point.

In other words, schemas not only give you control over your document structure, but also give you control over your document data. The secret to control of the kind of data an XML document includes is datatypes. A *datatype* indicates what kind of data you expect; the XML Schema specification supports 44 different datatypes. (Betcha didn't know there *were* that many types of data, huh?)

An exhaustive list of all datatypes would overflow this book (and maybe put you to sleep), but a sampling of them includes these:

- ✔ `string`: A collection of characters that is treated as a simple string of text.

- ✔ `decimal`: A number that includes a decimal point and some number of decimal places after the point. When you use the `decimal` datatype in your schema, you can specify how many decimal places the number in the element or attribute can include.

- ✔ `dateTime`: The date and time. You can specify what pattern the date and time should use.

- ✔ `anyURI`: A URI or URL.

- ✔ `integer`: A number without a decimal point. When you use this datatype, you can specify the total number of digits the number can include.

Each of the 44 datatypes has a list of *constraints* that you can use to further define the data described with an element or attribute. For example, the `string` datatype has both `minLength` and `maxLength` constraints that you can use to specify the minimum and maximum lengths for the string. If you want to be sure the value of a `firstName` element is a string with at least 1 character but no more than 20, you can specify that as part of the `string` datatype for the element.

Databases allow for similar datatype controls. The idea is to carefully guide the data stored in the different database fields. If you're creating XML documents whose data will eventually be moved into a database, you can use a schema to create rules for the data in the document that are compatible with the rules in the database.

Part 2 of the XML Schema Recommendation is entirely devoted to the particulars of datatypes. You can read about each of the 44 datatypes and their constraints at `www.w3.org/TR/xmlschema-2/`.

XML Prolog

The XML prolog is the housekeeping section of the document. It contains useful information about the document that is helpful to both people and computers — whoever/whatever may read the document.

Because a schema is simply an XML document, and the XML declaration is the first thing in an XML document, each schema starts with an XML declaration. Even though your schema is just an XML document with a particular purpose — to define a schema — you need to say, "Hello, this document uses XML Schema." You do that in the prolog. So at the very least, the prolog to your schema needs to include:

- **An XML declaration:** An XML declaration identifies the document as an XML document and specifies its version:

  ```
  <?xml version="1.0" encoding="UTF-8"?>
  ```

  For more information about XML declarations, see Chapter 5.

- **A schema element declaration:** The schema element is similar to the root element in a DTD; it contains all the other elements in the XML Schema document and includes an xmlns (*XML NameSpace*) attribute that specifies the namespace for the schema. The *namespace* is the URL that provides the details of XML vocabulary — in this case, the XML Schema vocabulary — that the document must adhere to. The resulting line of code looks like this:

  ```
  <xsd:schema xmlns:xsd="http://www.w3.org/2001/XMLSchema">
  ```

By using the format xmlns:xsd, you indicate that any elements or attributes with an xsd: prefix belong to this namespace (http://www.w3.org/2001/XMLSchema).

You don't have to use the prefix xsd: — xs: is also commonly used. You can actually use any prefix you choose, as long as you specifically associate it with the XML Schema namespace. It's not, however, valid to use xsd: or xs: to refer to namespaces other than the XML Schema namespace.

In fact, if you're only using one namespace, you don't have to use a prefix at all! Prefixes are used to distinguish between two or more namespaces. If you are only using elements and attributes as defined in the XML Schema specification — and, therefore, referencing only one namespace in your XML document — you can indicate that namespace without using a prefix, like so:

```
<schema xmlns="http://www.w3.org/2001/XMLSchema">
```

In this case, you don't need to prefix elements and attributes in your schema document with xsd: — it's assumed.

For more details on using namespaces, see Chapter 11.

This is what a complete prolog for an XML Schema looks like:

```
<?xml version="1.0" encoding="UTF-8"?>
<xsd:schema xmlns:xsd="http://www.w3.org/2001/XMLSchema">
```

What does *XSD* stand for? When XML Schema were first proposed by the W3C, they were called XSDs (XML Schema Definitions) — corresponding to the nomenclature for DTDs (Document Type Definitions). By the time XML Schema became an official W3C specification, however, Definition had been dropped from the official name, and these documents were called XML Schema.

Document Structures

Following the XML prolog is the meat of the schema that defines the schema's basic structures — elements and attributes. It also specifies how these structures work together — which elements are contained in other elements and which attributes belong to which elements.

Element declarations

XML Schema documents always include elements, and all elements included in a schema must be defined in an element declaration. (Write that down so you don't forget it.) The element declaration must include the element name and may also include the element datatype. There are two categories of element declarations:

- **Simple type definitions:** These declare elements that cannot contain any other elements and cannot include any attributes.

- **Complex type definitions:** These declare elements that can contain other elements and can also take attributes. The attribute declarations that go with these kinds of elements are part of the complex type definition.

Examples make this much clearer, so read on for a couple. In the following example, a *simple type* definition is used to specify an element named date that can contain only date information in the format YYYY-MM-DD — year-month-day:

```
<xsd:element name="date" type="xsd:date"/>
```

The type attribute specifies the datatype for the element, in this case, a date. The xsd: prefix before date (xsd:date) indicates that this datatype is part of the XML Schema vocabulary (namespace).

The date datatype (YYYY-MM-DD) is only one of several XML Schema datatypes for date and time information. Others include duration, dateTime, time, date, gYearMonth, gYear, gMonthDay, gDay, and gMonth. For details, see Part 2 of the XML Schema Recommendation at www.w3.org/TR/xml schema-2/.

In the following example, a *complex type* definition — the stuff between the <xsd:complexType> and </xsd:complexType> tags — specifies an element named book that includes a required attribute named format that uses the XML Schema string datatype:

```
<xsd:element name="book">
 <xsd:complexType>
  <xsd:attribute name="format" type="xsd:string" use="required"/>
 </xsd:complexType>
</xsd:element>
```

A content model defines what type of content — text, other elements, or some combination of the two — can be contained in an element. There are four basic content models for XML Schema elements. These four content models are:

✔ **Text:** The element can contain only text. The following example is a simple type definition for an element with text-only content. A string datatype is used, because text is a string of characters.:

```
<xsd:element name="author" type="xsd:string"/>
```

✔ **Empty:** The element cannot contain child elements or text — that is, the content of the element must be empty. Empty elements can include attributes, as in the following example of a complex type definition for an empty element:

```
<xsd:element name="source">
 <xsd:complexType>
   <xsd:attribute name="yearsInService" type="xsd:positiveInteger"/>
 </xsd:complexType>
<xsd:element>
```

When you create an element that's empty (or that can contain only text), you can use a simple type definition to declare it — as long as it doesn't contain any attributes. If your element's content model includes other elements (whether element content or mixed content) — or includes attributes — you have to use a complex type definition.

✔ **Element:** The element can contain child elements, like this:

```
<xsd:element name="bookInfo">
 <xsd:complexType>
  <xsd:sequence>
   <xsd:element ref="title"/>
   <xsd:element ref="author"/>
   <xsd:element ref="publisher"/>
   <xsd:element ref="isbn"/>
  </xsd:sequence>
 </xsd:complexType>
</xsd:element>
<xsd:element name="title" type="xsd:string"/>
...
```

The bookInfo element is a complex type element that can contain a sequence of four elements. It could be used in an XML document as follows:

```
<bookInfo>
 <title>London Bridges</title>
 <author>Patterson, James</author>
 <publisher>Little, Brown</publisher>
 <isbn>0316710598</isbn>
</bookInfo>
```

Notice the xsd:sequence element that encloses the list of child elements in the previous example. This element is a *compositor element,* and its job is to specify order and occurrence constraints for these child elements. The three compositors included in XML Schema are:

- sequence indicates that the elements must occur in the specified order in the XML document. Use this compositor if you want to be sure every instance of an element includes all of its child elements in a particular order.

- choice indicates that any one of the elements may occur in the XML document. Think of this compositor as the multiple-choice compositor. Use it if you want the element to contain only one of several possible children.

- all indicates that any or all of the elements may occur in the XML document. This is the free-for-all compositor. Use it if you don't care if the element contains one, none, some, or all possible children.

Elements referenced in the sequence must appear in this exact order in the XML document. That's because they're contained with the sequence compositor. If we change xsd:sequence to xsd:choice, the bookInfo element could contain only one of the elements listed. If we change it to xsd:all, the bookInfo element could then contain any number of the elements, or none, in any order. Small change; big effect.

✔ **Mixed:** The element can contain child elements and text, and uses compositor elements to define the structure for child elements:

```
<xsd:element name="confirmOrder">
  <xsd:complexType mixed="true">
    <xsd:sequence>
      <xsd:element ref="opening"/>
      <xsd:element ref="fullName"/>
      <xsd:element ref="date"/>
      <xsd:element ref="title"/>
    </xsd:sequence>
  </xsd:complexType>
</xsd:element>
```

The mixed attribute with a value of true in the complexType element indicates that character data can be used in between the child elements of the confirmOrder element.

Mixed content (as defined in the preceding example) could be used in an XML document as follows:

```
<confirmOrder>
<opening>To:</opening>
<fullName>Jolene Wilkes</fullName>,
This is to confirm that on <date>2005-01-24</date>,
we received your order for
<title>Whiteout</title>.
We expect to ship your title via media mail
within 2 business days of your order.
Thank you,
Best Seller Bookstores, Inc.
```

</confirmOrder> Attribute declarations

Attribute declarations are code snippets that include just a name and a type. They are always simple type definitions; they can't contain elements or other attributes. Complex type definitions, however, can contain one or more attribute declarations — which must be declared at the very end of the complex type, after all other components of the complex type have been specified. In the following example, the attribute custNumber is specified as part of the complex type definition of the element customer:

```
<xsd:element name="customer">
  <xsd:complexType>
    <xsd:sequence>
      <xsd:element name="firstName" type="xsd:string"/>
      <xsd:element name="lastName" type="xsd:string"/>
    </xsd:sequence>
    <xsd:attribute name="custNumber" type="xsd:positiveInteger"/>
  </xsd:complexType>
</xsd:element>
```

Attributes are always optional unless you include a use attribute with the value required, as in the following example:

```
<xsd:attribute name="custType" type="xsd:string" use="required"/>
```

Attribute groups

If you're all set to use the same set of attributes with more than one element in an schema, you can create an attribute group that can be accessed by as many elements as you choose. This following markup snippet combines several different geographical locations into a single attribute group. This group could be used over and over again with any element that would refer to location:

```
<xsd:attributeGroup name="location">
 <xsd:attribute name="US" type="xsd:string"/>
 <xsd:attribute name="Canada" type="xsd:string"/>
 <xsd:attribute name="Europe" type="xsd:string"/>
</xsd:attributeGroup>
```

An attribute group must be declared globally — that is, at the top level of your schema (right below the schema element declaration).

What about that white space?

Well, there's more to it than doesn't meet the eye. White space includes nonprinting characters such as tabs, carriage returns, spaces, or line feeds. White space is ignored by XML processors as long as it is included outside the XML markup itself. For example, an extra carriage return between two element declarations is ignored.

However, white space within the XML document content is not always ignored by XML Schema. Element or attribute content that includes white space is normalized according to the value declared for the whiteSpace facet in the element or attribute definition. The possible values for the whiteSpace facet are as follows:

- ✔ preserve indicates that no white-space normalization is done.
- ✔ replace indicates that tabs, carriage returns, and line feeds are replaced with spaces.
- ✔ collapse indicates that after tabs, carriage returns, and line feeds are replaced with spaces, sequences of spaces are collapsed to a single space.

For example, you could include a whiteSpace facet with value = "preserve" in the definition of the fullName element in the previous example of a mixed-content model. Doing so ensures that the space within the fullName content is preserved:

```
<xsd:element name="confirmOrder">
 <xsd:complexType mixed="true">
  <xsd:sequence>
   <xsd:element ref="opening"/>
   <xsd:element ref="fullName"/>
   <xsd:element ref="date"/>
   <xsd:element ref="title"/>
```

```
  </xsd:sequence>
 </xsd:complexType>
</xsd:element>
<xsd:element name="opening" type="xs:string"/>
<xsd:element name="fullName">
 <xsd:simpleType>
  <xsd:restriction base="xs:string">
   <xsd:whiteSpace value="preserve"/>
  </xsd:restriction>
 </xsd:simpleType>
</xsd:element>
...
```

A simpleType element and a restriction element are used here to specify a white-space preference for the fullName element. A simpleType element is used to create a simple type definition for an element that can't contain any other elements or any attributes. A simpleType element is used with either a restriction element or an extension element to constrain (restriction) or expand (extension) the properties of the element's datatype. In this case, a restriction element is used with a string datatype to create a new datatype that preserves any white space in the content of the fullName element. Why would you want to preserve the white space anyway? In this case, preserving the white space is a way to retain the space between the first and the last name in the fullName element content.

Listing 9-1 shows the full schema for our order-confirmation example of a mixed content model. This file (plus the XML file it validates — confirm. xml) is available on the Web site for this book at www.dummies.com/go/ xmlfd4e.

Listing 9-1:   confirm.xsd

```
<?xml version="1.0" encoding="UTF-8"?>
<xsd:schema xmlns:xsd="http://www.w3.org/2001/XMLSchema">
    <xsd:element name="confirmOrder">
        <xsd:complexType mixed="true">
            <xsd:sequence>
                <xsd:element ref="opening"/>
                <xsd:element ref="fullName"/>
                <xsd:element ref="date"/>
                <xsd:element ref="title"/>
            </xsd:sequence>
        </xsd:complexType>
    </xsd:element>
    <xsd:element name="opening" type="xsd:string"/>
    <xsd:element name="fullName">
        <xsd:simpleType>
```

```
            <xsd:restriction base="xsd:string">
            <xsd:whiteSpace value="preserve"/>
            </xsd:restriction>
        </xsd:simpleType>
    </xsd:element>
    <xsd:element name="date" type="xsd:date"/>
    <xsd:element name="title" type="xsd:string"/>
</xsd:schema>
```

This schema has several parts:

✔ The XML prolog and schema declaration comprise the first part. The
  schema element is the root element of the XML Schema document:

```
<?xml version="1.0" encoding="UTF-8"?>
<xsd:schema xmlns:xsd="http://www.w3.org/2001/XMLSchema">
```

✔ The second part is a complex type definition for the confirmOrder
  element — it requires a complex type definition because it contains
  other elements. The other elements are in a sequence, so they must
  occur in that specific order. Each of the other elements include a ref
  attribute that references the name of an element that's declared outside
  the sequence — actually, in the next part of the schema!

```
<xsd:element name="confirmOrder">
    <xsd:complexType mixed="true">
        <xsd:sequence>
            <xsd:element ref="opening"/>
            <xsd:element ref="fullName"/>
            <xsd:element ref="date"/>
            <xsd:element ref="title"/>
        </xsd:sequence>
    </xsd:complexType>
</xsd:element>
```

✔ The third part contains element declarations for each element in the
  sequence. Note that the declaration for the fullName element doesn't
  include a type attribute. Instead, a simpleType element is used to create
  a simple type definition that includes a restriction element. A specific
  but anonymous (unnamed) datatype is derived from the string datatype
  by putting a constraint on it. The new datatype is a string datatype with
  the additional feature that it preserves white space.

  You can also derive a new named datatype — the advantage of naming a
  datatype is that you can re-use it. You find out more about user-derived
  datatypes in the following section.

  The last line of the schema is the closing tag of the xsd:schema
  element — that's all, folks!

```
<xsd:element name="opening" type="xsd:string"/>
<xsd:element name="fullName">
   <xsd:simpleType>
      <xsd:restriction base="xsd:string">
      <xsd:whiteSpace value="preserve"/>
      </xsd:restriction>
   </xsd:simpleType>
</xsd:element>
<xsd:element name="date" type="xsd:date"/>
<xsd:element name="title" type="xsd:string"/>
</xsd:schema>
```

Datatype Declarations

A *datatype declaration* is markup that defines the data format for the content of an element or attribute and is included in the element or attribute declaration, as in the following example:

```
<xsd:element name="publisher" type="xsd:string"/>
```

The datatype declaration in this example is included in the element declaration for the element named publisher. The type attribute specifies that the type is equal to xsd:string, which is the string datatype from the XML Schema namespace.

XML Schema includes no less than 44 built-in datatypes — and allows you to derive your own datatypes by specifying additional constraints on the 44 basic types. XML Schema not only includes more datatypes than any other schema language, but it's also the only schema language that lets you define your own, reusable datatypes. This makes it the language of choice for validating XML documents that include a lot of data.

Simple datatypes

A datatype can be used in a simple type definition, where an element contains no attributes and no other elements, as in the following example:

```
<xsd:element name="itemNumber" type="xsd:integer"/>
```

This line of code specifies that the content of the itemNumber element in our XML document must be formatted according to the XML Schema definition for the datatype named integer.

Complex datatypes

A datatype can also be defined in a complex type definition, where an element contains other elements and/or attributes, as in the following example:

```
<xsd:complexType name="priceInfo">
 <xsd:sequence>
  <xsd:element ref="priceType"/>
  <xsd:element ref="priceN"/>
 </xsd:sequence>
</xsd:complexType>
<xsd:element name="priceType" type="xsd:string"/>
<xsd:element name="priceN" type="xsd:decimal"/>
```

This creates a new type named `priceInfo` that includes the sequence of two elements listed. But wait — where's the complex type element? Aaah, very good, grasshopper! The complex type element is the `price` element that include the `priceInfo` datatype, as follows:

```
<xsd:element name="price" type="priceInfo"/>
```

This datatype doesn't include an `xsd:` prefix because it's not part of the XML Schema namespace — of course not; we just created it!

Other elements in this XML Schema can also use this `priceInfo` datatype, as shown in the following example:

```
<xsd:element name="shipping" type="priceInfo"/>
```

Technically, you can use a complex type definition to create a new type — which can be used in an XML Schema document anywhere that a datatype can be specified. Remember, however, that the new type is actually a *content model* (described earlier in the chapter, in the discussion of element declarations); it isn't really a datatype.

Defining constraints and value checks

New datatypes can be derived from any of the 44 built-in datatypes through the use of simple type definitions and a `restriction` element. A `restriction` element creates a *restriction constraint* — a limit on a built-in datatype, which narrows the definition to be whatever you specify.

In the following example, a simple type definition with `totalDigits` and `fractionDigits` constraints is used to specify valid content for a `costNumber` element:

```
<xsd:element name="costNumber">
 <xsd:simpleType>
  <xsd:restriction base="xsd:decimal">
   <xsd:totalDigits value="6"/>
   <xsd:fractionDigits value="2"/>
  </xsd:restriction>
 </xsd:simpleType>
<xsd:element>
```

This snippet of code creates a new, anonymous, user-derived datatype with a base datatype of decimal, with constraints on the number of total digits (six) and the number of digits after the decimal point (two).

For additional information on the 44 built-in datatypes and on the use of the restriction element to create new datatypes, see Part 2 of the XML Schema Recommendation at www.w3.org/TR/xmlschema-2/.

Dealing with Entities, Notations, and More

Although *notations* (statements that tell a processor how to handle non-XML data, such as an image) and *entities* (structures that hold references to frequently used text or the location of external documents you want to include in your XML document) can be used in XML Schema, they can be used only in certain, very specific ways.

Using notations in XML Schema is a tedious process — this is one of the limitations of XML Schema — so if your documents don't need notations and entities, feel free to move on to the next section on annotations.

For starters, entities and notations in XML Schema can be used only as attribute values and can be used only if there's a preceding notation declaration in the schema, as shown in this example:

```
<xsd:notation name="gif" public="image/gif" system="GIFViewer.exe"/>
```

In this example, the notation declaration includes the name of the notation as well as values for the public and system attributes — attributes that define the location of external non-XML data as well as an external application to handle the data.

After you've declared a notation, you associate the notation declaration with an attribute. The way to do that is to derive a new datatype from the NOTATION datatype, as follows:

```
<xsd:simpleType name="imageType">
 <xsd:restriction base="xsd:NOTATION">
  <xsd:enumeration value="gif"/>
 </xsd:restriction>
</xsd:simpleType>
```

This creates an enumerated list — a list with one list item, in this case — for imageType that limits the value to gif.

Next, associate an attribute with the new datatype:

```
<xsd:complexType name="photos">
 <xsd:attribute name="imageFormat" type="imageType" use="required"/>
</xsd:complexType>
<xsd:element name="img" type="photos"/>
```

For more information on notations and entities, and how to use them in a DTD, see Chapter 8.

If your XML document includes references to external non-XML data or external entities, you may want to use a DTD for validation rather than an XML Schema.

Annotations

Annotations are used in XML Schema documents to provide additional information to humans who happen to read the document (and/or to other applications). You start with an annotation element and then include either a documentation element (if you want the information read by humans — then it works like a comment in XML and HTML) or an appInfo element (if you want the information read by computer applications — then it's similar to XML processing instructions). In this example, a documentation element is contained in the annotation element:

```
<xsd:element name="books">
 <xsd:annotation>
  <xsd:documentation xml:lang="en">
   This is a collection of best-selling books.
  </xsd:documentation>
 </xsd:annotation>
</xsd:element>
```

The documentation includes a comment for the reader between the `documentation` tags.

In the following example, we add an `appInfo` element to our markup to include information from another XML schema language (in this case, Schematron) in our XML Schema document:

```
<xsd:element name="books">
 <xsd:annotation>
  <xsd:documentation xml:lang="en">
   This element specifies book, sales, and customer information.
  </xsd:documentation>
  <xsd:appinfo>
   <assert test="totalCost &gt; cost">totalCost should be greater than
            cost</assert>
  </xsd:appinfo>
 </xsd:annotation>
</xsd:element>
```

Schematron is another schema language used to extend the capabilities of XML Schema documents. Schematron allows XML Schema documents to include conditional statements such as the one included in the preceding example.

Deciding When to Use a Schema

You don't have to use a DTD — or a schema, for that matter — to create and use XML documents. Validating your XML documents is a really good idea but entirely optional. When validity is important, however, you have to decide when to choose schemas or DTDs.

Use XML Schema when you want:

✔ **To make sure that your XML document includes all the needed information in a correct and consistent format.** An invoicing system is a good example. Invoices contain a lot of required information, and you want to be sure the different bits of information are in the right format and use the right datatype (`string`, `integer`, `dateTime`, and so on).

✔ **To create a large set of XML documents that all have the same document structure.** Payroll checks are a good example of this. Each check has the same format, and you need to closely control the structures and their data format.

✔ **To share your document structure rules with others when you've built an application that requires valid documents with particular data formats.** If you want people to send you data, you have to help them create and structure that data. In addition to being a validation tool, a schema can be a great communication tool.

Schemas *really* make sense when your XML document contains large amounts of data. In this case, you can ensure that the data in the XML document is as accurate as possible by validating it against a schema. If your document validates, you can be sure that all required data is present and in the correct format. The XML Schema specification allows you to create schemas that are as specific as they need to be about what that format should be.

If your document content consists of blocks of text rather than other types of data, it may be easier to use a DTD for validation instead of a schema.

Referencing XML Schema Documents

If you've based an XML document on a schema, you can reference that (separate) schema document — as well as public schema documents different from your own — from your XML document.

The inside view: Referencing a schema in an XML document

Although you can't include an entire schema inside your XML document, as you can with an internal DTD, you can reference a schema namespace within the root element of your XML document.

For example, suppose we create a schema named `bookstore.xsd` based on our hypothetical bookstore. We can reference that schema in the following way in our XML document:

```
<?xml version="1.0" encoding="UTF-8"?>
<books xmlns:xsi="http://www.w3.org/2001/XMLSchema-instance"
      xsi:noNamespaceSchemaLocation="bookstore.xsd">
```

In this example, we use the W3C Schema-instance namespace (`http://www.w3.org/2001/XMLSchema-instance`) and the `xsi:noNamespaceSchema Location` attribute to tie our XML document to the W3C XML Schema and to our XML Schema document (`bookstore.xsd`). This link is not required, but it does help XML Schema validators locate a schema.

Calling for outside support: Referencing external schemas in your schema

From within the depths of your own schema document, you can include references to multiple other schemas as long as they were written according to the XML Schema specification. Referencing multiple schemas enables you to include elements and attributes from other schemas in your own schema document.

To refer to other schemas from within your schema document, you use a *namespace* reference and create a prefix for this namespace. Some prefixes are standard. For example, W3C XML Schema components usually have the prefix xs: or xsd: (including the colons) in front of the component name. You don't have to use the prefixes from the W3C's recommendations. You can use whatever prefix you choose — as long as the prefix you use in the namespace reference is the same as the prefix you use in the schema document to identify the components of that namespace. But why reinvent the wheel? For some friendly pointers on using namespaces, we've included a handy sidebar (namely, "Namespaces are your friends").

You can also include new schema components that you create. For example, our schema, bookstore.xsd, could include references to as many namespaces as we choose to include. Here's what that looks like:

```
<?xml version="1.0" encoding="UTF-8"?>
<xsd:schema xmlns:xsd="http://www.w3.org/2001/XMLSchema"
            xmlns:bk="http://www.example.com/book.xsd"
            xmlns:wg="http://www.example.com/writersguild.xsd"
            xmlns:or="http://www.oregonbooksellers.com/Rbooklist.xsd">
```

Namespaces are your friends

Because everyone can build their own elements using XML, it's possible — and most likely probable — that two DTDs, schemas, or documents will use some elements with the same names.

A parser can deal with just about any set of XML elements. And a well-formed XML document can use elements from any DTD or schema. However, a special processor designed to work with documents written with one or two specific DTDs might not know what to do with a document that combines elements from several different DTDs, some of which may conflict because they have elements with the same names.

Namespaces let the parser know which DTD or schema you're using so you can use the markup from several different DTDs or schemas in one document. In the end, namespaces permit efficient sharing of vocabularies across documents and help eliminate confusion when two or more vocabularies use the same names for elements.

We cover namespaces in more detail in Chapter 11.

In this example, we include references to three namespaces in addition to the W3C XML Schema namespace. We assign these prefixes to the additional namespace: `bk`, `wg`, and `or`. If we use components from these namespaces in our schema document, we must use the appropriate prefix in front of each component. For example, to access a `title` element from the `www.example.com/book.xsd` namespace, we would create an element declaration that included the prefix we assigned to that namespace, like this:

```
<bk:element name="title">
```

Double-Checking Your Schemas and Documents

After you've created your XML document and defined all the elements and attributes in a schema, you're ready to parse!

Be sure that your XML document is well formed before you try to validate it. No mystery here: If your XML document isn't well formed, it won't validate. For more information on well-formed documents, see Chapters 4 and 5.

For more information on XML Schema

For more information on the details of using and writing XML Schema documents, see the W3C XML Schema Recommendation documents on the W3C Web site. The W3C XML Schema Recommendation has three parts:

✔ XML Schema Part 0: Primer Second Edition at

`www.w3.org/TR/xmlschema-0/`

✔ XML Schema Part 1: Structures Second Edition at

`www.w3.org/TR/2001/REC-xmlschema-1/`

✔ XML Schema Part 2: Datatypes Second Edition at

`www.w3.org/TR/xmlschema-2/`

The Second Editions are not new versions of the XML Schema recommendations — they were issued to provide corrections to the information in the First Editions. The W3C is currently working to develop a set of requirements for XML Schema 1.1.

Here's a list of the tools available to help you validate your XML document:

- **Validating parsers:** Compare your XML document to the referenced schema. Validating your XML document involves using the constraints defined in your schema to check the structure and hierarchy of the elements and attributes in your XML document, as well as to check the structure of the content contained in the elements and attributes.

- **Schema validity testers:** Compare your schema to the W3C's XML Schema recommendation to be sure it is valid. It doesn't do you any good to validate an XML document against an invalid schema. (You'd be surprised how many people forget that.)

- **Conversion tools:** Convert DTDs to schemas, and convert from one schema language to another.

In Chapter 10, we outline the steps for creating custom schema documents — and create another custom XML Schema document (books2.xsd) to validate an XML bookstore example (books2.xml).

Chapter 10

Building a Custom XML Schema

. . . .

In This Chapter

▶ Getting to know your data

▶ Defining elements

▶ Using content models

▶ Defining attributes

▶ Using datatypes

▶ Incorporating best practices

▶ Creating a simple XML Schema document

. . . .

*I*f you build custom XML documents, you probably want to create a map for the documents that defines how you intend to use markup to describe your content. (A wise move, that.) You also want to be sure all your custom XML documents play by the same set of markup rules, so you'll want to double-check them against your custom map — the process known as *validating*.

The two most popular and useful methods for defining the structure (map) for an XML document are Document Type Definitions (DTDs) and XML schemas. DTDs are most useful for defining the structure of XML documents with text-intensive content, although they can be used with any XML document. For more information on using and creating DTDs, check out Chapter 8. For data-intensive XML documents, schemas (which we also discuss in Chapters 9 and 11) have much more to offer in the way of data definition.

Doing the Validity Rag

An XML document is valid if it conforms to the rules you define in your schema. Validation against a schema is very useful if your XML documents contain a lot of data content that needs to be formatted in a particular way. For example, say the data content includes e-mail addresses, and you want to be sure that the addresses contain alphanumeric characters before and after the @ symbol. A schema lets you define a datatype to do just that!

Building a simple XML Schema requires these steps:

1. Understand your data.

2. Create element declarations.

3. Define content models.

4. Create attribute declarations.

5. Add datatype declarations.

This chapter takes you through the entire process of creating a custom schema that perfectly suits your XML document's every need. Whereas Chapter 9 described and gave examples of all the components of schemas, this chapter takes you through the process of actually building a schema document, piece by piece. You also get the word on how to use a schema to create an XML template in Word 2003 and use the template to create new XML documents.

We use the term *schema* throughout this chapter to refer to an XML document that has two specific characteristics:

✔ It's written according to the XML Schema specification.

✔ It's designed to describe the structure for other XML documents.

The XML Schema specification isn't the only option for writing schemas, but it's the one published by the W3C to work with XML, so it's probably your best choice. Look over Chapter 9 for more information on other schema options.

XML Schema basics are covered in detail in Chapter 9. To jog your memory, here's a quick review of the essential pieces of a schema:

✔ **Element declarations:** These statements are part of the basic structure of the schema document; they show how each component of the document is related to every other component. Elements can be simple (containing only text content) or complex (containing other elements, attributes, and/or text content).

✔ **Attribute declarations:** These statements are contained within the complex type definition for the element that contains the attribute. Attributes are always optional unless you specify in the attribute declaration that an attribute is required. A group of attributes that will be used in more than one element in an XML document can be defined as an attribute group and accessed by any elements you choose.

✔ **Content models:** These statements define what type of content can be contained in an element. There are four basic content models for XML Schema elements: element (can contain other elements), text (can contain only text), mixed (can contain other elements as well as text), and empty (contains no content).

✔ **Datatype declarations:** These statements tell the processor the valid format for an XML element or attribute. You can use any of the 44 built-in XML Schema datatypes or build your own custom datatypes. The datatype declaration is included within an XML Schema element or attribute declaration.

Schemas are just XML documents that use a specific set of markup defined by the XML Schema specification to define the structure for other documents. You use elements and attributes in a schema to define elements and attributes for use in other documents. (Cool, huh?)

The fact that XML schemas are XML documents is one of the advantages of using schemas — unlike using DTDs, you don't have to learn another language format to use schemas.

Step 1: Understanding Your Data

Before building a custom schema, you must understand the basic nature and function of your data. Is your data a collection of book titles, author names, and publishers? Or is your data a group of part numbers, phone numbers, and e-mail addresses? Take some time to look at the kind(s) of data you'll be using in your XML documents so you can use the right structures and datatypes to describe your content.

Before you design your schema, you also need to be clear about what you want to do with the data. Do you want to export data to a database from your XML documents, or do you want it available for access from wireless devices? Be sure your document structure matches up with the format you need for importing and exporting your data accurately and efficiently.

Step 2: Being the Root of All Structure: Elements

Elements define the basic structure for any XML document, including those created according to a schema. After you've got a good handle on your data and are ready to build a schema that fits it, you should first decide which elements will be included in your XML document.

As a first step in declaring the elements for your schema, map out the basic structure of the document: What elements do you think you'll need? How do they fit together? The best way to go about answering those questions is to gather up several sample documents and take a stab at defining markup to fit their content. After you have that basic structure down in a marked-up sample document or two, you have your map. For more details on content analysis, see Chapter 3.

A *map* makes deciding what kind of attributes, content models, and datatypes you need to define a lot easier. Listing 10-1 shows the `books2.xml` document (an adaptation of `books.xml` from Chapter 7 — we've changed two child elements of `book` to attributes of `book`) with just the elements listed — without the content or attribute values.

The `books2.xml` document (content included) can be downloaded at `www.dummies.com/go/xmlfd4e`.

Listing 10-1: books2.xml without the Content or Attribute Values

```
<books>
 <book contentType="" format="">
  <title></title>
  <author></author>
  <publisher></publisher>
  <price></price>
  <isbn></isbn>
 </book>
</books>
```

As you can see in Listing 10-1, identifying the underlying structure of an XML document makes building your schema a lot easier, because you can clearly see the relationships between the basic structural components (elements and attributes) before you start creating the document that describes this structure.

Only one `book` element is shown here, but the `books` element can contain any number of `book` elements as long as you specify that in the schema.

`books2.xml` is a very simple XML document — and that's deliberate on our part. Schema documents can get very complicated very quickly, so we're starting with a simple XML document to show the basics of schema creation. In Chapter 11, you get a chance to modify this schema into a more complex schema to validate `bookstore.xml`.

Elements that contain other elements and/or attributes are, by definition, *complex* types. We show you how to define complex type elements in the next section, "Step 3: Building Content Models." *Simple* element types contain only text content and can't contain attributes or other elements.

As you can see in Listing 10-1, `books` is the only complex type element in our document. The simple type elements are `title`, `author`, `publisher`, `price`, and `isbn`. You can add restrictions to these simple type elements to create user-defined datatypes, as detailed in Step 5.

Step 3: Building Content Models

A *content model* defines the type of content that can be contained in an element. The four content models for XML Schema elements are element (contains child elements), text (contains only text content), mixed (contains child elements and text), and empty (contains no content). For more details and examples of each of these content models, see Chapter 9.

For the schema you're building based on the books2.xml document, you need only two of these content models: element and text. (To see an example of a mixed-content model, see the files confirm.xml and confirm.xsd on the book Web site at www.dummies.com/go/xmlfd4e. If you get a hankering to add an empty content model to this schema, Chapter 11 shows you how.)

The books element in our XML document contain other elements, so you will need to create a complex type definition for this parent element.

Complex type definitions can include *compositor* elements, which specify order and occurrence restraints. The three compositors included in the XML Schema language are as follows:

- ✔ sequence indicates that the elements must occur in the specified order in the XML document.
- ✔ choice indicates that any one of the elements may occur in the XML document.
- ✔ all indicates that any or all of the elements may occur in the XML document.

For more information on compositors, see Chapter 9.

First, create a complex type definition for the books element. In the DTD you created in Chapter 8, the books element was the root element. In XML Schema, however, the schema element is always the root element and contains all the other elements of the document. The books element in this case contains all the other elements in the schema document except for the schema element. The following markup shows the complex type definition for the books element:

```
<xsd:element name="books">
 <xsd:complexType>
  <xs:sequence maxOccurs="unbounded">
   <xsd:element name="book" type="bookType"/>
  </xsd:sequence>
 </xsd:complexType>
</xsd:element>
```

The `xsd:` prefix indicates the namespace for our schema — namely, the XML Schema namespace. For more information on namespaces, see Chapters 9 and 11.

A sequence includes one or more element references.

Note that the sequence compositor element contains a `maxOccurs` attribute that specifies how many times the `book` element can occur in the document. Because you want the `books` element to contain any number of `book` elements, that value is unbounded.

The default values for occurrence of an element are a minimum of 1 and a maximum of 1. If you want to specify a different value, you need to use `minOccurs` and/or `maxOccurs` attributes.

When you use a sequence compositor, you specify child elements in one of two ways:

✔ By using a `ref` attribute with a value equal to the value of the `name` attribute in each child element's element declaration. The `ref` attribute must refer to an actual element declaration, though, and is not sufficient markup just by itself, so in this case you also need to add a separate element declaration for the `title` element in your schema:

```
<xsd:complexType>
 <xsd:sequence>
  <xsd:element ref="title"/>
 </xsd:sequence>
</xsd:complexType>
<xsd:element name="title"/>
...
```

✔ By using a `name` attribute with a value equal to the value of the child element's name along with a `type` attribute with the value of a user-defined complex type, as shown in this code from the complex type definition for the `books` element, listed earlier in this section. In this case, you don't need a separate element declaration for `book`, but you do need to add a complex type definition for `bookType`. It would look like this:

```
<xsd:element name="book" type="bookType"/>
```

Adding such a complex type definition for `bookType` is pretty easy, as can be seen in the following:

```
<xsd:complexType name="bookType">
 <xsd:sequence>
  <xsd:element ref="title"/>
  <xsd:element ref="author"/>
  <xsd:element ref="publisher"/>
  <xsd:element ref="price"/>
  <xsd:element ref="isbn"/>
```

```
  </xsd:sequence>
 </xsd:complexType>
 <xsd:element name="title"/>
 ...
```

The `title` element uses a simple element declaration that is included immediately after the complex type definition for `bookType`. The other elements referenced in the `bookType` definition (`author`, `publisher`, `price`, and `isbn`) also use simple type declarations — namely, these:

```
<xsd:element name="author"/>
<xsd:element name="publisher"/>
<xsd:element name="price"/>
<xsd:element name="isbn"/>
```

Congratulations! Here, you've created all the element declarations and complex type definitions that you need for your schema. All that's left is to add attributes, define datatypes, and put all the pieces together!

Step 4: Using Attributes to Shed Light on Data Structure

An *attribute declaration* is a declaration that describes an attribute for an element. Attribute declarations are always *simple* type definitions because they can't contain elements or other attributes. However, attribute declarations are *always* contained within a complex type definition.

Properly built schemas must declare attributes at the very end of a complex type definition, *after* all other components of the complex type have been specified.

The `book` element (for instance) contains two attributes: `contentType` and `format`. We want to limit the possible values for each of these attributes rather than letting the document author use just any text content willy-nilly. To build an attribute declaration that specifies exactly what values the attribute can take, you need to add the list of values to the attribute declaration and specify that the value of the attribute is restricted to those on the list.

In essence, you're making a list of values and saying that the attribute should take its values only from the list. Because markup often speaks louder than words, take a gander at the following markup:

```
<xsd:attribute name="contentType" use="required">
 <xsd:simpleType>
  <xsd:restriction base="xsd:string">
   <xsd:enumeration value="Fiction"/>
```

```
      <xsd:enumeration value="Nonfiction"/>
    </xsd:restriction>
  </xsd:simpleType>
</xsd:attribute>
<xsd:attribute name="format" use="required">
  <xsd:simpleType>
    <xsd:restriction base="xsd:string">
      <xsd:enumeration value="Hardback"/>
      <xsd:enumeration value="Paperback"/>
    </xsd:restriction>
  </xsd:simpleType>
</xsd:attribute>
```

The simpleType element inside of the attribute declaration indicates that you need to add some additional information about this attribute. The restriction element is a flag that says (in effect), *Choose only from the values in this list.* Each enumeration element lists the possible options to choose from. Even with the many layers of markup involved, it's still pretty simple.

Note that the restriction statement includes a base attribute with the value of the datatype that's being restricted. You'll find out more about datatypes in Step 5.

Attributes are always optional unless you specify that they're required. In this case, you want a value to be present for both attributes. Therefore, make sure the use attribute (with a value of required) is included in your attribute declarations.

Any XML Schema datatype can be further restricted to a certain set of valid content values. For example, you might want to restrict the valid content for an attribute to the set of integers that includes the values 23, 25, 27, and 29. You can do that pretty easily by using restriction and enumeration elements.

Step 5: Using Datatype Declarations to Define What's What

A *datatype declaration* is a statement added to an element or attribute in a schema that lets document creators (or validating parsers) know exactly what kind of data you're actually working with when you declare an element or attribute. Using XML Schema, you can get even more explicit than a run-of-the-mill built-in datatype: Using any of the 44 XML Schema datatypes, you can derive your own datatypes, adding further qualifications in your quest to make the datatype more specific to the demands of your work.

As you build your custom schema, you need to think carefully about the type of data each element and attribute will hold, and take advantage of datatype declarations to pass the specifics to document builders and processing applications. After you've created your initial set of elements and attributes, go back and add datatype declarations to them.

As we mention in Chapter 9, XML Schema offers 44 built-in datatypes — from strings to integers, to date and time stamps, and beyond — for you to use. XML Schema also has the unique feature of supporting reusable user-derived datatypes — in other words, you can derive your own datatypes from the built-in datatypes and reuse these datatypes throughout your schema document.

To find all you ever wanted to know about datatypes — including the gory details of every individual datatype and how you can use each one — refer to Part II of the XML Schema specification at

```
http://www.w3.org/TR/xmlschema-2
```

To create a simple type element whose data type is string, follow these steps:

1. **Create an element declaration.**

2. **Include an** xsd: **prefix to specify that this is an XML Schema** string **datatype.**

   The following markup is the element declaration for the title element, with an added type attribute:

   ```
   <element name="title" type="xsd:string"/>
   ```

In our books schema, each simple type element (title, author, publisher, price, and isbn) takes a string datatype.

You define datatypes for attributes in the same way. Create the attribute declaration, and add the following datatype declaration:

```
<attribute name="bookbinding" type="xsd:string"/>
```

If you're adding further restrictions to an attribute, you don't include a `type` in the attribute declaration statement. Instead, you use a `base` attribute in the `restriction` element that specifies the datatype, as in the `contentType` and `format` attributes for the `book` element.

Several XML Schema datatypes are derived from the `string` datatype. For that matter, you can use a `string` datatype as a base type for creating a user-defined type — such as a specific pattern of text or text with a specific number of characters.

Even if an XML element describes text-only data (such as a name or a copyright statement), you may want that text to follow a particular pattern. Using a custom datatype, you can specify, for example, that the `price` element must consist of a $ sign followed by one to four numeric digits, a decimal point, and two more digits, as in the following markup:

```
<xsd:element name="price">
 <xsd:simpleType>
  <xsd:restriction base="xsd:string">
   <xsd:pattern value="\$[0-9]{1,4}.[0-9]{2}"/>
  </xsd:restriction>
 </xsd:simpleType>
</xsd:element>
```

In this example, an element named `price` is defined using a simple type definition and a restriction of the `string` type to this particular pattern. An XML document based on this schema must include the `price` element content in this format to be valid.

XML Schema supports the use of regular expressions when you define a `pattern`. A *regular expression* is a specific pattern for a group of characters, such as the one we use in the previous example:

```
\$[0-9]{1,4}.[0-9]{2}
```

This pattern starts with a $, followed by one to four single digits (in the range 0 to 9), followed by a period — decimal point — followed by two single digits in the range 0 to 9.

Regular expressions are ideal for defining patterns of characters — their inclusion in XML Schema adds a very powerful feature for defining datatypes.

Basic regular expressions are not difficult to learn and give you a wealth of choices for formatting character data. To make it even easier, you can use an online regular expression tester, such as the one at `www.quanetic.com/regex.php`, to test that your regular expression matches the character data in your XML document. (Be sure to include a / at the beginning and end of your regular expression in the tester — this is the format for regular expressions in most other programming languages.)

We also used a regular expression to derive a more specific datatype from the `string` datatype for the `isbn` element:

```
<xsd:element name="isbn">
 <xsd:simpleType>
  <xsd:restriction base="xsd:string">
   <xsd:pattern value="[0-1][0-9]{9}"/>
  </xsd:restriction>
 </xsd:simpleType>
</xsd:element>
```

This regular expression denotes that the pattern must be a string that starts with 0 or 1 (`[0-1]`) — because ISBNs for books in English start with 0 or 1 — and be followed by 9 other digits (`[0-9]{9}`).

You can get much, much more specific about the pattern of an ISBN. See the ISBN simple type definition created by Roger Costello at `www.xfront.com/isbn.html`.

Tricks of the Trade

In this chapter and in Chapter 9, we cover the basics of building schemas. Here are some reminders and additional tips for building and using them:

- ✔ **Use** `annotation` **and** `documentation`**:** The `annotation` and `documentation` elements are similar to comments in HTML documents — they provide additional information for humans reading the schema document. (For more information, see Chapter 9.)

- ✔ **The** `schema` **element comes first:** The `schema` element is the root element of the schema document and is always the first element to appear after the XML prolog.

- ✔ **Tools do XML Schemas too:** See Chapter 19 for more details on XML editors that can create schemas from DTDs and vice versa.

- ✔ **Review your validation options:** Schemas are designed for data-intensive document or text content that includes many additional constraints (such as specific patterns of content). Otherwise, a DTD may be a better choice for validating your XML document. Visit Chapter 9 for more information on when to use a schema, and visit Chapter 11 for additional details on using schema for data-intensive documents.

Creating a Simple Schema

When you've created all the pieces of your schema, it's time to piece them all together to complete your little (or possibly huge) project. If you're ready to take that plunge, follow these steps:

1. **Create an XML prolog and a** `schema` **element.**

2. **Add an** `xmlns` **attribute to the** `schema` **element to specify that the document uses the XML Schema namespace and the** `xsd:` **prefix.**

   Here's an example:

   ```
   <?xml version="1.0" encoding="UTF-8"?>
   <xsd:schema xmlns:xsd="http://www.w3.org/2001/XMLSchema">
   ```

3. **Add the element and attribute declarations you created in the previous sections.**

   What you get looks similar to this example:

   ```
   <?xml version="1.0" encoding="UTF-8"?>
   <xsd:schema xmlns:xsd="http://www.w3.org/2001/XMLSchema">
    <xsd:element name="books">
     <xsd:complexType>
      <xsd:sequence maxOccurs="unbounded">
       <xsd:element name="book" type="bookType"/>
      </xsd:sequence>
     </xsd:complexType>
    </xsd:element>

    <xsd:complexType name="bookType">
     <xsd:sequence>
      <xsd:element ref="title"/>
      <xsd:element ref="author"/>
      <xsd:element ref="publisher"/>
      <xsd:element ref="price"/>
      <xsd:element ref="isbn"/>
     </xsd:sequence>
     <xsd:attribute name="contentType" use="required">
      <xsd:simpleType>
       <xsd:restriction base="xsd:string">
        <xsd:enumeration value="Fiction"/>
        <xsd:enumeration value="Nonfiction"/>
       </xsd:restriction>
      </xsd:simpleType>
     </xsd:attribute>
     <xsd:attribute name="format" use="required">
      <xsd:simpleType>
       <xsd:restriction base="xsd:string">
   ```

```
        <xsd:enumeration value="Hardback"/>
        <xsd:enumeration value="Paperback"/>
      </xsd:restriction>
    </xsd:simpleType>
  </xsd:attribute>
</xsd:complexType>

<xsd:element name="title" type="xsd:string"/>
<xsd:element name="author" type="xsd:string"/>
<xsd:element name="publisher" type="xsd:string"/>

<xsd:element name="price">
 <xsd:simpleType>
  <xsd:restriction base="xsd:string">
   <xsd:pattern value="\$[0-9]{1,4}.[0-9]{2}"/>
  </xsd:restriction>
 </xsd:simpleType>
</xsd:element>

<xsd:element name="isbn">
 <xsd:simpleType>
  <xsd:restriction base="xsd:string">
   <xsd:pattern value="[0-1][0-9]{9}"/>
  </xsd:restriction>
 </xsd:simpleType>
</xsd:element>

</xsd:schema>
```

Except for attribute declarations (which must occur at the end of complex type declarations), the declarations in your schema can occur in any order. In other words, you can list the declarations in any order you choose, as long as they're contained within the schema element. Remember, however, that when you define the structure of the parent–child relationships in your schema document, you also determine the order of elements in your XML document. (A document's underlying structure is often easier to view, however, if you list the declarations in the same order as the elements in the XML document.)

4. **Save your schema document with an** .xsd **file extension.**

   You can give your schema any name you like, but descriptive names make it easier to keep track of which schema document validates which XML documents. (For example, we decided to name this schema books2.xsd.)

The full schema document that we created in this chapter, books2.xsd, is available for download on the book's Web site atwww.dummies.com/go/xmlfd4e.

Using a Schema with an XML File in Word 2003

The professional version of Word 2003 allows you to add your own schema documents to Word's Schema library and attach these schemas to XML documents in Word.

You can start with a new XML file, add elements from your schema, add content, and then validate the content against your schema. This is an easy way to create new XML documents that conform to a schema.

When you've created a schema (or downloaded `books2.xsd` from the book Web site at `www.dummies.com/go/xmlfd4e`), you can use that schema to create new XML documents. Just follow these steps:

1. **Open Word 2003; then choose File⇨New⇨XML document.**

   The XML Structure pane will appear to the left of the new blank document.

   You can also open an existing XML document or start with a Word document (.doc) and mark up the document content according to the chosen schema.

2. **Click Templates and Add-Ins in the XML Structure pane to open the Templates and Add-Ins dialog box; then click the XML Schema tab.**

3. **In the XML Schema tab, click the Add Schema button; then use the Browse window to locate the schema document you want to add (in this case, `books2.xsd`).**

4. **After selecting the schema document you want, click the Open button in the Browse pane.**

   The Schema Settings dialog box opens, as shown in Figure 10-1.

5. **Enter `http://www.XMLFD.com/books2.xsd` for the URI and `books` for the alias.**

Figure 10-1:
The Schema Settings dialog box, open in Word 2003.

> **Schema Settings**
> Edit schema information
> URI: http://www.xmlfd.com/books2.xsd
> Alias: books
> Location: C:\Documents and Settings\Arundati\Desktop\   Browse...
> ☑ Changes affect current user only
> OK   Cancel

The URI specifies the namespace for the schema. Because the schema will be listed in the XML Schema tab by the name of the alias, the root element of the document is usually a good choice for the alias.

The names of the available XML elements now appear in the bottom of the XML Structure pane — to the left of your still-blank new document. You can add elements to the document by clicking each element's name.

6. **Add new elements to your blank document by clicking the element name in the XML Structure pane.**

Start with the root element of the document, books, and work your way down through all the elements, adding each in the correct order according to the schema (book, title, author, publisher, price, isbn).

Note the check box named *List only child elements of current element* in the bottom-left corner of the XML Structure pane. You'll need to uncheck this in order to add all the elements; most of them are siblings.

As you add elements, the upper part of the XML Structure pane shows the document structure.

7. **After you've added all the elements in order, add content — in other words, the data, such as book title and author name — to each element.**

   a. To add attributes, right-click the element that contains your chosen attribute(s) — in this case, book — and then choose Attributes from the context menu.

   The Attributes dialog box appears and shows available attributes for this element.

   b. Select the contentType attribute, choose a value from the Value drop-down menu (because a list of values is included in the schema), and then click the Add button.

   The new attribute is added to your element.

   c. Repeat for the format attribute and then click OK.

If any validation problems crop up, a yellow, diamond-shaped icon identifies them in the display.

8. **To deal with a validation problem, move the cursor over any such icon to view the specific error message.**

If the pane shows no icons, your XML document is valid! Figure 10-2 shows a (valid) sample XML file in Word 2003.

9. **Save your XML file.**

Next to the Save button is a check box named *Save data only*. Check this box if you want to save the file without any WordML (Word Markup Language). Unless you have added document-formatting features in Word or are starting from an existing Word document, check this box before you click Save.

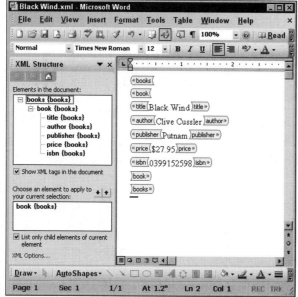

Figure 10-2:
An XML file
in Word
2003 with
XML tags
displayed.

XML schemas are a very effective validation method for XML files. You've discovered how to create a schema for a simple XML document in this chapter. In Chapter 11, you'll create a more complex schema and find out more about using namespaces.

Creating an XML template in Word 2003

You can easily make a template from any XML file in Word 2003. Just open an XML file; then choose File⇨Save As⇨Document Template. This creates a .dot file that you can use to create additional XML files.

This is a fast, easy way to make new XML files — and anyone can use this method in Word 2003 to create new (and valid!) XML content files, whether they understand XML structure or not.

To use your template file:

1. Choose File⇨New.

   The New Document task pane appears.

2. In the New Document task pane (to the left), select *On my computer* from the Templates section.

   If the New Document task pane isn't visible, choose View⇨Task Pane to display it.

3. Choose your template file from the Templates dialog box and then click OK,

4. Click any tag to highlight the content you want to replace and then replace it with new content.

5. Save as a new XML file.

Chapter 11

Modifying an Existing Schema

· ·

· ·

*T*his chapter grows right out of what you find in Chapters 9 and 10. In Chapter 9, you get to know the ins and outs of the basic structure of an XML Schema document; Chapter 10 walks you through building a custom schema step by step, according to the rules of the XML Schema specification. Here's where you get to try out the capabilities of a typical schema built using XML Schema.

If you're using a schema to guide the development of your XML documents, you have four possible basic approaches:

> ✔ **Work with an existing, off-the-shelf schema:** This is usually the fastest approach (but you knew that).

> ✔ **Create your own schema from scratch:** Laborious, sure, but what custom-built item isn't?

> ✔ **Customize an existing schema:** Tinker with it till it fits your content like a glove.

> ✔ **Convert a DTD to a schema:** This approach is the very thing if you already have a DTD but you want to take advantage of the XML Schema specification's strong datatyping capabilities.

In this chapter, you test-drive the XML Schema specification so you can construct a schema in different ways, depending on the type of data you're working with. In addition, you discover how to convert a DTD to a schema.

Trading Control for Flexibility

Schemas offer much tighter control of your content's format than do DTDs. This is a major advantage when you're using schemas to drive the creation of documents — and for validation when those documents are pulled into a processing system.

Of course, decisions about control and flexibility are best made at the beginning of the document design process. Examine your content closely, and make decisions about the most effective way to obtain and share the information in your XML document. After reviewing the content you want to include, you can make choices that determine how to structure that content to meet your requirements. Making these decisions at the beginning of the document's design cycle saves time in the end and reduces the amount of time spent revising and rewriting.

The basic structure of the content determines the flexibility of the document. You can make your schemas more versatile by using the `choice` compositor and enumerated lists of attributes. We show you how in the section "A matter of selection." later in this chapter. Add such flexibility with care, though — the price you pay may be a much more complex schema design.

Eliciting Markup from an XML Schema

In Chapter 10, you got the chance to create a simple XML schema (`books2.xsd`) to validate an XML file (`books2.xml`) that contains seven pieces of information about a book — five elements (`title`, `author`, `publisher`, `price`, and `isbn`) and two attributes (`contentType` and `format`). This schema could validate any XML file that conformed to this specific structure, whether it included information for 1 book or 1,000 books. So far, so good! However, in our (hypothetical) book business, we want to use XML to describe not only basic book information for one or more books, but also sales and customer information. For a closer look at how to go about that, flip over to Chapter 5 (`bookstore.xml`).

All the files mentioned in this chapter are available for download on the Web site for this book at

`www.dummies.com/go/xmlfd4e`

Comparing the structure of books2.xml and bookstore.xml visually will help guide the modification and expansion of the books2.xsd schema into the more complex bookstore.xsd schema. The following two figures show diagrams of the XML file structure for each of these documents as presented in XMLSpy — books2.xml in Figure 11-1 and bookstore.xml in Figure 11-2. The equal sign (=) indicates an attribute, and the brackets (<>)show an element.

Figure 11-1:
The
books2.
xml page in
Grid View in
XMLSpy.

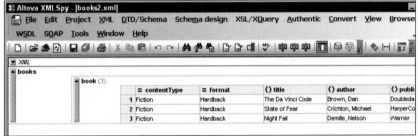

XMLSpy is a great tool for working with XML documents in general — and especially for creating documents that conform to the XML Schema specification. You find out how to generate an XML Schema in XMLSpy in the last section of this chapter, "Creating a schema With XMLSpy." Chapter 19 includes additional information on XMLSpy and other XML tools.

Figure 11-2:
The book
store.xml
page in Grid
View in
XMLSpy.

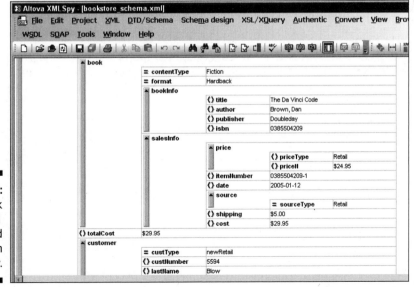

The second file is obviously more complex. As you'll see in the following section, however, the increased complexity is mainly in the outer levels of the document structure — the inner structure of `bookstore.xml` contains similar elements and datatypes to the simpler `books2.xsd`. We'll introduce some additional options later in this chapter.

Modifying a Schema

Comparing the two document structure diagrams in the previous section, you can see that the first document, `books2.xml`, has a very simple structure: All the information is contained within the `book` element. (There are three `book` elements, but the structure for each is the same.) The second document, `bookstore.xml`, uses the following three elements to structure the basic book stuff plus all additional information:

✔ A `book` element that contains book and sales information

✔ A `totalCost` element

✔ A `customer` element that contains customer data

This document has to have a relatively complex structure, for one simple reason: One customer can buy more than one book at a time. Our document has to include the option for multiple books, with book information and sales information for each book. We can use the basic format of the `books2.xsd` schema as a starting point, adding to it and modifying it to create a schema for the bookstore document.

After you compare the schema you've targeted for re-use with your new XML document, your next step in creating or modifying a schema is to look at how you want the structures defined in the schema to describe your content. The basic structure of your XML document is specified by the complex type definitions in the schema — in other words, which elements contain other elements and attributes. You need to have a good understanding of the pieces and parts of your content before you can create a set of structural components to accurately describe them.

A quick look at `bookstore.xml` confirms that you will need to create complex type definitions for the `books`, `book`, and `customer` elements.

Start by creating a complex type definition (if you're shaky on what terms like "complex type definition" mean, see Chapter 10) for the root element of the `bookstore.xml` document, `books`:

```
<xsd:element name="books">
 <xsd:complexType>
  <xsd:sequence>
   <xsd:element name="book" type="bookType"/>
```

```
    <xsd:element ref="totalCost"/>
    <xsd:element name="customer" type="customerType"/>
  </xsd:sequence>
 </xsd:complexType>
</xsd:element>
```

You'll need to add a simple type definition for the `totalCost` element, but here's a timesaver: The format of the data is the same as the `price` element in the `books2.xsd` schema, so you can just change the name and use the same definition, like this:

```
<xsd:element name="totalCost">
 <xsd:simpleType>
  <xsd:restriction base="xsd:string">
   <xsd:pattern value="\$[0-9]{1,4}.[0-9]{2}"/>
  </xsd:restriction>
 </xsd:simpleType>
</xsd:element>
```

As we're sure you've noticed, "simple" type definitions aren't necessarily that simple! The term just means they don't contain other elements.

You'll also need two complex datatypes for `bookType` and `customerType`. You'll find out how to create complex datatypes later in this chapter.

Using Datatypes Effectively

You can use XML Schema datatypes in your schemas whether your document content is data intensive or text intensive. (Not sure about the distinction, grasshopper? Read on and become enlightened!)

Using datatypes with data-intensive content

For data-intensive content such as e-mail addresses, time and date information, and floating-point numbers — numbers with a decimal point, XML Schema offers built-in datatypes for most datatypes used in common programming languages such as Java.

For a graphic presentation of the built-in datatype hierarchy, see the diagram "Built-in datatypes" in the W3C Schema Recommendation at

```
www.w3.org/TR/xmlschema-2/#built-in-datatypes
```

The schema definition of each datatype can be found in the W3C Schema for Datatype Definitions at

```
www.w3.org/TR/xmlschema-2/#schema
```

In addition, XML Schema offers the capability to further customize these built-in datatypes by defining new ones. For example, numeric data of any type can be restricted to

✔ A minimum value, either exclusive or inclusive
✔ A maximum value, either exclusive or inclusive

You don't have to use minimum values and maximum values together; you can use one or the other, or both. For example, if you want to be sure that a telephone number has at least ten digits (the seven-digit number plus the area code), you can set the minimum value to 10.

If you want to leave the maximum size of the phone number open so folks can include an extension or even an international number, just don't set the maximum size. Or if you want to be safe, you can cap the phone number at 50 characters or so, just so you don't get a 1,000-digit phone number.

Sometimes, of course, your minimum value and maximum value are the same. Say what? You read right: If you want to be sure a value is made up of a specific number of digits (nine of 'em for a Social Security number, for example), you'd set both the minimum value and maximum value to 9. A Social Security number has to be *at least* 9 digits but *no more than* 9 characters; setting the minimum and maximum values to the same number ensures that you get *exactly* 9 digits. It may look silly, but it works.

You could do something similar by using totalDigits, as in the following simple type definition for the custNumber element:

```
<xsd:element name="custNumber">
 <xsd:simpleType>
  <xsd:restriction base="xsd:integer">
   <xsd:totalDigits value="6"/>
  </xsd:restriction>
 </xsd:simpleType>
</xsd:element>
```

You can also further restrict numeric data that includes a decimal point. You can specify

✔ The total number of digits in the data (includes digits on both sides of the decimal point)
✔ The number of digits to the right of the decimal point

For example, if you want to include the price for a book, you could require that your datatype specifies four total digits, with two digits after the decimal place, like this:

```
<xsd:element name="price">
 <xsd:simpleType>
  <xsd:restriction base="xsd:decimal">
   <xsd:totalDigits value="4"/>
   <xsd:fractionDigits value="2"/>
  </xsd:restriction>
 </xsd:simpleType>
</xsd:element>
```

This datatype is derived from the `xsd:decimal` type. The value for `totalDigits` specifies the total number of digits in the content of the `price` element. The value for `fractionDigits` specifies the number of the total digits that must occur after the decimal point.

Using datatypes with text-intensive content

For text-intensive content such as technical manuals or textbooks, XML Schema offers the `string` datatype and other built-in datatypes for text content, including time and date formats. You can heavily customize the content of your string by creating custom datatypes — so valid string content can contain goodies like these:

- ✔ Specific patterns of alphanumeric characters
- ✔ A minimum and/or a maximum length (number of characters)
- ✔ One of a list of valid values
- ✔ Instructions for preserving or converting white space in content

For example, to allow `zip` to be either a five- or a nine-digit number, we used a modification of the `string` datatype that includes a specific pattern that (in turn) includes both possibilities. Here's what it looks like:

```
<xsd:element name="zip">
 <xsd:simpleType>
  <xsd:restriction base="xsd:string">
   <xsd:pattern value="\d{5}(-\d{4})?"/>
  </xsd:restriction>
 </xsd:simpleType>
</xsd:element>
```

This specifies a pattern of five single digits, followed by four more optional single digits — the ? means the part contained in parentheses can occur zero or one times.

Making Elements Work Wisely and Well

One of the first steps in designing an effective schema is to define elements and attributes. Your XML document will include elements and attributes in a particular pattern — and you have to specify every one of them in the schema if you want the document to be valid.

The basic structure of your schema is based on the structure of the content you want to describe in an XML document. The content itself will tell you which elements are complex types (contain other elements and/or attributes) and which elements are simple types (contain only text content).

When it's clear which elements are complex types and which are simple types, you can create the schema type definitions to specify these elements and attributes.

Creating crafty content models

Content models define what type of content can be contained in an element. The four types of content are:

- ✔ **Element:** The element can contain child elements.
- ✔ **Text:** The element can contain only text.
- ✔ **Mixed:** The element can contain child elements *and* text.
- ✔ **Empty:** The element cannot contain child elements or text but can include an attribute.

See Chapters 9 and 10 for detailed examples of each content model.

Both element content and text content are pretty straightforward. An element-content model requires a complex type definition. A text-content model can be defined with a simple element declaration, as here:

```
<xsd:element name="date" type="xsd:date"/>
```

where name specifies the element name (date) and type specifies an XML Schema datatype (xsd:date).

If your content lends itself to elements that can contain other elements as well as text content, use a mixed-content model. As you'd expect, such a model is generally more useful for text-intensive content than for data-intensive content. (See Chapter 9 for a detailed example of a mixed-content model.)

Using an empty content model is (believe it or not) a useful way to include attributes without specifying any element content. Basically, the empty element acts as a container for attribute content. For example, the source element is an empty element used to contain the sourceInfo attribute, as shown in the following markup for a complex datatype named sourceInfo:

```
<xsd:complexType name="sourceInfo">
 <xsd:attribute name="sourceType" use="required">
  <xsd:simpleType>
   <xsd:restriction base="xsd:string">
    <xsd:enumeration value="Retail"/>
    <xsd:enumeration value="Wholesale"/>
   </xsd:restriction>
  </xsd:simpleType>
 </xsd:attribute>
</xsd:complexType>
```

The empty element is the source element, which is declared like so:

```
<xsd:element name="source" type="sourceInfo"/>
```

A matter of selection

You can build flexibility into your XML document by including options for selecting element and/or attribute content in your schema. You can choose what attributes work with an element or which elements make up the content model for an element. You use the enumeration compositor for attributes and the choice compositor for elements. By adding flexibility to the schema and the content it can describe, built-in selection mechanisms help you create a schema that fits a wider range (or bigger collection) of content. If you aren't sure exactly what the content model for an element will be, down to the last element, or you want to allow some flexibility in the attributes and values an element takes, use a selection.

You use the choice compositor element to make a choice between child elements. For example, you could specify a choice of customer types in the XML Schema document, as shown here:

```
<xsd:element name="priceType">
 <xsd:complexType>
  <xsd:choice maxOccurs="unbounded">
   <xsd:element ref="Retail"/>
   <xsd:element ref="Wholesale"/>
  </xsd:choice>
 </xsd:complexType>
</xsd:element>
<xsd:element name="Retail" type="xsd:string"/>
<xsd:element name="Wholesale" type="xsd:string"/>
```

where the `priceType` element can contain either a `Retail` element or a `Wholesale` element — either a `Retail` element or a `Wholesale` element is a valid option in an XML document that conforms to this schema.

The `choice` compositor element in the preceding example includes a `maxOccurs` attribute with the value `unbounded`. The `unbounded` occurrence constraint means this choice can occur an unlimited number of times in the XML document — which means you can include any number of `Retail` elements *and* any number of `Wholesale` elements. That's a handy way to give your document structure some flexibility.

The following components are required when you want to provide a choice between attribute values:

- ✔ A complex type definition for the element containing the attribute
- ✔ An attribute declaration
- ✔ A simple type definition
- ✔ A restriction on the simple type definition
- ✔ A series of enumeration elements to define the possible attribute values

Although creating attribute choices might seem complex, it's actually quite simple. For example, to include a choice of values for the `custType` attribute, you could use this markup:

```
<xsd:element name="customer">
 <xsd:complexType>
  <xsd:attribute name="custType" use="required">
   <xsd:simpleType>
    <xsd:restriction base="xsd:string">
     <xsd:enumeration value="newRetail"/>
     <xsd:enumeration value="prevRetail"/>
     <xsd:enumeration value="newWholesale"/>
     <xsd:enumeration value="prevWholesale"/>
    </xsd:restriction>
   </xsd:simpleType>
  </xsd:attribute>
 </xsd:complexType>
</xsd:element>
```

The `custType` attribute of the `customer` element includes a `simpleType` element that creates a simple type definition that includes a `restriction` element. The `restriction` element creates a constraint on the string content of the `custType` attribute. The four `enumeration` elements spell out the four valid choices for the value of the `custType` attribute.

Mixing up the order

You can also make your schema more flexible by using a `choice` compositor to include a selection of elements that contain different child elements (or that contain different sequences of the *same* child elements).

For example, to give your schema an option to specify the `author` and `title` in different sequences, you could include a choice of `format1` and `format2` elements, as shown here:

```
<xsd:element name="book">
 <xsd:complexType>
  <xsd:choice>
   <xsd:element ref="format1"/>
   <xsd:element ref="format2"/>
  </xsd:choice>
 </xsd:complexType>
</xsd:element>
<xsd:element name="format1">
 <xsd:complexType>
  <xsd:sequence>
   <xsd:element ref="author"/>
   <xsd:element ref="title"/>
  </xsd:sequence>
 </xsd:complexType>
</xsd:element>
<xsd:element name="format2">
 <xsd:complexType>
  <xsd:sequence>
   <xsd:element ref="title"/>
   <xsd:element ref="author"/>
  </xsd:sequence>
 </xsd:complexType>
</xsd:element>
<xsd:element name="author" type="xsd:string"/>
<xsd:element name="title" type="xsd:string"/>
```

It's certainly possible to include flexibility in your schemas by using selections of elements and attributes. As you can see in this example, though, your schema can quickly become complex.

Using Complex Datatypes

XML Schema offers extensive support for custom (user-derived) datatypes. Using these custom datatypes gives you tight control over the structure of the content in your XML document.

Both simple and complex types can be used for custom datatypes. Simple types are used to put further restrictions on a datatype. You could, for example, put constraints on the format of the `email` element in the bookstore schema. For example, the following markup restricts the content to any number of alphanumeric characters followed by an @, followed by any number of alphanumeric characters, a period, and any number of alphanumeric characters (Now, *there's* a long description of an e-mail address!):

```
<xsd:element name="email">
 <xsd:simpleType>
  <xsd:restriction base="xsd:string">
   <xsd:pattern value="(\w+)@(\w+).(\w+)"/>
  </xsd:restriction>
 </xsd:simpleType>
</xsd:element>
```

Complex datatypes can be named — and that allows you to reuse a datatype (even a complex one) in your schema. As a result, you can write more efficient (and less complex!) schemas. Take a look at the following markup:

```
<xsd:element name="books">
 <xsd:complexType>
  <xsd:sequence maxOccurs="unbounded">
   <xsd:element ref="book"/>
  </xsd:sequence>
 </xsd:complexType>
</xsd:element>
<xsd:element name="book">
 <xsd:complexType>
  <xsd:sequence>
   <xsd:element ref="author"/>
   <xsd:element ref="title"/>
   <xsd:element ref="publisher"/>
   <xsd:element ref="price"/>
   <xsd:element ref="isbn"/>
  </xsd:sequence>
 </xsd:complexType>
</xsd:element>
<xsd:element name="author" type="xsd:string"/>
...
```

This portion of the schema document uses a `book` element with a complex type definition but doesn't name the type. Although you can include as many `book` elements as your heart desires, you can't reuse the structure of the `book` element for another element without rewriting the entire complex type definition. (D'oh!)

In the following example, a complex type definition is used to create a complex datatype named `bookType`:

```
<xsd:element name="books">
 <xsd:complexType>
  <xsd:sequence maxOccurs="unbounded">
   <xsd:element name="book" type="bookType"/>
  </xsd:sequence>
 </xsd:complexType>
</xsd:element>
<xsd:complexType name="bookType">
 <xsd:sequence>
  <xsd:element ref="author"/>
  <xsd:element ref="title"/>
  <xsd:element ref="publisher"/>
  <xsd:element ref="price"/>
  <xsd:element ref="isbn"/>
 </xsd:sequence>
</xsd:complexType>
<xsd:element name="author" type="xsd:string"/>
...
```

The complex datatype is named `bookType` — otherwise, these schemas are exactly the same. The advantage of using a complex datatype is that you can reuse it an unlimited number of times. This datatype definition is not limited to any particular element. You could, for instance, include a new element named `childrensBook` with the `bookType` datatype with just an element declaration, like this:

```
<xsd:element name="childrensBook" type="bookType"/>
```

You can download the entire `bookstore.xsd` schema file at `www.dummies.com/go/xmlfd4e`. (You can also view it in Listing 10-2 in Chapter 10.) You have all the necessary techniques under your belt to create this schema file.

When XML Schemas Collide: Namespaces

You can use namespaces to include references to as many other schemas as you want from within one master schema document. Doing so enables you to use elements and attributes from more than one schema within your XML document.

A *namespace* is a collection of all the names of elements, types, and attributes in a specific schema. Because you can use components from multiple schemas in your master schema document, it's nearly inevitable that conflicts arise — and that they're mainly a result of namespace issues. Collisions can occur, for example, if an element in one schema has the same name as an element in another schema. The more elements you have, the likelier that is.

Namespaces enable you to associate prefixes with specific schemas. You can then reference the elements, types, and attributes from a specific schema quickly and easily. For example, names from XML Schema documents usually have an xs: or xsd: prefix.

Namespaces are also called *vocabularies* because they consist of a collection of names and definitions.

For example, you could include components from other bookstore schemas in your XML document by first identifying the namespaces and defining prefixes for those namespaces in the schema element of your schema document, as in the following:

```
<?xml version="1.0" encoding="UTF-8"?>
<xsd:schema xmlns:xsd="http://www.w3.org/2001/XMLSchema"
            targetNamespace="http://xmlfd.com/ns/bookstore"
            xmlns:ob="http://www.oregonbooksellers.com/oregonBooks"
            xmlns:nwb="http://www.northwestbooks.net/new"
            xmlns:fic="http://www.fictionwriters.org/fiction"
            elementFormDefault="qualified">
```

Then add xsd:import elements to indicate where the schema documents for these namespaces can be found, like so:

```
<xsd:import namespace="http://www.oregonbooksellers.com/oregonBooks"
 schemaLocation="books.xsd"/>
<xsd:import namespace="http://www.northwestbooks.net/new"
 schemaLocation="newbooks.xsd">
<xsd:import namespace="http://www.fictionwriters.org/fiction"
 schemaLocation="fiction.xsd">


 <xsd:element name="books">
. . .
```

The first line of the schema element declares the default namespace for the schema — the XML Schema namespace — and associates the xsd: prefix with this namespace so you can use names such as schema, element, attribute, as defined by the XML Schema specification:

```
xsd:schema xmlns:xsd="http://www.w3.org/2001/XMLSchema"
```

The second line creates a namespace for the elements defined in this schema document — for example, `books`, `book`, `customer`. Specifying a *target name-space* allows you to use these components in other schema documents:

```
targetNamespace="http://xmlfd.com/ns/bookstore"
```

The next three lines in the `schema` element associate prefixes with additional namespaces, so you can use components from those schemas in your schema document:

```
xmlns:ob="http://www.oregonbooksellers.com/books.xsd"
xmlns:nwb="http://www.northwestbooks.net/newbooks.xsd"
xmlns:fic="http://www.fictionwriters.org/fiction.xsd">
```

The final line in the schema element is added because, by default, only glob-ally declared elements and attributes are associated with the target name-space. (Global elements and attributes are children of the `schema` element.) To add local elements to the target namespace, you add:

```
elementFormDefault="qualified"
```

The next three lines in the schema document indicate the location of the schemas associated with the three imported namespaces:

```
<xsd:import namespace="http://www.oregonbooksellers.com/books.xsd"
 schemaLocation="books.xsd"/>
<xsd:import namespace="http://www.northwestbooks.net/newbooks.xsd"
 schemaLocation="newbooks.xsd">
<xsd:import namespace="http://www.fictionwriters.org/fiction.xsd"
 schemaLocation="fiction.xsd">
```

To access elements from other namespaces, you create components that include the prefix you assigned to that namespace. You could, for example, define new elements to include in the `book` element in the following way:

```
<xsd:element name="book">
 <xsd:complexType>
  <xsd:sequence maxOccurs="unbounded">
    <xsd:element ref="author"/>
    <xsd:element ref="ob:title"/>
    <xsd:element ref="nwb:publisher"/>
    <xsd:element ref="fic:price"/>
  </xsd:sequence>
 </xsd:complexType>
</xsd:element>
<xsd:element name="author" type="xsd:string"/>
```

The `book` element is a complex type element — it contains other elements. The complex type definition defines a sequence of four elements. The `author` element is defined in this schema. The next three elements in the sequence are defined in other schemas. By using a `ref` attribute with a prefix associated with an imported namespace in the element declaration, the name and definition for that element are imported into this schema document. The `title` element definition is imported from the namespace associated with the prefix `ob:`, the publisher element from the namespace associated with the prefix `nwb:`, and the price element from the namespace with the prefix `fic:`.

Namespaces are one of the most complex areas in XML — especially in XML Schema. For more details on using namespaces in schemas, see "Working with Namespaces in XML Schema" at

```
http://msdn.microsoft.com/library/default.asp?url=/library/en-
              us/dnexxml/html/xml08192002.asp
```

Including External Data

If you're using a Document Type Definition (DTD) to drive the creation of your XML documents, it" easy to include external data by using entities and notations. Alas, a major weakness of XML Schema is its meager support (so far!) for entities and notations — you can use them in your schemas, but only in very specific and limited ways.

If your XML document includes references to external non-XML data or external entities (any nontext file, like a picture or an XML file), consider using a DTD rather than a schema — and also check out Chapter 8 for more details on DTDs and Chapter 9 for more information on using entities in schemas.

XML Schema only provides for entities and notations to be used as attribute values, rather than as elements. This severely limits the use of external data in your schemas. Better support for entities and notations in XML Schema is at the top of the wish list for improvements in the next version of the XML Schema specification.

Including/Excluding Document Content

XML Schema includes two methods for including or excluding content in an XML document. The first method is using a `choice` group, which allows you to use either/or choices between two elements. as well as choices among several elements. For example, you could extend the bookstore schema to include a choice between child elements of the book element. In this example, the choice is between the publisher and the isbn elements:

```
<xsd:element name="book">
 <xsd:complexType>
  <xsd:choice>
   <xsd:element ref="publisher"/>
   <xsd:element ref="isbn"/>
  </xsd:choice>
 </xsd:complexType>
</xsd:element>
<xsd:element name="publisher" type="xsd:string"/>
<xsd:element name="isbn" type="xsd:string"/>
```

The second method uses a substitution group, which allows you to substitute one element for another element of the same type (or one derived from the same type). One element acts as the head of the substitution group; you can replace this element with other elements from the group as needed.

If the bookstore schema included a location element, and you wanted to replace it with a more specific element (such as OakwayCenter, RiverValleyMall, or GatewayMall), you could create a substitution group so you could use one of these more specific elements.

To create a substitution group in the bookstore schema, follow these steps:

1. **Add a location element.**

   ```
   <xsd:element name="location" type="locationType" abstract="true"/>
   ```

   The location element declaration includes an abstract attribute with the value true. Because the location element is abstract, it can't appear in an XML document; instead, it's represented in the document by a member of the substitution group. The location element is the head element of the substitution group.

2. **Include a substitutionGroup that consists of three other elements:** OakwayCenter, RiverValleyMall, **and** GatewayMall.

   All of them use the same datatype: locationType.

   ```
   <xsd:element name="OakwayCenter" type="locationType"
    substitutionGroup="location"/>
   <xsd:element name="RiverValleyMall" type="locationType"
    substitutionGroup="location"/>
   <xsd:element name="GatewayMall" type="locationType"
    substitutionGroup="location"/>
   ```

   Each of these element declarations includes a substitutionGroup attribute with the value location to identify it as a member of this group.

3. **Define the** `locationType` **datatype.**

It includes a sequence of four elements: `address`, `phone`, `fax`, and `email`:

```
<xsd:complexType name="locationType">
 <xsd:sequence>
  <xsd:element name="address" type="xsd:string"/
  <xsd:element name="phone" type="xsd:string"/>
  <xsd:element name="fax" type="xsd:string"/>
  <xsd:element name="email" type="xsd:string"/>
 </xsd:sequence>
</xsd:complexType>
```

Your XML document can now use an `OakwayCenter`, `RiverValleyMall`, or `GatewayMall` element in place of a `location` element.

Converting DTDs to Schemas

If you've been using DTDs to drive the development of your XML documents, you may want to convert the DTD to a schema to provide tighter control of your document content.

Tools for DTD-to-schema conversion are available both separately and as part of XML editor packages (such as XMLSpy and Turbo XML). Doing the conversion yourself, however — without any additional software — is easy. Just keep in mind as you do the conversion that a DTD is usually a *less*-specific structure than a schema. You'll definitely have to modify the DTD structure to change it from a general document-description tool to a much more specific, datatype-focused tool that utilizes the features of XML Schema. No instant transformation here.

Even if you use a tool for DTD-to-schema conversion, you'll still need to tweak the resulting schema by hand in order to make it more specific. (You'll need to add in things like complex datatypes and simple type definitions, for example.)

Take a look at a DTD (`books2.dtd`) to validate `books2.xml` (Listing 11-1); then we look more closely at how to transform this DTD into a schema. (See Chapter 8 to refresh your memory about DTD syntax.)

Listing 11-1: Books2 DTD

```
<!ELEMENT books (book+)>
<!ELEMENT book (title, author, publisher, price, isbn)>
<!ATTLIST book
 contentType CDATA #REQUIRED
```

```
 format CDATA #REQUIRED>
<!ELEMENT title (#PCDATA)>
<!ELEMENT author (#PCDATA)>
<!ELEMENT publisher (#PCDATA)>
<!ELEMENT price (#PCDATA)>
<!ELEMENT isbn (#PCDATA)>
```

The first line specifies that the books element includes one or more book
elements:

```
<!ELEMENT books (book+)>
```

To create the same specification in an XML Schema, use a complex type definition and a sequence compositor with unlimited occurrence:

```
<xsd:element name="books">
  <xsd:complexType>
   <xsd:sequence maxOccurs="unbounded">
    <xsd:element ref="book"/>
   </xsd:sequence>
  </xsd:complexType>
```

The next DTD line indicates that the book element contains five other elements in a specific order:

```
<!ELEMENT book (title, author, publisher, price, isbn)>
```

To convert this DTD element declaration to a schema declaration, we create
a complex type definition and a sequence, as follows:

```
<xsd:element name="book">
  <xsd:complexType>
   <xsd:sequence>
    <xsd:element ref="title"/>
    <xsd:element ref="author"/>
    <xsd:element ref="publisher"/>
    <xsd:element ref="price"/>
    <xsd:element ref="isbn"/>
   </xsd:sequence>
  </xsd:complexType>
```

The book element in the DTD includes two attributes:

```
<!ATTLIST book
 contentType CDATA #REQUIRED
 format CDATA #REQUIRED>
```

These attributes each have two possible values, so we include them in the schema's complex type definition for the book element:

```
<xsd:element name="book">
 <xsd:complexType>
  <xsd:sequence>
   ...
  </xsd:sequence>
  <xsd:attribute name="contentType" use="required">
   <xsd:simpleType>
    <xsd:restriction base="xsd:string">
     <xsd:enumeration value="Fiction"/>
     <xsd:enumeration value="Nonfiction"/>
    </xsd:restriction>
   </xsd:simpleType>
  </xsd:attribute>
  <xsd:attribute name="format" use="required">
   <xsd:simpleType>
    <xsd:restriction base="xsd:string">
     <xsd:enumeration value="Hardback"/>
     <xsd:enumeration value="Paperback"/>
    </xsd:restriction>
   </xsd:simpleType>
  </xsd:attribute>
 </xsd:complexType>
</xsd:element>
```

You use the general DTD definitions for book attributes and transform them into very specific schema definitions.

The attribute declarations for the two attributes are included at the end of the complex type definition for this element. The DTD uses CDATA to specify that the content is any combination of characters; by contrast, the schema invokes specific restrictions on the XML Schema string datatype: Both the DTD and the schema define the attribute content as a string, but the DTD allows the content to include any string, while the XML Schema only allows specific strings.

```
<!ATTLIST book
 contentType CDATA #REQUIRED
 format CDATA #REQUIRED>
```

#REQUIRED specifies that the attribute is required and is replaced with use="required" in the schema, which looks like this:

```
<xsd:attribute name="format" use="required">
```

The following lines of the DTD declare elements with PCDATA content. PCDATA stand for parsed character data — text that the document processor actually looks at and interprets to display both content and markup. For example, the character entity < would be interpreted by the processor as <. PCDATA content can include numbers, letters, symbols, and entities.

```
<!ELEMENT title (#PCDATA)>
<!ELEMENT author (#PCDATA)>
<!ELEMENT publisher (#PCDATA)>
<!ELEMENT price (#PCDATA)>
<!ELEMENT isbn (#PCDATA)>
```

In this case, the schema uses the string datatype for the first three elements:

```
<xsd:element name="title" type="xsd:string"/>
<xsd:element name="author" type="xsd:string"/>
<xsd:element name="publisher" type="xsd:string"/>
```

You can use more specific XML Schema datatypes for PCDATA content, such as date and time formats. XML Schema also allows you to further restrict the string datatype if you want to control other attributes (such as the pattern of the characters, minimum and maximum length, and instructions for dealing with white space). For the bookstore example, we want to create more specific definitions for the price and isbn elements, so we add datatypes for these elements with simple type definitions:

```
<xsd:element name="price">
 <xsd:simpleType>
  <xsd:restriction base="xsd:string">
   <xsd:pattern value="\$[0-9]{1,4}.[0-9]{2}"/>
  </xsd:restriction>
 </xsd:simpleType>
</xsd:element>
<xsd:element name="isbn">
 <xsd:simpleType>
  <xsd:restriction base="xsd:string">
   <xsd:pattern value="[0-1][0-9]{9}"/>
  </xsd:restriction>
 </xsd:simpleType>
</xsd:element>
```

Schemas are designed to be more specific than DTDs. If you convert a DTD to a schema, convert the general DTD markup to specific XML Schema markup whenever possible. Fortunately, both built-in and user-derived XML Schema datatypes make this conversion possible.

As you can see, it's really not difficult to convert a DTD to an XML schema. What you gain is a much more specific validation tool for your XML documents.

This chapter introduces all the essential techniques for modifying schema documents so they meet your document validation requirements. In addition, it covers how to convert a DTD to a more specific schema document. That's a start. In the next chapter, you discover the art of transforming XML documents with XSL (Extensible Style Language).

Part IV

Transforming and Processing XML

The 5th Wave   By Rich Tennant

SNOW GLOBE DATA STORAGE

Okay let's shake this thing and see what we come up with.

In this part. . .

By itself, XML doesn't look like much in a Web browser. But there's a lot more to XML than making it look pretty for human reading or consumption. Part IV delves into packaging and delivering XML content for all kinds of uses. Chapter 12 covers how the eXtensible Stylesheet Language (XSL) works with XML, not only to turn XML into HTML, but also to turn it into just about any format you might need.

Chapter 13 introduces XPath, a powerful tool for mapping elements, attributes, and content in an XML document. But wait, there's more: The XPath Analyzer in XMLSpy helps you fine-tune your use of XPath for even mightier results.

Chapter 14 gives you pointers in handling XML for data delivery, explains how XML processors read and internalize XML content (as well as other aspects of internalizing and handling XML content for reuse, delivery, or transformation), then calls it a day and orders out for pizza (just kidding).

Chapter 12

Handling Transformations with XSL

XSL (eXtensible Stylesheet Language) helps you do something meaningful with your XML. Though XSL is the stylesheet language created specifically for XML, it's more than just a tool for creating display templates. XSL is also a powerful tool for converting your XML document from one set of markup (vocabulary) to another — a key component of many solutions that use XML for data exchange. This capability is equally important if you want to turn your XML into a format that a display device can understand — say, eXtensible HyperText Markup Language (XHTML) or Portable Document Format (PDF).

One great thing about XSL is that (surprise!) it's really just XML. An XSL document is simply an XML document written according to a particular set of rules. The really good news is that you don't have to learn a new language to learn XSL — just the particular rules that apply to the creation of transformations or the use of formatting objects. Learning to use XSL is just like learning to use any other XML vocabulary. Neat, huh?

An XML vocabulary is a set of names and definitions for XML elements, attributes, and datatypes. A vocabulary is defined in an XML Schema or a DTD.

In this chapter, you'll find out how XSL's two sides, transformation and formatting, make it a powerful tool for manipulating your XML for a variety of purposes.

The Two Faces of XSL

XML's style needs are pretty extensive. Clean XML document structures are rarely in the form you need for presentation, and you may need to present the same XML document in several ways — in print, on the screen, or even in a multimedia presentation. In addition, for those who want to take full advantage of XML's power as a tool for sharing data across systems, there should be an easy way to convert documents from one vocabulary to another.

The architects of XML have you covered. They decided that the responsibility for display and for document conversion should be handled by a separate mechanism rather than XML proper, so they developed XSL as a special vocabulary of XML, designed to describe stylesheets for XML documents. During development, these same architects realized that creating one mechanism for both display and conversion was a Herculean task. So they split the style and conversion mechanisms of XSL into two different but related mechanisms:

- **XSL Transformations (XSLT)** handles the conversion from one set of markup to another.

- **XSL Formatting Objects (XSL-FO)** helps you format XML for devices that want to display XML.

XSLT

The first and most well-developed face of XSL is a conversion tool known as XSLT. The *T* stands for *transformation,* and that's exactly what this part of XSL is designed to do — use a set of rules to *transform* (that is, convert) documents described by one set of elements into documents described by another set of elements. The two sets of elements don't even have to look anything alike.

You can use XSLT in a couple of especially intriguing ways:

- **To transform documents described using XML elements into HTML or XHTML for display in a Web browser.** This nifty trick overcomes the dilemma created by the overall lack of consistency in browser support for XML and its friends, such as XSL-FO and even CSS. One day, browsers will all be XML savvy, but until then, XSLT lets us have our cake and eat it too — with XSLT, you can describe data with XML for storage and manipulation and transform it into HTML or XHTML to display it on the Web for all the world to see.

- **In XML-based data exchange systems.** Systems need to exchange data regularly, and many use XML for that exchange. More often than not, the two systems don't use the same XML internally, so they have to spit out and receive data written in an XML vocabulary they aren't ready to work with. These systems use XSLT to convert data from their internal XML vocabulary to one that another system can work with, and vice versa.

To write an XSLT stylesheet, you simply identify an element in one document and specify how it should be described using a different element or set of elements in the new document. You can grab entire elements or just an element's content. You can even reference attribute values and turn them into element content (or turn element content into attribute values). All in all, XSLT is really cool. You'll learn to create a simple XSLT stylesheet later in this chapter.

The ins and outs of data exchange

It's entirely possible that two (or more) systems exchanging data don't use the exact same schema or DTD. One possible solution to this quandary is for one system to change its internal programming to work with the other's DTD or schema. As much as this fosters a cooperative spirit, often it simply isn't practical. If a system is built around a particular DTD or schema, you can't just come along and rebuild it.

A more practical solution is for each system to support data transformation so that each can continue to use the format it needs. Here's how that solution works:

1. When My Business, Inc., gets data from Your Company, Ltd., that's described with markup based on Your Company's schema or DTD, My Business simply transforms that data into its own data formats (described with markup based on My Business's schema or DTD) before pulling it in.

2. Alternatively, Your Company, Ltd., may be nice enough to transform its data to My Business's XML format before sending it along to My Business.

   Either way, a data transformation has to take place.

The mechanism XML uses for defining how data should be transformed from one flavor of XML markup to another is XSL, and specifically the transformation functionality of XSL known as XSL Transformations (XSLT).

See Chapter 17 for more information on data exchange with XML.

The role of XPath

Without XPath, XSLT simply wouldn't work. Before you can transform an element, attribute, or even a chunk of content using XSLT, you have to be able to identify its exact location. For example, if you want to do something special to every third instance of a list item, you have to be able to point to it — and that's what XPath makes possible. XPath is the mechanism XSLT uses to point to a piece of an XML document so that it can be transformed. If you can't find it, you can't change it.

XPath is a very sophisticated set of rules for identifying the most specific pieces of an XML document. You can not only specify particular elements or attributes or their content, but you can also find individual pieces of content — *strings* — based on the elements and letters around them.

XPath is such a helpful specification that it's not only used by XSLT to guide transformations, but it's also what the XML Linking (XLink) specification uses to make very specific pieces of an XML document into links — and the XML Query language uses XPath for data exchange. Because XPath is so important, we've devoted Chapter 13 to it.

XSL-FO

XSL-FO is used to specify how the structured content of an XML document should be displayed — how content should be styled, laid out, and paginated for presentation on a Web page, a handheld device, or a set of pages in a catalog or book.

As XSL-FO's name indicates, formatting objects are the key to making your XML ready for display.

If you're familiar with CSS, many of these formatting objects will be very familiar, as will the general concepts of formatting.

The different XSL-FO formatting objects are organized into these eight categories:

- ✔ **Declaration, Pagination, and Layout** formatting objects include all the things you need to set up the basic layout of a document, including pages, master pages, and a title.

- ✔ **Block** formatting objects create paragraphs, block quotes, and the other building blocks of a document.

- ✔ **Inline** formatting objects create styles such as boldface, italics, specific colors, and even special individual characters (or strings) inside a block.

- ✔ **Table** formatting objects create and control tables.

- ✔ **List** formatting objects create and control lists of all kinds.

- ✔ **Links and Multi** formatting objects handle — and style — links and multimedia components.

- ✔ **Out-of-line** formatting objects create and style floating areas and footnotes.

- ✔ **Other** formatting objects are catch-alls for the objects that don't fit in other categories.

Knowing which XSL you're dealing with

If you're just getting into XSL, figuring out which *version* of XSL is the topic of a particular book or article can be difficult. Generally, information about XSLT involves the word *transformation,* and anything that involves the word *formatting* probably refers to XSL-FO. The W3C uses the term *XSL* to mean the general XML stylesheet standard that includes both XSLT and XSL-FO. In this book, when we use the term *XSL,* we're also using the W3C definition. But if we're talking about XSLT or XSL-FO specifically, we use their proper names.

When you go looking for information about XSL — whether it's lurking in books, magazines, or online — look for the most recent information. Although XML itself has been stable for quite a while now, XSL is only just now starting to slow down from the blur of changes. The more recent your information is, the more likely it refers to the latest developments of XSL.

For a complete history of XSL, XSLT, and XSL-FO, as well as links to the current XSL recommendation that includes both XSLT and XSL-FO, visit the W3C's XSL page at

`www.w3.org/Style/XSL`

Though the basic concepts behind XSL are fairly straightforward, the syntax for creating XSL documents is complex. Although we'll introduce some basic XSLT syntax later in this chapter, it's not something we can cover in detail in this book. For more detailed information on XSLT, see *XSLT For Dummies,* by Richard Wagner.

Every formatting object has properties that can be applied to it. For example, the object that creates a table (`fo:table`) can take properties that specify how thick its borders are, what color they are, and so on. You can use properties to control just about every aspect of a particular object.

XSL-FO is intended to do more than just specify how XML documents should appear on-screen; it's also designed to make the content easier for computers to read aloud. The aural part of the XSL-FO specification focuses on how to make XML content accessible to everyone, including those who can't see the content.

The specifics of using XSL-FO are beyond the scope of this book. For an excellent introduction to the details, see "What is XSL-FO?" at `www.xml.com/pub/ a/2002/03/20/xsl-fo.html`.

XSL Stylesheets Are XML Documents

If you're a little perplexed by all this alphabet-soup terminology, don't worry: XSL stylesheets (whether XSLT or XSL-FO) are really just XML documents. They use elements, attributes, and all the other standard XML syntax tools; the rules they must follow are what set them apart from other XML documents.

Because XSL stylesheets are XML documents, technically, any system that can process XML can process an XSL stylesheet. For a stylesheet to be useful, however, the system has to know what to do with the results of the processed stylesheet.

The best way to keep up with XSL and new XSL tools is to visit the W3C's XSL Web page (www.w3.org/Style/XSL).

A Simple Transformation Using XSLT

An XSLT stylesheet consists of instructions that tell the computer how to convert a document described by a particular schema or DTD to a document described by a second, *different* schema or DTD. Each instruction focuses on one element in the source document and specifies how it should be changed to fit the second schema or DTD. The stylesheet doesn't replace or change the elements in the source file but instead builds a new file to hold the results of the transformation. When you're working with XSLT, all you're really doing is using XSLT elements to transform a document using one set of elements into a document that uses another set of elements.

The best way to show you how XSLT works is by example. In the following section, we show a simple XSLT stylesheet that transforms books2.xml into an HTML document. After that bit of magic, we break the XSLT stylesheet into its component parts so you can see what's really going on — and how the transformations occurred in each part.

An XSLT Stylesheet for Converting XML to HTML

If we open books2.xml in Internet Explorer, the program ignores all the elements it doesn't recognize — which is all of them — and simply displays the text within the markup, as shown in Figure 12-1.

If you want people to see the books2 document in a useful and meaningful way while they're using a Web browser, you have to describe the document with something the Web browser can recognize and handle — namely, HTML.

If you use the following XSLT stylesheet with books2.xml and then open it in Internet Explorer, as shown in Figure 12-2, you have a much more user-friendly and functional document for the Web.

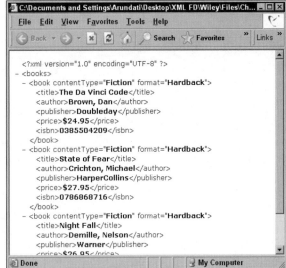

Figure 12-1:
books2.
xml in
standard
XML as
displayed in
Internet
Explorer.

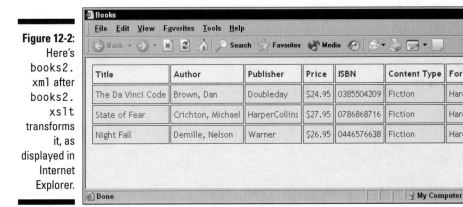

Figure 12-2:
Here's
books2.
xml after
books2.
xslt
transforms
it, as
displayed in
Internet
Explorer.

Listing 12-1 shows all the code for books2.xslt. You'll learn about each part of the code in the following sections.

At www.dummies.com/go/xmlfd4e, you can download the code for books2_xslt.xml (which is books2.xml with a link to the XSLT stylesheet), books2.xslt, and books2_xslt.css.

Listing 12-1: The books2.xslt Stylesheet

```
<?xml version="1.0" encoding="UTF-8"?>
<xsl:stylesheet version="2.0" xmlns:xsl="http://www.w3.org/1999/XSL/Transform">
 <xsl:template match="/">
  <html>
  <meta http-equiv="Content-Type" content="text/html; charset=UTF-8" />
  <head>
  <title>Books</title>
  <link rel="stylesheet" type="text/css" href="books2_xslt.css"/>
  </head>
  <body>
<xsl:for-each select="books">
 <table>
  <tr>
   <th>Title</th>
   <th>Author</th>
   <th>Publisher</th>
   <th>Price</th>
   <th>ISBN</th>
   <th>Content Type</th>
   <th>Format</th>
  </tr>
<xsl:for-each select="book">
  <tr>
   <td>
    <xsl:for-each select="title">
     <xsl:apply-templates />
    </xsl:for-each>
   </td>
   <td>
    <xsl:for-each select="author">
     <xsl:apply-templates />
    </xsl:for-each>
   </td>
   <td>
    <xsl:for-each select="publisher">
     <xsl:apply-templates />
    </xsl:for-each>
   </td>
   <td>
    <xsl:for-each select="price">
     <xsl:apply-templates />
    </xsl:for-each>
   </td>
   <td>
    <xsl:for-each select="isbn">
     <xsl:apply-templates />
    </xsl:for-each>
   </td>
   <td>
    <xsl:for-each select="@contentType">
     <xsl:value-of select="." />
```

```
      </xsl:for-each>
    </td>
    <td>
     <xsl:for-each select="@format">
      <xsl:value-of select="." />
     </xsl:for-each>
    </td>
   </tr>
  </xsl:for-each>
  </table>
  </xsl:for-each>
  </body>
  </html>
 </xsl:template>
</xsl:stylesheet>
```

In a nutshell, this stylesheet specifies exactly how each element in our XML document should be changed to HTML. Each style rule identifies one element from the XML document — and provides instructions for converting it to a similar or equivalent HTML element (or set of elements).

The pieces of the stylesheet puzzle

In this section, we break up an XSLT stylesheet into its component parts to see what makes it do its stuff. XSLT is a robust conversion tool and has many facets; an attempt to describe them all would take us too far afield. Instead, we focus on the most basic structures that make up an XSLT stylesheet. Getting all the pieces of the XSLT puzzle right means creating and using XSLT *templates* to transform one set of markup (vocabulary) to another.

The instructions in an XSLT stylesheet that control how an element and its content should be converted are called *templates*. These instructions identify which element in a document should be changed — and then specify exactly how the element should be changed. The template element goes by a distinctive (if obvious) name: xsl:template.

Using patterns

A template in an XSLT stylesheet focuses on a single node in a document. To identify the node to which the template applies, XSLT uses the match attribute with the xsl:template element to point to a specific node. The value of match is called a *pattern*. The XSLT processor looks at the pattern, works its way through the source document to find the pattern, and then applies the template to every node that matches the pattern. Pretty neat.

The structure of XML documents can be described as a tree. Anywhere that the tree branches is a node. Nodes can be described using family relationships; for example, *this* node is a parent of *that* node; *this other* node is a sibling of *those other* two nodes, and so forth. XSLT uses the nodes of XPath (see

Chapter 13 for more on XPath), which include element, attribute, comment, document element, root, processing instruction, namespace, and text nodes — that should cover it!

Our XSLT document begins with an XML declaration, followed by a namespace declaration that includes the `xsl:` prefix and the URI for the XSLT namespace:

```
<?xml version="1.0" encoding="UTF-8"?>
<xsl:stylesheet version="2.0" xmlns:xsl="http://www.w3.org/1999/XSL/Transform">
```

A namespace is a vocabulary — it's a collection of names and definitions of elements, attributes, and types. A namespace declaration associates a specific namespace (vocabulary) with a document. In this case, any component in the stylesheet that uses an `xsl:` prefix belongs to the XSL namespace (`http://www.w3.org/1999/XSL/Transform`). For more information on namespaces, see Chapter 11.

This is followed by a template:

```
<xsl:template match="/">
```

This template matches the XML document root (/) to the HTML document root — and (as spelled out in Listing 12-1) adds the following HTML markup:

```
<html>
 <meta http-equiv="Content-Type" content="text/html; charset=UTF-8" />
 <head>
 <title>Books</title>
 <link rel="stylesheet" type="text/css" href="books2_xslt.css"/>
 </head>
 <body>
```

This procedure is an easy way to include whatever markup we choose for the head section of the HTML document. Our markup includes a meta tag to specify the character encoding, a title to display in the browser title bar, and a link to an external CSS stylesheet, but any legitimate HTML markup for the head section of an HTML document could be included here.

In our XSLT document, this `xsl:template` element contains the entire HTML document — but we could also use an XSLT stylesheet that uses a separate template element to match each XML element. Here's an example:

```
<xsl:template match="publisher">
 <td>
  <xsl:apply templates/>
 </td>
</xsl:template>
```

The td element creates a table cell in an HTML table — the XSLT stylesheet applies a template to the publisher element and then includes it in an HTML table cell.

Because our XML document can include any number of book elements, our XSLT stylesheet uses one xsl:template element that contains instructions for the transformation of repeating XML elements, as detailed in the following sections of this chapter.

Using instructions to get results

In addition to using a pattern to identify which node(s) in the source document to transform, the template specifies how to transform each node. These instructions guide the XSLT processor through content transformation. For example, we use a value-of instruction with the book attributes to tell the processor to convert the result to text and place it in an HTML table cell:

```
<td>
 <xsl:for-each select="@contentType">
 <xsl:value-of select="." />
 </xsl:for-each>
</td>
```

This snippet says (in effect), "For each contentType attribute node (@), take the text content of that node (. specifies the current node) and make it the content of an HTML table cell — in other words, place the content between an opening (<td>) and closing (</td>) HTML table cell tag."

Processing element content

You use the xsl:apply-templates instruction when you want to return the content and text nodes of the current element and its children — but not the surrounding element tags. For example, to put the content of each XML price element into an HTML table cell without including the surrounding <price></price> tags, we use:

```
<td>
 <xsl:for-each select="price">
 <xsl:apply-templates />
 </xsl:for-each>
</td>
```

Unless you add a select attribute to apply-templates to limit its scope, the template will be applied to the current node *and* to all its child nodes, including any text nodes that are children of the current node.

Choosing templates

Well, okay, what template gets applied here? It depends; the XSLT processor looks for the best template to apply and makes a choice:

- If a select attribute is used with apply-templates, then the processor looks for the best template for that node.
- If no select attribute is used, the template rule that contains the apply-templates instruction is chosen as the current node — in this case, the XML price element.

We've included style instructions for td elements in our CSS stylesheet, so that style is applied to the content of the price element.

So when you create XSLT style rules, you have to think about not only the way you're transforming an individual node, but also how to deal with its content. Does the content from the source document need its own transforming? Should it be nested in a particular set of markup in the new document? Or do you even want to transform the content at all? If you don't specify xsl:apply-templates, the resulting document won't include any of the content from within any element — text, markup, or otherwise.

Adding external CSS

You may have noticed that we included a link to an external CSS stylesheet in our XSLT markup:

```
<link rel="stylesheet" type="text/css" href="books2_xslt.css"/>
```

You can include style information directly in the XSLT markup if you choose, but we find it faster and more efficient to use external CSS and XSLT. Need convincing? Here's why . . .

First, here's the code that sets up an HTML table cell to hold the content of the author element from our XML document:

```
<td>
<xsl:for-each select="author">
 <xsl:apply-templates />
</xsl:for-each>
</td>
```

The following code is concise because we use an external CSS stylesheet to define the display style for the content of a table data <td> tag:

```
td {
    background-color: #ffff80;
    color: #800000;
    text-align: left;
    vertical-align: text-top;
```

```
    padding: 5px;
    font-family: "Trebuchet MS", Verdana, sans-serif;
    font-size: small;
    border-color: #800000;
    border-width: 1px;
    border-style: solid;
}
```

We know you can't tell colors apart in our black-and-white screenshots, but this page actually displays in color: background color, text color, and border color. The style information also includes vertical alignment, padding, and border style instructions.

Okay, now look at the alternative. Here's the same XSLT stylesheet *without* any external CSS:

```
<td style="background-color:#FFFF80; color:#800000;border-color:#800000;
            border-width:1px;border-style:solid;
            font-family:Trebuchet MS, Verdana, sans-serif; font-size:small;
            padding:5px; text-align:left; vertical-align:text-top;">
 <xsl:for-each select="author">
  <xsl:apply-templates />
  </xsl:for-each>
</td>
```

We haven't really changed the XSLT here; we've just used the HTML `style` attribute to write out the style info. And to really ice the cake? We have to change this spec for *every one of the table cells* — every time we want to change the way the information is displayed. Thanks, but we have a life; we choose to use an external CSS stylesheet instead.

Dealing with repeating elements

Our XSLT stylesheet (`books2.xslt`) deals with repeating elements by using a single template element that contains all the instructions for transforming each instance (`xsl:for-each`) of these elements in our XML document. That's one way — but not the only way — to deal with repeating elements. What if your XML document includes a list? A single list might have 50 items — what if you want each of those items transformed the same way? That may sound difficult, but actually, you can handle the task pretty easily if you write a template that loops through the items one at a time, applying the same transformation to each instance of the element — as in the following style rule:

```
<xsl:template match="books/book">
  <ul>
   <xsl:for-each select="publisher">
    <li>
     <xsl:apply-templates/>
```

```
    </li>
   </xsl:for-each>
  </ul>
</xsl:template>
```

Here the xsl:for-each element points at a specific element that is repeated —
and applies the same transformation to each instance of that element. In this
template, every publisher element nested within <books><book> . . .
</book></books> is changed to an HTML list item (li) within an unordered
list (ul).

The XSLT elements we discuss are only a few of the XSL elements that you
can use to transform an XML document from one schema or DTD to another.
You can sort through elements, point to attribute values, create attributes,
and assign attribute values in the results document — and that's only the
beginning.

Creating an XSLT Stylesheet with XSLT Editors

If hand-coding is not your favorite art form, you can also use an XSLT editor
to create your XSLT stylesheets instead. One of the friendliest WYSIWYG
(What You See Is What You Get) XSLT editors is Altova StyleVision. (We'll talk
more about another Altova product, XMLSpy, in Chapter 19.)

StyleVision enables you to open an XML schema document and use a GUI
(Graphic User Interface) to add CSS style rules to your XML elements and
attributes to create an XSLT or XSL-FO stylesheet. Seriously easy.

Altova offers a 30-day trial version of all its products, including StyleVision.
See the link to the trial version of StyleVision on the Web page for this book
at www.dummies.com/go/xmlfd4e. After getting StyleVision on your hard
drive, go ahead and download the books2.xsd file from the same Web page,
and take StyleVision for a spin. Here's how:

1. **Open** books2.xsd **(or any schema document) in StyleVision.**

   At the top left of the StyleVision window, you'll see the document diagram. Under the heading / DocumentRoot, find the books element. Click
   on the + next to books to expand it and display all the elements in
   books2.xsd. You'll see the document diagram on the left above two
   tables of style properties, as shown in Figure 12-3.

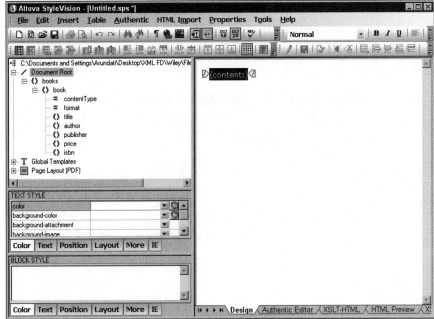

Figure 12-3:
Opening
books2.
xsd in
StyleVision.

2. **Select the** book **element from the document diagram, and drag it onto the pane on the right, onto the area labeled** *(contents)*.

A menu appears, as shown in Figure 12-4.

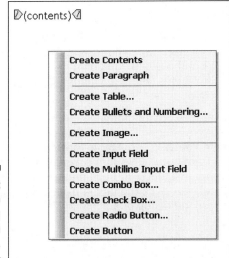

Figure 12-4:
The
Formatting
menu in
StyleVision.

3. **Choose Create Table from the displayed menu.**

The Create Dynamic Table dialog box, shown in Figure 12-5, opens. All the attributes and child elements of the book element are automatically selected.

Figure 12-5:
The Create
Dynamic
Table dialog
box in
StyleVision.

4. **In the Create Dynamic Table dialog box, deselect any attributes or children you don't want to include in the table display and then click OK.**

This action creates table cells for each of the selected attributes and child elements of the book element.

You can specify additional table formatting features in this dialog box:

- **Table Growth** specifies whether the cells of the table are displayed as a column (Top/Down) or as a row (Left/Right). Use the default choice (Top/Down).

- **Display Cells As** specifies how to format the table cells. You can choose Contents to format the cell content as plain text or choose formatting options: Combo Box (drop-down menus), Field (text input fields), Multiline Fields (text area fields), Check Box, or Radio Buttons. Use the default choice (Contents).

- **Header/Footer** is used to create table headers and footers. **Create Header** creates table header cells from the names of the elements or attributes. **Create Footer** creates table footers for tables with multiple columns (Top/Down). The sum of numeric contents in cells can be displayed in a footer if the Summary for Numeric Fields option is checked. Check the box in front of Create Header; then click OK to close the dialog box.

The selected elements and attributes are now displayed on the StyleVision canvas in columns with three rows. The top row is the table header; the middle row contains the opening and closing tags for elements and attributes, with a (Contents) label in between these tags.

You can preview the table display by selecting an XML document to work with. Choose File➪Assign Working XML File and then browse to the location of the XML file. Click OK. Then click on the HTML Preview tab in the bottom right of the StyleVision window to see a preview of the display.

5. **To add formatting properties, place the cursor inside the table, row, column, or cell that you want to format.**

   You choose Table➪Table Properties to open the Table Properties window. You can choose table formatting properties such as alignment, width, and background color for the entire table or for individual rows, columns, or cells.

6. **Select additional formatting properties for individual cells on the StyleVision canvas.**

   You can do so by placing the cursor in the cell to be formatted and then choose styles from the Block Style window at the lower left. Here, you click through the tabs to choose styles from each group of style properties in the Block Style window.

7. **Click the XSLT-HTML tab at the bottom of the canvas on the right side to view the source code for the XSLT document.**

   Click the HTML Preview tab to get a preview of how your XML page appears in a browser after transformation with XSLT.

8. **Choose File➪Save Generated Files➪Save Generated XSLT-HTML File.**

   Sure enough, doing so saves the XSLT stylesheet.

Voilà! You've got a full-fledged XSLT stylesheet! But don't let it just sit there. Attach it to your XML file by adding this line after the XML declaration:

```
<?xml-stylesheet type="text/xsl" href="books2.xslt"?>
```

You now have a stylesheet that can transform any XML document that's based on the schema you started with (books2.xsd) to create a dynamic HTML table from the XML document content.

In the next chapter, you find out all about using XPath to locate elements, attributes, and content in an XML document.

FrontPage 2003 and XSLT

StyleVison is not the only XSLT editor in town — although we do think it's pretty neat. FrontPage 2003 also includes a WYSIWYG XSLT editor that is very easy to use. However, there are several requirements for using XSLT in FrontPage 2003:

✔ Windows Server 2003

✔ IIS 6.0

✔ ASP.NET

✔ Windows SharePoint Services

All of the live data-driven features of FrontPage 2003 require Windows SharePoint Services — basically, a Web-services intranet. You can find a SharePoint hosting service (just use your favorite search engine), or Microsoft offers a free, 30-day trial of SharePoint Services (visit `www.sharepointtrial.com/default.aspx` for more details).

Windows Server 2003, Enterprise edition, and SharePoint Services are included in the FrontPage 2003 trial CD, available for purchase at

```
www.microsoft.com/office/
    frontpage/prodinfo/trial.
    mspx
```

There are lots of XSLT editors to choose among these days — see Chapter 19 for more details. If you don't have a need for the full gamut of SharePoint Services, we recommend you download trial versions of several XSLT editors and see which one works best for you.

If you already own FrontPage 2003, however, be sure to check out the XSLT features. For more information on creating a Web page to display XML data in FrontPage 2003, see

```
http://office.microsoft.com/
    enus/assistance/HA011123381
    033.aspx
```

Note: FrontPage 2003 is no longer included in the Microsoft Office suite, so you must purchase this software as a separate product if you want to use it.

Chapter 13

The XML Path Language

*N*obody creates XML just for the fun of creating XML. The idea is to actually DO something with the XML, and for that you need software to manipulate the XML (software that uses XML document content to populate a database, for example, or software that manages online financial transactions). Software, as smart of some of the programs may be, usually can't figure out XML on its own.

You need some way to tell software where to go in an XML document — you need a language that describes the paths built into a document as well as how to follow a route through that document. XML Path Language (XPath) does just that, providing a concise language describing the location of specific elements, attributes, and their values in an XML document.

Here's how you might describe a path through an XHTML document:

```
"Starting at the top of the document, go to the root element <html>,
then go to the <body> element, and then find the third <p> element."
```

This is quite simple and understandable to a human reader, but what you really want is a common simple language that you can use to describe this path to software. XPath is such a language.

The XPath 1.0 specification (available at www.w3.org/TR/xpath) is all about naming the XML paths that run through a document — its mission in life is to provide a concise language to describe directions for how to get from one place to another in an XML document. XPath 2.0 is a W3C working draft specification (www.w3.org/TR/xpath20/) as of October 2004. For more details on the features in XPath 2.0, see "What's New in XPath 2.0," later in this chapter.

In this chapter, you find out how XPath creates paths to help computer systems find every little piece of markup or content in your XML document. You also discover where those paths lead, what markup to use to describe them, and how to correctly document them.

Why Do You Need Directions?

In XML, you need to know how to get from point A to point B only if there's some purpose to your journey. XML has no equivalent to the Sunday afternoon drive to see the fall colors. XML gurus navigating XML documents are like stern Puritans who travel only when they have a purpose. In other words, if you don't need to worry about paths, hooray — don't bother. But if you do need to know your document's path, then you need the right tool for the job: a specific, XML-based language.

To do some of the higher-end tasks that are possible with XML, you need a language to describe how to move about a document, for two primary reasons:

- ✔ **To find your way to and describe a section of a document that needs to be transformed or formatted for display.** This task involves XSL Transformations (XSLT) or XSL Formatting Objects (XSL-FO). See Chapter 12 for more information.

- ✔ **To be able to point to a certain part of the document.** This task involves the use of XPointer or XML Query (XQuery) language. Visit www.w3.org/TR/xptr-framework/ for more information on XPointer and www.w3.org/XML/Query for information on XQuery.

For example, if you want to transform every paragraph element that contains the word W3C into an indented block with a purple background for display, you have to be able to find those specific paragraphs, which you can do with XPath. Or if you want to create a link from the W3C to every paragraph element that contains the word *W3C*, you have to be able to locate those paragraphs so that you can link to them.

XPath may be used for other purposes as well, but these two tasks were tricky and complex enough that they provided the motivation for writing the XPath specification.

XPath document trees

To understand how XPath describes paths and directions, we use the clients.xml document — an example of an XML document that we could use to keep track of clients:

```
<?xml version="1.0"?>
<!-- Clients.xml-->
<Clients>
<!--This is the root element of Clients.xml-->
 <Client id="c1">
  <Name>Jon Smith</Name>
  <Phone type="home">440-123-3333</Phone>
  <Fax>440-123-3334</Fax>
  <Email>jon@acme.com</Email>
 </Client>
 <Client id="c2">
  <Name>Bill Jones</Name>
  <Phone type="cellphone">330-124-5432</Phone>
  <Fax>440-123-5433</Fax>
  <Email>bjones@someinc.com</Email>
 </Client>
 <Client id="c3">
  <Name>Matt Brown</Name>
  <Phone type="work">220-125-1234</Phone>
  <Phone type="cellphone">233-344-4455</Phone>
  <Phone type="home">234-567-8910</Phone>
  <Fax>220-125-1235</Fax>
  <Email>matthew@hotstuff.com</Email>
 </Client>
</Clients>
```

This document can be laid out like a tree, as shown in Figure 13-1.

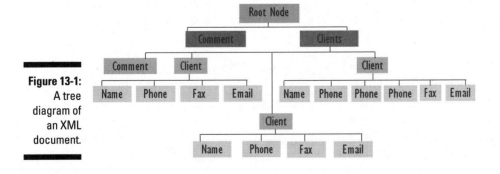

Figure 13-1: A tree diagram of an XML document.

Figure 13-1 shows the *root node,* comments, and elements in the `clients.xml` file (we haven't included the text or attributes in this diagram). These components are called *nodes* in XPath terminology. XPath uses nodes to create a map of an XML document based on family relationships: child, parent, sibling, descendant, ancestor, and so on.

Understanding XPath nodes

Understanding XPath nodes is essential to successfully using XPath in your documents. The XPath document tree is very similar to the DOM (Document Object Model) tree we discuss in Chapter 14 but isn't exactly the same — we'll point out differences as we go along.

The name *node* is borrowed from biology. When a tree or a plant branches, the place where it does so is a node. Sometimes this comparison is carried even farther — a node with no children is called a *leaf.*

There are seven kinds of nodes in the XPath data model:

✔ **Root node:** A single node that is the root of the document tree and contains the entire document. The root node is a concept — there is no visible element or text in a document that represents the root node. A root node contains the element node for the *document element* and can also contain processing instruction nodes and comment nodes.

✔ **Element node:** There is an element node for every element in the document. Element nodes can contain other element nodes, comment nodes, processing instruction nodes, and comment nodes.

The document element node is a single node that contains the entire contents of the document except for any processing instruction nodes or comment nodes that are children of the root node.

The document element is comparable to the root element in an XML document — but be careful! The document element node is not the root node of the document.

✔ **Attribute node:** Each element node has an associated set of attribute nodes. The element is considered the parent of these nodes, but the attribute node is not considered the child of the element node.

The W3C Document Object Model (DOM) considers an attribute to be a *property* of the element that contains it. (For more information on the DOM, see Chapter 14.)

✔ **Namespace node:** Each element has an associated set of namespace nodes — one for each namespace prefix for that element and one for the default namespace. As with attribute nodes, the element node is the parent of the namespace nodes, but the namespace nodes are not considered the children of the element node.

The reason for this contorted reasoning about attribute nodes, namespace nodes, and family relationships in XPath is nerdy stuff that has to do with XML namespaces. If you want a beginner's guide to namespaces, take a peek at Chapter 11. To read even more about the topic of namespaces and how they relate to all manner of XML goodness, we suggest reading Ronald Bourret's "XML Namespaces FAQ" at

```
www.rpbourret.com/xml/NamespacesFAQ.htm
```

If you want to read about it in hard copy, pick up a copy of *XML 1.1 Bible,* 3rd Edition, by Elliotte Rusty Harold (Wiley Publishing).

✔ **Processing instruction node:** There is a processing instruction node for every processing instruction in a document unless the processing instruction is part of a DTD.

The XML declaration is not a processing instruction — therefore, there is no processing instruction node that corresponds to the XML declaration.

✔ **Comment node:** There is a comment node for every comment in a document unless the comment is part of a DTD.

✔ **Text node:** Character data — strings of characters — is contained in text nodes. Each text node contains at least one character, and as much character data as possible is grouped into a single text node — in other words, no text node has a text-node sibling directly before or directly after it.

Reserved characters can't be included in strings in XML documents unless they are part of a CDATA section or unless they're escaped with a character entity For example, to include a <, it must be replaced by < — otherwise, an XML processor interprets the < as the start of a tag.

Characters inside comments, processing instructions, and attribute values are considered part of the comment, processing instruction, or attribute node — they don't make up a separate text node.

Here are some examples of the XPath relationships among the various nodes in clients.xml:

✔ A single node, called the *root node,* is the root of the document tree and contains the entire document.

✔ The root node in clients.xml contains two children: a comment node and the document element node (Clients). These two very different nodes are siblings.

✔ The Clients node is the document element node of the document.

✔ The Clients node has four child nodes: a comment node and three Client element nodes.

✔ The parent of the second comment node in the document is the document element node. The comment node has no children (the text of a comment is considered part of the node) but has three siblings in the form of `Client` element nodes.

✔ Each `Client` element node has children of its own. For example, the third `Client` node has six children elements: a `Name` element node, three `Phone` element nodes, a `Fax` element node, and an `Email` element node. All these element nodes are siblings of one another.

✔ Each of these element nodes has a text node as a child.

✔ The parent of every `Phone` element node is a `Client` element node.

XPath Directions and Destinations

In this section, you take a look at the language that XPath uses to describe a route through a document. We need to clarify that *an XPath* is a terse set of directions presented as a string — which is read by suitable software and then returns a *destination node* or a set of nodes.

A *string* is a term for a line of text. Similarly, when we talk about something being *returned,* we're talking about the *answer* that a piece of software gives if you ask it a question.

Different software systems can use the set of directions in XPath in various ways. For example, a transformation system takes what it finds at the end of the path and applies transformation rules to create new markup from it. The XPointer specification uses this set of directions in its fragment identifier, and the XSL specification uses it as an attribute.

XPath says nothing about what to do with a destination after it's been reached. Again, this is left up to the individual system that uses XPath for its own purposes.

Every trip has three parts, and here is what XPath has to say about each part:

✔ **The starting point** is called the *context node.* It can be the root node of the document or another node in the document.

✔ **The journey itself** consists of both a direction and a number of steps. XPath describes each of these steps using its syntax. Each step is separated by a forward slash (/). Sometimes, a journey consists of one step; at other times, a journey may involve many steps. In the following section, we look at several examples of these steps.

✔ **The destination** can be either a single node or a collection of nodes. This concept shouldn't be too difficult. For example, in a real journey, you could say that your destination is 27 Palace Court, London, W1; or Europe; or England; or London, UK (or, if you're just landing here, Earth). All these statements are correct.

XPath says nothing about what to do when you reach your destination: It just describes the destination and how to get there.

XPath Syntax

XPath uses two types of syntax: an abbreviated form and an unabbreviated form. In this section, we show you both forms. We start with the unabbreviated syntax because it's a little more descriptive and easier to follow.

XPath calls the most important of its set of directions a location step. A *location step* searches for a node depending on the information that you give it. The general syntax for a location step is as follows:

```
axisname :: nodetest[expression1] [expression2] ...
```

Here's a closer look at the parts of this syntax:

✔ axisname is the type of selection that you want to perform. It also tells you the direction in the document that you need to travel. If you select child, descendant, or following-sibling as an axis, you travel forward in the document. If you select parent, ancestor, or previous-sibling, you travel backward in the document. If you select self, you stand still.

✔ nodetest tests for the type of node that you want to select. This is usually the name of a node.

✔ expression appears in square brackets and further refines your selection process for a node or set of nodes. You can use more than one expression (which may also be called a *predicate*).

A *location path* is made up of one or more location steps. A / is used to separate each step.

Before getting into more of the details of XPath, here are a few simple examples of location steps using the clients.xml document. In the examples in the following sections, the starting point (the context node) is the root node of clients.xml, unless otherwise stated.

Got any (XPath) axes to grind?

Here are the various axes that XPath provides, along with a brief description of each:

- ✔ `child` selects the children of the context node.

- ✔ `descendant` selects from any of the descendants of the context node.

- ✔ `parent` selects the parent of the context node.

- ✔ `ancestor` selects the parent of the context node, and the parent of the parent, and so forth, up to the root node.

- ✔ `following-sibling` selects from all the following siblings.

- ✔ `preceding-sibling` selects from all the preceding siblings.

- ✔ `following` is any following node other than attribute or namespace nodes.

- ✔ `preceding` is any preceding node other than attribute or namespace nodes.

- ✔ `attribute` contains all attributes of the context node.

- ✔ `namespace` contains all namespace nodes of the context node.

- ✔ `self` contains just the context node itself.

- ✔ `descendant-or-self` contains the context node and all of its descendants.

- ✔ `ancestor-or-self` contains the context node and all of its ancestors.

Some simple location paths

Here are some simple examples of location steps and location paths using the `clients.xml` document. First, we show you the code, followed by a brief description:

- ✔ **Handy Example #1**

  ```
  child::Clients
  ```

  The axis is `child`, and the node test is `Clients`. This selects all the `Clients` element children of the root node.

- ✔ **Handy Example #2**

  ```
  child::*
  ```

  The axis is `child`, and the node test is `*`, which represents a wildcard selection. This selects all the element children of the context node (the root node, in this case).

✔ **Handy Example #3**

```
child::node()
```

The axis is `child`, and the node test is `node()`, which selects all the child nodes of the root node, including the comment node and the element node `Clients`.

The `child` axis is the default axis for a location step. You can omit `child::` from a location step, if you want — the result will be identical.

Adding expressions

Here are some simple examples of expressions, which further refine the selection process. As before, first we show you the code and then we give a brief description:

✔ **Additional Handy Example #1**

```
child::Clients[position()=1]
```

The axis is `child`, and the node test is `Clients`. We add an expression, `[position()=1]`, which selects the first node that is a child of the root node and is also named `Clients`. You can also abbreviate this to the following format:

```
child::Client[1]
```

In this case, you could also use the `last()` function to return the last node in the list:

```
child::Clients[position()=last()]
```

Or you could do the same thing in abbreviated form, like this:

```
child::Client[last()]
```

Because there's only one `Clients` node, the last `Clients` node is identical to the first `Clients` node.

Taking steps along the XPath

Having taken one step on the path, take another one and step into the document properly. XPath uses a forward slash (/) to tell you when to take another step. The new context node is the node that's selected in the preceding step:

```
child::Clients[position()=1]/child::Client
```

After the first step, you make a new location step from a new context node. In other words, the first step selects the first node that is a child of the root node and is also named `Clients` — and that node becomes the context node for the second step. The second step selects all the nodes that are child nodes of the `Clients` node and that are named `Client`.

Looking at attributes

You can use the value of attributes to narrow your selection of a destination node. For example:

```
Clients/Client[attribute::id="c3"]
```

The first step selects all the nodes that are a child of the root node and are also named `Clients` — the `Clients` node becomes the context node for the second step. The second step selects all the `Client` nodes that are children of the `Clients` node and also have an attribute named `id` with a value of `c3` — which is to say, the last `Client` element.

Going backward

You can also step backward through an XML document. Of course, if you start from the root node, you have nowhere to go. It's like the old joke about taking a picture of someone at the edge of the Grand Canyon ("Just take *one* more step back . . ."). If you want to step backward, you have to start farther forward.

For these next examples, we assume that the context node is the last `Email` element of the third `Client` — that is, the `Email` element with the content `matthew@hotstuff.com`. Here's the first example:

```
preceding-sibling::Fax
```

Using this code returns all the preceding sibling elements called `Fax` — in this case, just one element. The next example returns all the preceding sibling elements called `Phone`:

```
preceding-sibling::Phone
```

When you apply this to the `clients.xml` file, it describes the three `Phone` elements.

Finally, the following path returns the parent element, provided it's named Client:

```
parent::Client
```

When applied to the clients.xml file, this path indeed returns its parent. In this case, the context node is the Email element node of the third Client element node, so this path returns the third Client element node.

Reversing direction

When you start going backward, you also reverse the direction of counting for the position() function. If (for example) you assume the same context node as in the preceding section, what's returned is the Phone element node with a type attribute with a value of home:

```
preceding-sibling::*[position()=1]
```

The following example returns the Name element node:

```
preceding-sibling::*[position()=last()]
```

Null results

Sometimes you ask for something, and nothing is there! For example, the following command returns the preceding parent element if it's called MoneyBags:

```
parent::MoneyBags
```

Alas, there's no parent called MoneyBags, so XPath returns a null value.

Null is one of those nerdy terms that crops up from time to time, and it means there is no value. Null is different from empty, different from zero. It's the black hole of XML — it doesn't suck you in but does just sit there, stubbornly being nothing. Okay, it's weird, hard to explain, and plain old goofy. A *null value* is something that is "completely devoid of any value" (no cheap jokes, please). It's different from an empty string — it's not something that's empty; it's just happy being nothing. (How strange is that??)

Getting back to your roots

You can always go back to the root node of a document by using the forward slash (/). If the context node is still the Email node, the following selects the root element of the document (Clients):

```
/child::*
```

The / takes you back to the root of the document (think of it as the top of the document); child is an axis that selects the children and * makes sure that you select only the element children. Because of the rules of XML, there can only be one document element node, which means that this construct always selects the document element node.

XPath functions

XPath also includes several handy functions — these, for example:

- ✔ **String functions** such as starts-with() compare a particular substring to a string and return true if the string starts with that substring.

- ✔ **Node set functions** such as count() return the number of nodes in a node set.

- ✔ **Boolean (true/false) functions** such as lang() return true if the language matches the language of the xsl:lang element.

- ✔ **Number functions** such as round() modify numbers (for example, this one rounds to the nearest integer value).

Using XPath with XMLSpy

XMLSpy is a multifaceted XML tool (you can find more about it in Chapter 19). In this section, you give XMLSpy's XPath Analyzer tool a test drive.

You can download a free, full-featured, 30-day trial version of XMLSpy (either the Enterprise or Professional Edition) or a free, time-unlimited version of XMLSpy Home Edition. Here's where:

```
www.altova.com/download.html
```

XMLSpy 2005 includes a built-in XPath Analyzer tool to help you build and test XPath expressions. To use the XPath Analyzer, follow these steps:

  1. Open an XML file in XMLSpy.

2. **Choose XML⇨Evaluate XPath.**

   The Evaluate XPath dialog box opens, as shown in Figure 13-2.

3. **Enter an expression in the Input pane.**

   Presto! The destination node(s) is listed in the Results pane.

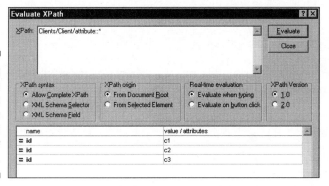

Figure 13-2:
The
Evaluate
XPath
dialog box in
XMLSpy
2005.

The features of the XPath Analyzer include three especially useful ones:

✔ **The Input pane:** You enter an XPath expression in the Input pane. The expression is displayed in black type if the syntax is correct and in red type if the syntax is not correct. Correct syntax doesn't guarantee that the expression is error free — any errors are shown in the Results pane at the bottom of the dialog box.

✔ **Evaluator options:** You have several choices regarding the evaluation of your XPath expression.

- **XPath Syntax options:** For XPath 1.0 expressions, you can choose the full XPath 1.0 grammar, the XML Schema Selector grammar, or the XML Schema Field grammar. (Schema selectors and fields are used to specify constraints if your XML document is an XML schema.)

- **XPath Origin options:** You choose the context node, either the Document Root (root node) or a Selected Element. You can specify the selected element via your XPath expression, or you can high-light the selected element in the XML file that's open in the main XMLSpy window. The file should be opened in Text view or Grid view.

- **Real-Time Evaluation options:** The expression can be evaluated as you type it, or you can choose to evaluate the expression only when you click the Evaluate button.

• **XPath Version options:** You can select either XPath 1.0 or XPath 2.0. The XPath evaluator uses a different engine for each version.

✔ **The Results pane:** When an expression is evaluated, the Results pane displays a list of items in sequence, along with their corresponding attributes and/or values.

Okay, here's a look at what some of these can do for you. In Figure 13-2, the expression

```
Clients/Client/attribute::*
```

returns all the attributes of the Client element nodes and displays them in sequence in the Results pane.

Watch what happens if we change the context node to the Fax element node of the second Client element node and then evaluate this expression:

```
preceding-sibling::*
```

As shown in Figure 13-3, the result is both the Phone element node and the Name element node of the second Client element node. (We're moving backwards in the document, so the Phone element is listed first.)

Make sure you've selected From Selected Element as the XPath origin — otherwise, your result will be null.

Figure 13-3: Using a selected element in the XPath Analyzer in XMLSpy 2005.

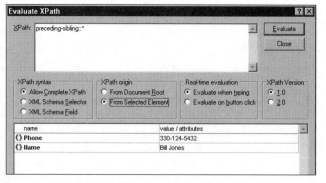

The Short Version

XPath is designed to be used with other applications such as XPointer, XSL, and XQuery. To limit the resulting complexity, it makes sense to provide less verbose syntax. This is called *abbreviated syntax* for XPath.

The most important (and compact) abbreviation is `child::`. This abbreviates to . . . wait for it . . . nothing!

Child-axis abbreviations

For other compact ways to show a child axis, here are some of the previous examples from this chapter, set out with their abbreviated equivalents:

- `child::Client` abbreviates to `Client`.
- `child::*` abbreviates to `*`.
- `child::node()` abbreviates to `node()`.
- `child::text()` abbreviates to `text()` and selects all text nodes of the context node.

Attribute-axis abbreviation

The `attribute::` axis abbreviates to the @ symbol. So the example

```
child::Client[attribute::id="c3"]
```

abbreviates to

```
Client[@id="c3"]
```

Predicate and expression abbreviations

XPath offers several useful abbreviations for common expressions that can make your coding go faster and take up less space. The `position` expression (for example) abbreviates to nothing; therefore

```
Client[position()=1]
```

abbreviates to

```
Client[1]
```

This simply selects the first `Client` element of the context node.

The next expression selects the last child of the context node:

```
Client[position()=last()]
```

It must retain the empty parentheses; otherwise, it looks for other child elements. Therefore, it abbreviates to

```
Client[last()]
```

Here are some other handy abbreviations:

- ✔ `Client[>1]` selects all the client nodes other than the first `Client` node.
- ✔ `Client[< last()]` selects all the `Client` nodes other than the last `Client` node.
- ✔ `Client[last()-1]` selects the `Client` node immediately before the last `Client` node.
- ✔ `Client[position()=1]/phone` abbreviates to `Client[1]/phone`.

Some more abbreviations

Here are a few more abbreviations, just so you can't claim that we're not working you hard enough.

The `descendant` axis abbreviates to two forward slashes, as when

```
descendant::Name
```

(which selects all the `Name` elements in the document) abbreviates to

```
//Name
```

The context node abbreviates to a dot (`.`), so

```
.//Fax
```

is a compact way to select all the `Fax` element nodes that are descendants of the context node.

The parent node abbreviates to two dots (`..`), so

```
..
```

selects the parent of the context node.

More XPath abbreviations and functions are possible, but the examples just given are the ones you're likeliest to use in most cases. To see the other examples, consult the specification at www.w3.org/TR/xpath.

Let's face it: All by themselves, XPath expressions aren't very useful. They're just part of a language that describes how to select a set of nodes or a single node from a document. You have to *make* them useful by combining them with some other application. For instance . . .

- In XSL, XPath expressions are used to select a node or a whole series of nodes so that they can either be transformed from one XML element set to another element set or have styles applied to them.
- In XML Query language, XPath expressions are used for retrieving hunks of data from an XML document.
- In XPointer, the expressions of XPath are used to point software to a particular spot in the document.

What's New in XPath 2.0?

XPath 2.0 is at the W3C Working Draft stage at the time of this writing. XPath 2.0 is used with both XSLT 2.0 and XQuery 1.0, and introduces several new features not available in XPath 1.0, including:

- **XML Schema datatypes:** XPath 1.0 processes everything as string data, but XPath 2.0 supports the 19 XML Schema primitive datatypes so that you have access to decimal, float, double, and date and time datatypes.
- **New features for nodes:**
    - Element and attribute nodes can now be associated with XML Schema datatypes.
    - The root node is now called the *document node.*
    - XPath1.0 expressions return a node set, which is an unordered collection. XPath 2.0 expressions return an ordered sequence of nodes.
- **Aggregation:** XPath 2.0 offers aggregation functions such as min() and avg() that allow functions to be applied to data in groups. This capability expands the new grouping features of XSLT 2.0, including these:
    - the xsl:for-each-group element

- new attributes for grouping that can be used with the `xsl:for-each-group` element include `group-by`, `group-adjacent`, and `group-starting-with`

- a `current-group ()` function for referring to a group

✔ **Programming constructs:** XPath 2.0 adds support for several common programming constructs, including these:

- `for` loops

- conditional expressions

- regular expressions

✔ **User-defined functions:** `xsl:function` allows you to create user-defined functions to use in XPath 2.0 expressions.

✔ **A wide variety of new functions,** including these:

- numeric functions such as `absolute value`, `floor`, `ceiling`, and `round`

- string functions such as `concatenation`, `length`, `uppercase`, and `lowercase`

- substring functions such as `contains`, `starts-with`, and `ends-with`

- pattern matching functions that support regular expressions

- a multitude of date and time functions

✔ **New operators,** including these:

- operators on numeric values, including `add`, `subtract`, `multiply`, `divide`, and `modulus`

- operators for comparison of numeric values, such as `greater than` and `lesser than`

- operators for comparison of date and time values

This is by no means an exhaustive list! For more details on all the new functions and operators in XPath 2.0, see "XQuery 1.0 and XPath 2.0 Functions and Operators" at `www.w3.org/TR/xpath-functions/`.

XPath 2.0 supports many features of programming languages — and document-mapping capabilities are much more powerful than what you get with XPath 1.0. True, XPath 1.0 can be expanded with proprietary extensions, but these are tied to specific XSLT processors — and that can easily lead to a swarm of incompatibilities. XPath 2.0 — in combination with XSLT 2.0 — enables you to

create stylesheets that are compatible with multiple processors and multiple platforms. (Think of the savings on aspirin alone.)

Also, XQuery is an extension of XPath 2.0. Okay, XQuery is not quite ready for prime time yet — but learning XPath 2.0 will speed you right up the learning curve when it comes time to implement XQuery. That could happen soon; XQuery is expected to become the standard method for querying XML documents.

Where to Now?

There are many resources online for finding out more about XPath. Check out the tutorials at these sites:

- ✔ www.zvon.org/xxl/XPathTutorial/Output/
- ✔ www.topxml.com/xsl/tutorials/intro/
- ✔ www.w3schools.com/xpath/default.asp

One fun way to apply XPath occurs in a language called Schematron (an alternative to XML Schema, in fact). Schematron uses XPath (and some XSL) to describe document structures. To get the goods on Schematron, visit

www.ascc.net/xml/resource/schematron/schematron.html

In this chapter, you found out about using directions and paths to locate nodes in the XML document tree. In the next chapter, you find out more about the document tree and the DOM (Document Object Model). XML processors use the DOM to make your XML document available to programming applications.

Chapter 14

Processing XML

● ●

● ●

*P*rocessing XML means putting your document to work. That usually means changing it so an application (whatever its function) can do something with your XML document.

The key to the "something" that an application can do with your XML is the *Document Object Model (DOM)* — a structure that breaks up your XML document into a form that an application can get at and work with. This chapter explains how applications use the DOM to work with the content in your XML documents.

To process your XML documents, you need an XML processor. An *XML processor* takes in XML files — along with any stylesheets — and makes their structure and content available (in a format that's useful to a programming language) so the XML document can be used in an application. In this chapter, we take an in-depth look at what's involved in processing XML, and we give you some insight into how a program can access and work with the data in an XML document.

Frankly, My Dear, I Don't Give a DOM

A *Document Object Model (DOM)* is a programming interface that allows programs and programming languages to access and update the content, structure, and style of documents in a standard way. The DOM does this by using a standard syntax to describe a document as a series of objects. When an XML document is passed through an XML processor, the processor creates a DOM for that document. Programming languages (such as C++ and Java) and scripting languages (such as JavaScript and VBScript) can access the DOM, reach out and grab a particular object, and manipulate it. We take a different view of the `bookstore.xml` document to show its DOM. In case you haven't already downloaded this XML file, it's available at www.dummies.com/go/xmlfd4e.

To really understand what a DOM is, you need to get a mental picture of how XML documents actually work with the DOM. This Zen approach to understanding may be a little, um, Zenlike (After all, how can you know how a DOM works without knowing what it is?), but trust us on this one, and you'll feel much more balanced. Keep in mind that although there's a sense of hierarchy to how a DOM works, you shouldn't confuse it with the hierarchy of a filing system (such as Windows Explorer or another filing cabinet application), because the DOM is *not* a filing system or data-storage hierarchy. It's a programming hierarchy and a method for exposing data for manipulation.

You can describe the `bookstore.xml` document as a series of elements and their content. You can also describe the document as a series of objects — after all, each element in the document is an individual object. The following piece of the document (for example) includes five different objects:

```
<bookInfo>
 <title>The Da Vinci Code</title>
 <author>Brown, Dan</author>
 <publisher>Doubleday</publisher>
 <isbn>0385504209</isbn>
</bookInfo>
```

The five objects are:

- ✔ The `bookInfo` element
- ✔ The `title` element that contains the content "The Da Vinci Code"
- ✔ The `author` element that contains the content "Brown, Dan"
- ✔ The `publisher` element that contains the content "Doubleday"
- ✔ The `isbn` element that contains the content "0385504209"

The DTD and XML schema we have used to validate this document in previous chapters allow more than one `book` element per document, so there could be more than one `title` element, `author` element, and so on. In that case, even though individual elements use the same markup tags, they're all separate objects in the document — the first `title` element is a different object from the second `title` element, and so forth.

All these individual objects are part of the DOM for the `bookstore.xml` document. In addition to identifying each element in an XML document as an individual object, a DOM shows how each element relates to the others hierarchically. In fact, the DOM identifies each unique object in a document according to its position in the document's hierarchy.

As in any hierarchy, the DOM consists of a fairly complex system of relationships that must be adhered to. (We introduce these relationships in Chapters 5 and 12.) See "Keeping in touch with the family" (the section coming up) to get a better picture of siblings, parents, and the rest of the gang.

A *processor* is an application that makes your documents do something. XML processors create a DOM each time they process an XML document so that the programming code can get and work with the content in the document. Figure 14-1 is a grid view of `bookstore.xml` in XMLSpy. It illustrates how the DOM for this document might look to an XML processor. (See "What Goes In Must Come Out: Processing XML" for more information about how processing works.)

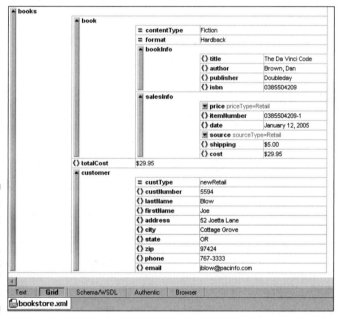

Figure 14-1:
The book
store.
xml DOM,
as an XML
processor
sees it.

Of course, if you don't plan to program an application that reads and processes XML documents, then you can probably live the remainder of your life happily without the brief review of document-family relationships, trees, and nodes in the next two sections of this chapter. Remember, however, that many XML resources — especially the more technical ones — tend to assume you're hip to at least the basics of trees and nodes. If you're already comfortable with these concepts — or if you're not planning to program applications for XML — you can skip ahead to the section called "Using the DOM and XSL."

Keeping in touch with the family

To understand how the DOM works and how applications use programming commands to access individual objects in a document, first you need a good grasp of how the document's elements relate to each other. As you found out in previous chapters, the terms *parent, child,* and *sibling* are all used to describe element relationships. These relationships have to do with how the elements are nested. For example, in the following bit of markup, the street, city, and state elements are nested within (and children of) the address element:

```
<address>
 <street>1312 Wilshire Blvd</street>
 <city>Santa Monica</city>
 <state>California</state>
</address>
```

street, city, and state are also siblings of each other, and address is their parent. The concept of parents and siblings doesn't extend past one level of nesting. You can refer to parents, children, and siblings but not to grandparents, grandchildren, great-aunts, or second cousins. Fortunately.

Understanding DOM structure

Ultimately, this whole discussion comes down to a common terminology that explains how this relates to that. A *tree* is a diagram of an XML document's structure that shows the order of elements and illustrates the relationships between elements in exactly the same way that a family tree illustrates genealogy. A tree is a visual representation of the DOM. If you refer back to Figure 14-1, the tree's root is the books element. The book, totalCost, and customer elements are branches under the books element, and both the book and the customer elements contain child elements.

Notice that the tree includes things other than the elements in the document — for example, attributes and element content. The objects included in a DOM are more than just the elements; they're called *nodes* when displayed on the DOM tree. Figure 14-2 illustrates some additional types of nodes that a DOM tree can include.

If you're familiar with basic XML structures, you probably recognize the majority of node types, because they're common XML elements. The ones in bookstore.xml are:

✔ **Root node:** This node contains the whole document, including the prolog and the document element node.

✔ **Document element node:** This node contains the entire contents of the document except for any processing instruction nodes or comment nodes that are children of the root node. For this example, it's `books`.

✔ **Element nodes:** `book`, `bookInfo`, `title`, `author`, `publisher`, `isbn`, `salesInfo`, `price`, `itemNumber`, `date`, `source`, `shipping`, `cost`, `totalCost`, `customer`, `custNumber`, `lastName`, `firstName`, `address`, `city`, `state`, `zip`, `phone` and `email`.

✔ **Text nodes:** The text content of any element. For example, `Joe` is the text node of the `firstName` element.

✔ **Attribute nodes:** `contentType`, `format`, `priceType`, `sourceType`, and `custType`.

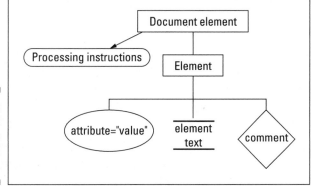

Figure 14-2:
Additional node types in a DOM tree.

Node types that aren't included in `bookstore.xml` but that are discussed in other chapters of the book are:

✔ **Namespaces** (Chapter 11)

✔ **Processing instructions** (Chapter 8)

✔ **Comments** (Chapter 8)

As you can see, there's not much in any given XML document that you can't access by using the DOM. Not surprisingly, that's what the members of the W3C had in mind when they created the DOM specification.

Using the DOM and XSL

XSL-FO and XSLT stylesheets are XML documents. When an application uses a stylesheet, it processes the stylesheet like any other XML document. The only difference is that the application applies the stylesheet to the XML document. The stylesheet has its own DOM, as does the XML document; the final transformation or display guided by the stylesheet takes information in both DOMs into account. (For more on XSL-FO and XSLT stylesheets, see Chapter 12.)

The DOM recommendation

As you might have guessed, the way a DOM is laid out adheres to a specific syntax, and that syntax is defined in W3C recommendations. DOM Level 1, Level 2, and Level 3 are all now W3C specifications. To find out more details on each of these DOMs, visit the W3C DOM Activity Statement page at

`www.w3c.org/DOM/Activity`

As always, keep your eye on the W3C Web site to keep up with the latest versions of all specifications.

Web browsers and the DOM

A good example of an application that uses XSLT stylesheets and the DOM to process XML documents is a Web browser. To display XML documents in Web browsers (as something other than a list of elements, attributes, and/or content, anyway), you actually have to apply an XSLT stylesheet to the XML document — which converts XML to HTML or XHTML. Or you can use an XSL-FO stylesheet with the XML document for display in the browser. For example, when Internet Explorer 6 displays content using an XSL-FO stylesheet, two processes actually occur:

1. Internet Explorer accesses the DOM that's created when its processor — Microsoft XML (MSXML) — reads and processes both the XML document and the related XSL-FO stylesheet.

2. The browser uses the document and stylesheet together to determine the final display of the content.

As you found out in Chapter 7, you can also use a CSS stylesheet for displaying an XML document in a browser.

What Goes In Must Come Out: Processing XML

In Chapter 12 and the chapters in Part V of this book, we look closely at what you have to do to make your XML do something for you. XML DTDs, schemas, and documents are almost always part of a larger solution, such as the XML solution used by an online loan-refinancing system. Stylesheets can also be important tools — both for the transformation of data from one set of markup to another and for controlling the display of data in an XML document.

For all the different pieces in a solution to work together, you need programming code of some kind, and that programming code needs a way to access the content you've described with XML and any stylesheets you've written to go with it. Enter the XML processor. A processor takes the code and makes it do something. A processor may be part of a simple Web browser (such as Internet Explorer or Mozilla), or it can be a whole other kind of program — such as a utility that takes in an XML document, grabs the info it's carrying, and populates an Oracle database.

XML processors and the DOM go hand in hand. The processor creates the DOM; without the DOM, you can't use programming code to get your XML content and do something with it. All things considered, that makes the XML processor a seriously important tool in your XML arsenal.

All Web browsers have HTML processors built into them, and those that can work with XML also have XML processors built into them. Because a browser is really designed for display, when you view an XML document in a browser, the browser uses the information the processor feeds it to drive the display of your document.

If you create a stylesheet in either XSL or CSS, an XML-enabled browser can also open and process that stylesheet. It then uses the processed XML and processed stylesheet to present a final display. The browser is programmed to look for information provided by the processed document — and then to do something with it.

Although we use a display-driven solution (to display XML documents in a browser) as an example, remember that putting stuff on-screen is just *one* use for XML. All XML solutions have processors involved in them; the programming code behind the solution's XML processor just does something different — whatever the solution calls for — with the processed XML. For example, if the solution takes data from a document and plugs it into a database, the document is processed and then the processor uses the processed data to insert the document's content into the database.

Many different processors are available for you to choose among. This is a Good Thing because it means you don't have to write your own processor; you can use one that someone else wrote. You probably don't want to pick the first processor you trip over on a Web page — it helps to know a little bit about your processor options so you can find one that's right for you.

Although the job of every XML processor is approximately the same — to expose the structure and content of the document to a program for manipulation — processors are written in a variety of languages. Processors may also be validating or nonvalidating (more about these in just a bit). Throughout the rest of this section, we take a look at different kinds of processors and give you the information you need to find the processor that best meets your requirements.

We use the terms *processor* and *processing* in our discussions of making your XML do something useful. You often see the words *parser* and *parsing* used in the same context. Okay, an XML parser and an XML processor are really the same thing — a tool you use to make your XML content and structure available to programming code for manipulation. For the sake of consistency, we stick with *processor*. As you check out other sources of information, keep in mind that parsers and processors do the same thing.

So many processors, so little time

Browse the XML Parsers/Processors section of xmlsoftware.com (the full address is www.xmlsoftware.com/parsers.html), and you see more than three dozen processors listed (and this isn't even a complete listing, just a good start). So what makes all these processors different from one another? Each processor has four distinct characteristics:

- ✔ **The programming language it was written in:** For each of the many different programming languages, there's at least one processor. Each language needs its own processor because the processor has to be programmed to work seamlessly with that language and to run on the same system as the code written in that language. For example, if you're creating a C++ application, it doesn't make sense to use a processor written in Java. You'd waste a lot of time trying to get the two to communicate when you can get a C++ processor that's already designed to play nice with your C++ code.

- ✔ **Whether or not it validates documents:** A key difference among processors is whether they validate your XML documents. Every XML document needs to be well formed, and if it isn't, any processor (validating or not) spits it (or an error message) right back at you — no DOM, no content, no nothing. On the other hand, some processors also validate your documents against a DTD or schema. Invalid documents are spat out just like malformed ones.

  The benefit of a validating processor is that you know the data coming into your system adheres to a DTD or schema, so you can be sure that you get the data you need for the system to work properly. The downside to a validating processor is that it takes longer to process the XML document; it has to check the document for well-formedness, and then for validity, before doing anything else. (In the next section, we talk a little more about determining whether you need a validating processor.)

- ✔ **The version of the different specifications (DTD, schema, and so on) that it supports:** For example, most processors support XML 1.0 DTDs, but some don't support XML Schemas. When you read the description of a processor, check to be sure it supports the standards you're using.

✔ **If it was written to accompany a particular software or database application:** Some processors are built to work with specific applications or databases; MSXML (for example) is the processor built by Microsoft for Microsoft solutions. Oracle offers a range of processors written in various programming languages, each specifically designed to work with Oracle database applications. Such a processor is a kind of tradeoff: Usually, it has utilities or functionality designed to use a specific application or database — but will those features limit compatibility? Your call.

Which processor is right for you?

When you're trying to pick a processor, you should ask yourself the following questions to help narrow your search:

✔ **What programming language is the rest of your solution using?**

Generally, you can avoid some compatibility headaches if you go with a processor that's written in the same language.

✔ **Do your documents need to be validated during processing?**

If you've created a solution that revolves around a particular DTD or schema, you want valid documents coming into that system — but you don't necessarily have to validate during processing. If you control the document-creation process, you can set up standards for valid documents. If you don't control that process (as when, say, data comes in via a Web page or from someone else's system), validating during processing may make more practical sense. You can do some testing to find out which is the greater tradeoff — the slower processing time you get with a validating processor or the number of errors you have to handle when invalid data gets into your system.

✔ **Which XML versions and standards are you using?**

If you're using schemas, be sure that your processor supports them. As a general rule, you want the most up-to-date processor you can lay your hands on.

✔ **Does the application framework or database you're using have a processor?**

If you're working with an Oracle database, it pays to look into the Oracle processor. If you're working with any of Microsoft's products, look into MSXML. Whatever you wind up with, read the documentation for your database or application, and find out what kind of processor it offers. Be sure the processor meets other essential criteria: proper programming-language support, validating capability (if necessary), and proper standards support.

The best person to help you pick out your processor is probably an experienced programmer who can help you answer the questions just listed. Good programmers have worked with XML, know the pitfalls of the various processors for each language, and can help you work through validation issues.

The next part of this book (Part V) focuses on XML application development. Chapter 15 starts off Part V by introducing the use of XML for Web services.

Part V

XML Application Development

The 5th Wave   By Rich Tennant

Oh come on— how fatal can it be?

FATAL ERROR

In this part. . .

"**I** tell you, we can use the power of XML to capture, organize, and represent data of many different kinds, to make it available for all kinds of uses, and rule the galaxy . . ."

Chapter 15 invades the world of Web services with a potent combination of XML applications to advertise, describe, and broker connections between service providers and the consumers who (hopefully) love them. Chapter 16 offers fishing tips for gathering information with XML forms — some of which you create with the W3C XForms technology and with InfoPath (the Microsoft XML Forms editor). Chapter 17 ushers you into the use of XML with databases; before you know it, you'll be importing and exporting XML data using Word 2003, InfoPath, XMLSpy, and Access. Chapter 18 introduces RSS, an XML application for creating news feeds and weblogs (blogs) — complete with a how-to for creating an RSS feed and syndicating your Web content. That galaxy had just better look out.

Chapter 15

Using XML with Web Services

● ●

In This Chapter

▶ Understanding the vision behind Web services

▶ Unstacking the Web Services Architecture

▶ Explaining the ubiquitous role of XML in Web services

▶ Moving messages for Web services

▶ Exchanging information to support Web services

▶ Describing or advertising Web services

▶ Discovering Web services

▶ Understanding where Web services can lead

● ●

*T*he Internet and the Web are remaking and reshaping the world of computing in fundamental ways — and (of course) XML plays a key role in
this reshaping. That's because XML documents — at least, those governed by
Document Type Definitions (DTDs), XML Schemas, or other alternative forms
of documentation — are sufficiently self-describing to carry their descriptions along with their content and make themselves understood to any XML-
capable software program.

Web services are remote applications (accessed via a Web page) that carry
out specific tasks or functions. They allow different applications from different sources to communicate with each other by using XML. Through the use
of Web services technology, the Web can be accessed not only to share information, but also to share services.

From the view of Web services, there are two broad classes of computer
users: those who have specific information-gathering or -processing needs to
fulfill (we dub them *service consumers*) and those who have specific information resources or processing capabilities to offer *(service providers)*. Basic
supply and demand.

A service provider can also be a service consumer because, in addition to
providing its own unique data, the provider may provide content that it
digested from another resource. For example, say an accounting firm offers
access to IRS tax code information. The service provider passes on the

content to end users, along with useful tips on reading and interpreting the code. This is what Web services are fundamentally about: the use, reuse, augmentation, and dissemination of information.

This chapter gives you a bird's-eye view of how XML plays a role in the exchange and storage of data for consumers and providers.

What's Up with Web Services?

In the Web services world, service consumers — individuals, corporations, organizations, associations, and institutions — seek the best resources and the best deals for their information and processing needs. In this same world, service providers seek to advertise and promote their services so that service consumers can take a look at the wealth of resources and pass these services on to their customers.

For example, most people run an e-mail client on their desktop, downloading and managing e-mail messages locally. When you're ready to read your e-mail, you click the Receive button (or something similar) to signal your e-mail server that you'd like to receive all your e-mail messages. The server complies and sends them to you. Your e-mail client handles all this for you (that's what clients are supposed to do, after all). When you're ready to send an e-mail message, you type it into your e-mail client's editor and click the Send button. Your client shoots the message off to the outgoing mail server, and the mail is off and running. Figure 15-1 illustrates how an e-mail client on the desktop sends and receives messages via mail servers on the Internet.

The e-mail software and the entire store of downloaded e-mail messages reside on your desktop machine, but these e-mail messages made their way to your desktop via the Internet. As evidenced by the collection of e-mail piling up in your mailbox, service providers have created elaborate systems to make it possible for you to send and receive e-mail seamlessly from a server on the Internet.

A Web services model for e-mail (of which many implementations are already available, including Hotmail, Yahoo! Mail, and others) takes a different approach to e-mail access. To use one of the Web-based e-mail services, you set up an e-mail account and use your Web browser to send and receive e-mail. The brains that drive the e-mail software are split between your desktop and the remote e-mail server that holds your messages and folders. Figure 15-2 shows how the Web service e-mail approach is different from the desktop client e-mail approach.

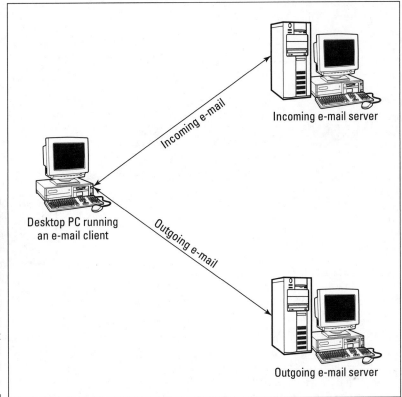

Incoming e-mail server

Incoming e-mail

Outgoing e-mail

Figure 15-1:
Desktop
e-mail
clients com-
municate
directly with
e-mail
servers on
the Internet
to send and
receive
messages.

Desktop PC running
an e-mail client

Outgoing e-mail server

In this e-mail scenario, you manage the e-mail interface, decide what to do with incoming e-mail messages, and create outgoing e-mail messages just as you do with a desktop e-mail client. However, a server somewhere on the Web handles all the dirty work: requesting and sending messages, storing messages, filing messages, and so on. With most of these Web-based e-mail services, you get the same functionality as you do with your favorite desktop client, and as a bonus, you can access your e-mail from any location through any computer with a Web browser and Internet connection.

You have to access a Web page and provide an account name and password to supply proof of identity before you can access the stored data (the collection of folders and saved messages in the case of e-mail) of the Web application service — the Web-based e-mail service you use to send and receive, read and write, and otherwise manage e-mail messages.

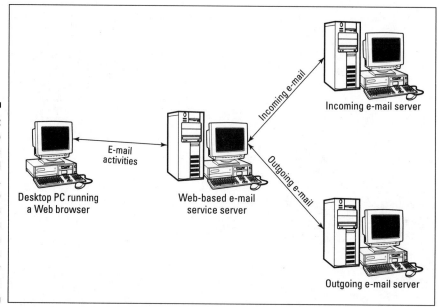

Incoming e-mail server

Outgoing e-mail server

E-mail
activities

Desktop PC running
a Web browser

Web-based e-mail
service server

But the concept of Web-based applications goes way beyond e-mail. Word processing applications, spreadsheet programs, database management systems, and presentation systems can become service based. The great benefit of Web services is that they aren't tied to any single computer, like traditional software applications are. A centralized server stores both the application functionality and the data. This makes the functionality and content more accessible and encourages online collaboration.

But how? Patience, Grasshopper. If a service provider maintains a current copy of the Web-based application and gives you access to all the necessary data (e-mail messages for e-mail services, documents for word processing, spreadsheets for spreadsheet services, and so on), just about any conceivable form of computing could fall into the Web services model. We think this explains why many software vendors are moving away from selling software outright and are instead beginning to license software on a renewable term.

Okay, but what does all this have to do with XML? We're glad you asked. In the following sections, you find out about the key role of XML in providing Web services.

A Web Services Architecture

Because XML is well suited to describing all kinds of documents and data, and because such descriptions are easy to exchange across the Internet, XML is a natural foundation on which to construct a model for Web services in general. In fact, XML experts have constructed a general model for how XML Web services should work; this model is known as the *XML Web Services Architecture.*

The Web Services Architecture is divided into four layers, each of which depends on access to one or more XML applications to support that layer's specific functions. In this particular section, we examine the entire model and provide (admittedly brief) explanations of the layers involved. In the following sections, we explore each layer in more detail and introduce some of the many XML applications that various Web services implementations require at each layer.

In addition, the following list is presented top-down, so that the highest layer in this stack represents the most abstract functions and the lowest layer in this stack represents the least abstract functions. As is the case with many layered models for communications (and that's a big part of what Web services is about), higher layers depend and build on the capabilities supplied at lower layers. Here's the list:

- ✔ **Discovery** is the part of the Web services environment in which service providers can supply descriptions of the information and services that they have to offer. This is also where would-be service consumers can make inquiries about what services are generally available or request details about specific services. This layer generally addresses the question "What's available out there?"

- ✔ **Description** is the part of Web services in which available services and information are described in detail, along with the mechanisms necessary for prospective service consumers and service providers to exchange information with one another. This layer generally addresses questions like "For Service *X,* what are the details involved in accessing this service, and what kinds of messages and data objects must be exchanged to take advantage of that service?"

- ✔ **Packaging/Extensions** is the part of Web services that handles issues related to managing, packaging, and securing exchanges of information between a service consumer and a service provider. This layer generally addresses questions like "What kinds of requests and replies are reasonable for consumers and providers to exchange, and how will that message traffic be managed, controlled, secured, packaged, and represented?"

✔ **Transport** is the part of Web services that implements protocols related to moving messages from a sender to a receiver. (Note that both consumers and providers can be senders and receivers; this changes as needed to maintain a working consumer/provider relationship.) This layer addresses questions like "What kinds of messages will be sent or received across the network, and what kinds of requests and replies do those messages represent?"

If you're familiar with the construction of network protocol stacks, you'll notice an intentional resemblance between the names and definitions we list here and the OSI (Open System Interconnection) layers model.

In the following sections, we tackle the Web Services Architecture from the bottom up, starting with the Transport layer and working up to the Discovery layer.

Transport: Moving XML messages

At the Transport level — the bottom of the stack — software clients (like Web browsers) and service delivery software on Web servers communicate with each other. In general, browsers and servers talk to each other at this level without requiring much user knowledge or interaction, if any.

Bottom line? The Transport layer acts like the highway that carries messages from senders to receivers; as long as the messages are suitable for the underlying road, the messages move along just fine.

SOAPing it up

Nearly every major XML player has endorsed SOAP — the XML application known as Simple Object Access Protocol (SOAP) — as a basic mechanism for exchanging XML messages between senders and receivers (or providers and consumers, if you prefer) across the Internet. SOAP is independent of platform and language. A SOAP message is an XML document that is sent via a transport protocol.

Underlying protocols in SOAP include not only the HyperText Transport Protocol (HTTP) already used for everyday Web communications, but also other implementations of HTTP, including secure HTTP implementations and a newly minted *reliable HTTP* (also known as HTTPR). The newest version of the SOAP specification, SOAP 1.2, also supports protocols in addition to HTTP, including SMTP (Simple Mail Transfer Protocol) and TCP/IP (Transmission Control Protocol/Internet Protocol).

SOAP revisited (version 1.2)

SOAP 1.2 is a World Wide Web Consortium (W3C) Recommendation and consists of four basic parts:

✔ An envelope that describes what's in a message and how to process it

✔ A set of encoding rules for application-defined data types

✔ A convention for remote procedure calls (RPCs) and responses

✔ A binding convention for exchanging messages via an underlying protocol

SOAP allows applications to invoke object methods on remote servers. Because SOAP is platform- and language-independent, the application and the server can use different languages as long as they both use the SOAP protocol.

For more details on using SOAP, see "Getting Your Feet Wet with SOAP" at `http://webmonkey.wired.com/webmonkey/02/08/index0a.html`.

For more information about the SOAP specification, visit the W3C XML Protocol page at `www.w3.org/2000/xp/Group`. You can find links to all the parts of the SOAP 1.2 specification about halfway down that page.

Packaging/Extensions: Managing information exchange

One layer up from the Transport layer in the Web Services Architecture is the *Packaging/Extensions layer.* This layer is primarily concerned with establishing, managing, securing, and packaging information for exchange between service consumers and providers.

The functions associated with this layer are aptly named. *Packaging* permits text information, images, and other kinds of binary data to be neatly encapsulated and sent to another party over a network.

Extensions address enhancements to basic messaging services for the following reasons:

✔ To increase the level of security through encryption

✔ To strengthen the credentials that establish consumer and provider identities (such as digital signatures or certificates, which act the same way for virtual proofs of identity that inspections of driver's licenses or passports act for visual proofs of identity)

✔ To manage how messages are delivered from sender to receiver

SOAP provides packaging and extensions for Web services by specifying a binding. A *binding* is a protocol — usually HTTP — and data-format specification for a specific port type. (A *port* associates a network address with a binding.)

For more information on packaging and extensions, see "SOAP Version 1.2 Part 1: Messaging Framework" at `www.w3.org/TR/soap12-part1` and "XML-binary Optimized Packaging" at `www.w3.org/TR/xop10`.

Description: Specifying services and related components

The Description layer is where things start to get more interesting from the overall perspective of what Web services are and can do (as compared to how they're packaged, delivered, and addressed). In fact, the Description layer encompasses a number of XML applications designed to describe the following:

✔ How services are composed

✔ How services may be used

✔ How services can interact with other services

✔ How services must behave

✔ What services can offer potential consumers

Many languages are available for Description layer services, but some are tailored for specific IBM or Microsoft views of Web services. Others are designed to make it easier for multiple service providers to interact and exchange data on behalf of shared service consumers.

Of greatest interest at present is the Web Services Description Language (WSDL), which describes what kinds of information and services a specific service provider has to offer. Yep, that's right: a service that lists the services you can provide. Think about how many services a company like Yahoo! has to offer: e-mail, chat, bill pay, shopping, and more. WSDL can provide a catalog of Yahoo!'s many services and the particulars of each of them.

To access a Web service application, your Web page needs a way to communicate with the application to determine the *programmatic interface* — the available methods and parameters. WSDL is the proposed standard for this communication. WSDL is an XML format that describes the basic form of Web service requests with different network protocols. It can be extended to any network protocol or message format.

Each Web service includes a WSDL file that describes the bindings, methods, and data inputs and outputs.

For more information on WSDL, see "Web Services Description Language (WSDL) Explained" at

```
http://msdn.microsoft.com/library/default.asp?url=/library/en-
            us/dnwebsrv/html/wsdlexplained.asp
```

WSDL 2.0 is a W3C Working Draft in four parts (`www.w3.org/TR/wsdl20-primer`, `www.w3.org/TR/wsdl20`, `www.w3.org/TR/wsdl20-extensions`, and `www.w3.org/TR/wsdl20-bindings`). The W3C Working Drafts describe bindings (protocol and data-format specifications) with SOAP 1.2, HTTP 1.1 GET/POST, and MIME (Multipurpose Internet Mail Extensions) but are not limited to these bindings. More information about current W3C work in the Web services area is available on the W3C Web Services Activity Page at `www.w3.org/2002/ws`.

Discovery: Finding what's available

At the top of the Web Services Architecture, you find XML applications geared to registering Web services for discovery by searching for services, inquiring about specific services, or inspecting what services a particular service provider offers. Think of this as Google for Web services consumers. The customers can go out and search for which providers have what services (how many e-mail or shopping services are out there, for example).

Providers readily understand that providing information to assist the discovery process is essential. Providers also recognize that documenting how they can interact with other services is similarly important. In a sense, the Discovery layer is the public face that drives the Web services environment. The remaining layers of the Web Services Architecture make it possible to request and obtain services; to handle matters of payment, identity, and security; and to make sure that consumers and providers can communicate seamlessly and successfully with one another.

For example, a user asks his or her online bill-paying service to request and pay bills from billers. This request launches the discovery that sends the service out to find out if it can get the bill and if it can pay the bill online. The results of the discovery drive what the user sees in the online system. If Web service communication is possible, the bill-paying system displays the bill, prompts the user to pay the bill, and manages the electronic funds transfer (EFT) from the user's bank account to the biller's bank account (yet another example of Web services). If the Web service communication isn't possible, then the online bill-paying service has to use another tool to display bills and make payments (such as scanning in printed bills and mailing printed checks for payment).

The major XML application used for discovery is *UDDI* (Universal Description, Discovery, and Integration). UDDI enables businesses to discover one another, to define how they can interact, and to share service descriptions in a global registry.

UDDI is a method for finding Web services. UDDI is built upon SOAP and is independent of platform and implementation. A UDDI interface is used to connect to services provided by external partners. A UDDI registry provides a place for businesses to publish services, as well as a place for clients to obtain services. Three types of information are provided in a UDDI registry:

- ✔ Contact and general business information (services, categories, URLs)
- ✔ Information about Web services a business provides and how an application finds a particular service
- ✔ Technical details and binding information

For more information on UDDI, see "About UDDI" at www.uddi.org/about. html. To find products and services in the UDDI Business Registry, start at www.uddi.org/find.html.

Where Will Web Services Lead?

Those who build Web services applications must master the details of numerous XML languages, as well as know a scripting and/or programming language. But unless you plan to join their ranks, all you need to know as a Web services consumer is how to use the discovery process.

Regardless of how deeply you dig into the details of Web services, the discovery process enables you (and every other Web user out there) to find Web service providers. Both free and commercial services are available. For a commercial service, you need to satisfy the requirement that you can prove your identity as well as your ability to pay for information and/or services before you can access their Web services.

If you want to check out some Web services, here are some Web sites of interest:

- ✔ **XMethods:** XMethods (`www.xmethods.com`) provides a list of publicly available Web services that you can try out.

- ✔ **SOAPMethods:** Tony Hong of XMethods (and an occasional contributor to XMLhack) has a UDDI browser with a sample repository ready for immediate access at `www.soapclient.com/uddisearch.html`.

- ✔ **Microsoft UDDI Registry:** The Microsoft UDDI registry is free, but you must register to use it at `http://uddi.microsoft.com/default.aspx`.

- ✔ **Web Services List:** The Web Services List offers a list of over 1,000 Web services. This list is updated very frequently and can be accessed at `www.webservicelist.com`.

You access a Web service from a Web page. In order to create a Web page that accesses a Web service application, you need to know the server implementation and the protocol used by the application. This information is available as part of the online registry listing or directly from the service provider.

We honestly believe that Web services will remake the computing landscape in the next five years. After that, the way we interact with computers, software, and data is going to change dramatically and radically.

After going out on that limb, it's time to move on. In the next chapter, you find out all about using XML with forms.

Chapter 16

XML and Forms

*F*orms are an easy and efficient way to collect information. Almost every business uses some type of form to gather data about their customers — via a printed form, an online Web form, or an interactive form displayed in a kiosk.

XML is an obvious choice for collecting data with forms, and two very different options are now available for using XML with forms:

▶ **XForms** is an XML application created by the World Wide Web Consortium (W3C) to provide "the next generation of Web forms." XForms is not a freestanding document type — it's used with XHTML or other XML languages to create XML forms.

▶ **InfoPath** is part of Microsoft Office 2003. It's a visual XML forms editor that you can use to create forms from an XML document or XML Schema. You can also use it to design an XML form from scratch — InfoPath automatically creates an XML Schema document for your form.

In this chapter, we take a close look at creating forms with XForms and with InfoPath.

Collecting Information with Forms: The Basics

Most of us are used to filling in blanks and checking boxes to provide requested information on a printed form. Since the advent of e-commerce, Web users have also become very familiar with completing online HTML forms, including typing text in boxes, choosing radio buttons, checking boxes, and selecting options from scrolling lists.

Most interaction on the Web takes place through the use of forms, though it's not always obvious that a form is involved. In addition to data collection and submission with forms, HTML form elements can create interactivity via scripting languages such as JavaScript.

HTML Forms

You can use HTML to create forms for display on Web pages. HTML includes elements for creating text boxes, text areas (larger boxes), radio buttons, check boxes, and menus. These forms have a standard look and structure, which makes it easy for Web users to use them to enter data. Figure 16-1 shows a standard HTML form.

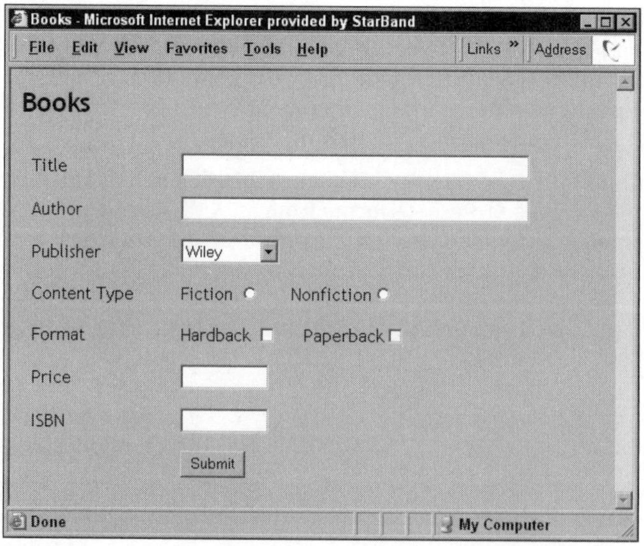

Figure 16-1: An HTML form for collecting book information.

HTML form elements, however, can create only the *structure* of a form for display on a Web page. Actually collecting the data that's entered on an HTML form requires the use of a scripting or programming language in addition to HTML. Perl, PHP, and Java are programming languages commonly used for forms processing. Form data is submitted to a Web server and processed by a server-side script that conforms to the CGI (Common Gateway Interface) specification. The form results can then be returned to a Web page, sent in an e-mail message, saved as a data file, or submitted to a database.

You now have other options for using and gathering data — you can use XML files to create XML forms and collect data with XForms or InfoPath.

XML Forms

XML and forms go together well — both XML and forms have to do with collecting and exchanging data. Although you can use Extensible Stylesheet Language Transformation (XSLT) to generate HTML forms code, two new options (XForms and InfoPath) provide easier solutions for XML data exchange.

XForms

XForms is an XML application created by the W3C. XForms allows the separation of presentation and content, expanded form capabilities, and a decreased reliance on scripting for forms validation and processing.

Why use XForms?

Using XForms for your XML data has several advantages over using HTML forms:

- ✔ Form data can be collected and submitted as XML.
- ✔ External XML documents can be loaded as initial form data.
- ✔ XPath expressions and XML Schema datatypes can be used with XForms.
- ✔ XForms can be integrated with Web services.
- ✔ XForms is device independent — the same markup can be used in Web browsers, speech-enabled Web browsers, mobile phones, and PDAs.

XForms properties

XForms markup resembles HTML forms markup and is not difficult to learn and use. XForms markup is shown in Listing 16-1.

Listing 16-1: `book_XForms.html`

```
<h:html xmlns:h="http://www.w3.org/1999/xhtml"
        xmlns="http://www.w3.org/2002/xforms">
<h:head>
<h:title>Books</h:title>
 <model>
  <submission action="http://example.com/books"
   method="get" id="bk"/>
 </model>
</h:head>
<h:body>
<h:p>
 <input ref="bk"><label>Title</label></input>
 <submit submission="bk"><label>Enter</label></submit>
</h:p>
</h:body>
</h:html>
```

XForms does not include a `form` element; the form markup is divided between the `head` section and the `body` section of the document. The `head` element contains a `model` element with a `submission` element that includes the attributes that are usually contained in an HTML `form` element: `action`, `method`, and `id`. (Form controls such as `input` and `select` are included in the `body` section.)

```
<model>
  <submission action="http://example.com/books"
   method="get" id="bk"/>
 </model>
```

XForms uses XML namespace prefixes so that the XML processor knows which elements to associate with which languages:

```
<h:html xmlns:h="http://www.w3.org/1999/xhtml"
        xmlns="http://www.w3.org/2002/xforms">
```

In this case, XForms is the default namespace, and the XHTML namespace uses an `h:` prefix. For more information on using namespaces, see Chapter 11.

The `input` element doesn't include a `name` attribute as in HTML — a `ref` attribute is used instead. The value of the `ref` attribute can be an identifier (as in an HTML `name` attribute) or an XPath expression:

```
<input ref="bk"><label>Title</label></input>
```

There's no `type` attribute in the `input` element; the type is `string` by default.

Styling in XForms is done with Cascading Style Sheets (CSS). For example, rather than specifying the number of rows and columns in a `textarea` element, you use CSS to define the size of the text area:

```
<textarea ref="comments"><label>Comments</label></textarea>
...
textarea[ref="comments"] {font-family: serif;
                          height: 100px;
                          width: 50%;}
```

XForms includes all the form control elements of HTML forms. HTML forms markup, however, controls the appearance of form elements. In the case of XForms, markup is used to control the action of form elements. For example, XForms includes a `select` and a `select1` element. You use the `select` element when there are zero or more choices (such as with check boxes) and the `select1` element when only one choice can be selected (such as with radio buttons). An `appearance` attribute specifies the appearance of `select` or `select1` elements, as in

```
<select1 appearance="full" ref="bk1">
 <label>Content Type</label>
   <item><label>Fiction</label><value>F</value></item>
   <item><label>Nonfiction</label><value>NF</value></item>
</select1>
```

for radio-button markup and

```
<select appearance="full" ref="bk1">
 <label>Shipping Options</label>
   <item><label>Gift Wrap</label><value>GW</value></item>
   <item><label>Gift Card</label><value>GC</value></item>
</select>
```

for check-box markup.

XForms includes the following built-in features that require scripting when used in HTML forms:

- **Required values:** A required value must be entered in the form before the form can be submitted.

- **Value constraints:** A value must be within a certain range of values. An XPath expression is used to evaluate this constraint.

- **Datatypes for values:** An XML Schema datatype can be specified for a value.

- **Values that are calculated from other values:** An XPath expression is used to calculate a new value from other values in the form. The XPath expression can include XPath functions and mathematical operators.

XForms also provides these additional features:

- The capability to specify an initial value for form data.
- p3ptypes for privacy-related values: P3P (the W3C *P*latform for *P*rivacy *P*references) datatypes can be used for privacy monitoring.

  For more information on P3P, visit the P3P Project page on the W3C site at www.w3.org/P3P/.
- A switch element for creating wizard-like behavior for form completion (as shown in Figure 16-2).
- A repeat element that allows items to be added and deleted, as in a shopping cart.
- Functions galore — including arithmetic functions, string manipulation, date handling, and conditional statements using if.

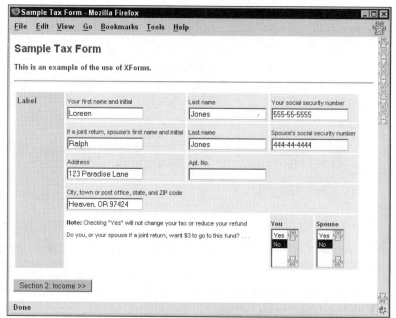

Figure 16-2: An XForms form with a switch element to create wizard-like behavior.

Submission options

XForms includes several options for the method of submitting form data. These are specified in a method attribute in the submission element. Three of these methods are similar to those available with HTML forms:

✔ `method="get"`

✔ `method="urlencodedpost"`

✔ `method="form-data-post"`

In addition, XForms offers

✔ `method="post"` (posts the results as an XML document)

✔ `method="put"` (puts the results in an XML document)

Figures 16-3, 16-4, and 16-5 show the use of the `"put"` method. Figure 16-3 shows an XML document with content. Figure 16-4 shows an XForms form to edit this content, and Figure 16-5 shows the same XML document with new content.

Figure 16-3:
An XML document and content.

To find out more about using XForms, see the XForms tutorial at `http://xformsinstitute.com/lesson1.php`.

Although special browsers are available for viewing XForms, Mozilla has created an XForms project to implement XForms in the Mozilla and Firefox browsers. To find out more about the XForms project and to download an XForms extension for Mozilla or Firefox, visit `www.mozilla.org/projects/xforms`. (This Web page also includes sample XForms documents; some of these documents were used to create the XForms screen shots in this chapter.)

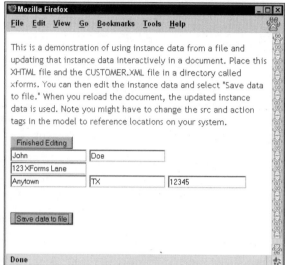

Figure 16-4:
An XForms form that edits content in the XML document in Figure 16-3.

Figure 16-5:
The XML document with new content.

The XForms 1.0 specification can be viewed at www.w3.org/TR/xforms. Several other XForms documents are available via the W3C XForms Activity page at www.w3.org/MarkUp/Forms.

InfoPath

Now, for a completely different approach to XML forms, take a look at Microsoft's InfoPath. (You can order a free 60-day trial version on CD at `www.microsoft.com/office/infopath/prodinfo/trial.mspx`.) InfoPath is a WYSIWYG (What You See Is What You Get) XML forms editor that can create an XML form from an XML document or XML Schema document. You can also create your own form — and InfoPath will create the XML Schema to accompany it — or use any of InfoPath's sample form designs.

InfoPath forms can be used online or downloaded and completed offline. Users must have InfoPath on their computers to use these forms, however.

Why use InfoPath?

You should consider using InfoPath for several reasons:

- ✔ InfoPath is easy to use and doesn't require any knowledge of XML.
- ✔ Form data from InfoPath can be exported to other Microsoft applications, such as Excel 2003.
- ✔ InfoPath allows you to select multiple forms and combine the data into one form.
- ✔ You can use an existing XML Schema document and automatically create a form based on the structure of the schema.
- ✔ InfoPath can be integrated with Web services.
- ✔ InfoPath includes data validation and conditional formatting features.

Automated form design from an XML Schema

You can easily design a form from an existing XML Schema in InfoPath:

1. **Open InfoPath, and select File⇨Design a Form.**

   The Design a Form task pane opens on the right side of the InfoPath window.

2. **From the Design a New Form list in the task pane on the right side of the page, select New from XML Document or Schema.**

   The InfoPath Data Source Wizard window opens.

3. **Click the Browse button in the Data Source Wizard window, and browse to the location of the** `bookstore.xsd` **file.**

   That's the file we created in Chapter 9. (By the way, you can download the `bookstore.xsd` file at `www.dummies.com/go/xmlfd4e`.)

4. **Select the** `bookstore.xsd` **file, click Open, and then click Next in the Data Source Wizard window.**

   The Data Source Wizard window displays a question: *Do you want to add another XML document or schema to the data source?*

5. **Choose No in response to the question and then click the Finish button.**

   InfoPath displays a blank template document, and the Data Source task pane opens on the right. The XML document tree is visible in the Data Source task pane.

6. **Select the Layout task pane from the list at the top of the task pane and then select Two Column Table from the Insert Layout Tables menu in the task pane.**

7. **Select the Data Source task pane, highlight the** `book` **element in the task pane, and then drag the** `book` **element into the left column of the table.**

   A contextual menu appears in the left column of the table.

8. **Choose Section with Controls from the contextual menu.**

   Doing so adds all the elements contained in the `book` element as form controls and automatically binds the form controls to the corresponding schema elements.

9. **Select and drag the** `totalCost` **element into the bottom of the left column, below the repeating section. Then select and drag the** `customer` **element into the lower-right cell.**

   A contextual menu appears.

10. **Choose Section with Controls from the contextual menu.**

    The bottom of your form should now resemble Figure 16-6.

    You don't have to include all the elements from the schema in your form. You can select and drag individual elements into the template window.

11. **Choose File⇨Save As⇨Save⇨ to open the Save As dialog box. Enter** `bookstore.xsn` **for the file name and then click the Save button.**

    This saves your file as an InfoPath template document (`.xsn`).

12. **Choose File⇨Preview Form. Then choose With Data File from the submenu.**

    This opens the Choose Data File to Preview window.

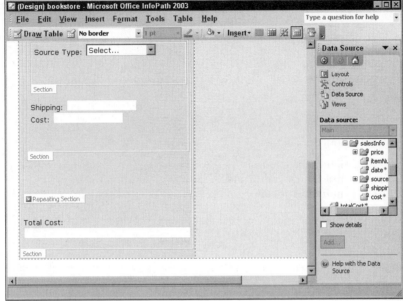

Figure 16-6:
The `total
Cost`
element
goes below
the
repeating
section on
the left.

13. **Browse to the location of** `bookstore_schema.xml` **from Chapter 9, select it, and then click Preview.**

    Check out your Preview file; then close the Preview window to return to the main InfoPath window. (Figure 16-7 shows the InfoPath Preview file.) You can also preview the file without data by choosing Default from the submenu.

14. **Publish your file to a folder, and put your form to work.**

    You can publish your file to a folder on your computer or on a network, to a Web server, or to a SharePoint form library by choosing File⇨ Publish.

    You can open the form template in InfoPath and fill in new data by choosing File⇨Fill Out a Form and then selecting the form template file from the menu on the left side of the Fill Out a Form dialog box that appears.

Now you can see why we included InfoPath in this chapter — it's fast, and it's easy to

✔ Create a working XML form document that can be populated with data from any XML document that corresponds to the XML Schema the form is based on.

✔ Fill out new data in a blank form based on a form template document.

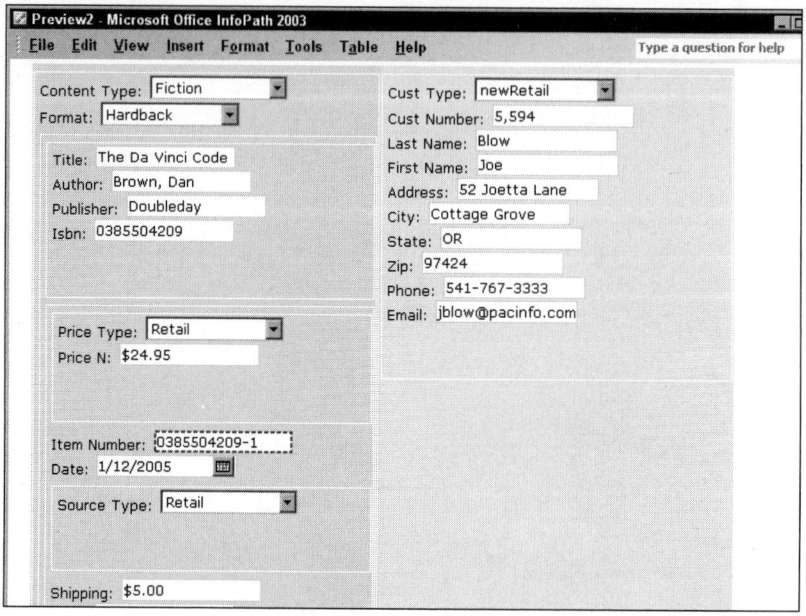

Figure 16-7:
Preview file
in InfoPath.

For more information on InfoPath, see `http://office.microsoft.com/en-us/assistance/HA011221251033.aspx`.

In Chapter 17, you find out more than you probably want to know about using XML with databases.

Chapter 17

Serving Up the Data: XML and Databases

*T*hese days, data exchange makes the world go 'round. Online billing systems receive electronic bills and send out electronic statements. Colleges and universities exchange student data without the hassle of printouts or data entry. Loan underwriters receive credit reports electronically, instead of by fax, and incorporate that information directly into their systems. If one business needs to share data with another — for any reason — it can be done electronically with XML.

We can't talk about XML data exchange without restating what we hope is indelibly ingrained in your head by now: XML is simply text, and it works on any platform and with just about any application that can read a text file.

In this chapter, you have the opportunity to get some hands-on practice with XML and databases. Using three different software applications (Word, InfoPath, and XMLSpy), you find out how to import data from a database to an XML document and how to export data from an XML document to a database. You also discover how to export data directly from Access 2003 in several different file formats.

Using Databases with XML

The connection between databases and XML is a logical one: Both store data in a structured manner. A very common use for XML is to take data stored in XML documents and move it into a database so that the data can be accessed and manipulated by an application. All the major database systems — from Oracle to Microsoft SQL (Structured Query Language) Server and beyond — have XML utilities that help you work with XML in the context of the database.

Another common use of databases with XML is to let the database serve as an index to the content described with XML. For example, an online article archive uses XML as the format for describing articles. When a new article comes into the system, the tool that pulls the article into the archiving system populates a database with some basic data about the article, such as the author, date, title, and topic. The rest of the article is stored as a flat text file on the system's hard drive for later access. You can then use the database to search for articles by the information stored in the database: author, date, title, and topic.

This particular solution, an online article archive, takes advantage of the individual strengths of both XML and databases:

✔ XML provides detailed structural information about the articles, which a database can't handle very well.

✔ The data about the articles (the article metadata) stored in the database can be searched and filtered according to all manner of criteria — something XML isn't particularly suited for.

For example, if you want to find all articles written by John Doe between January and February of 2005 that include *XML* in the subject line, this system helps you find them and then makes their content available to you (or a display system) for further manipulation.

If your solution includes a database, you need to think about how, if at all, your XML documents will interface with the database.

Text-intensive XML

XML documents usually fall into one of two broad categories:

✔ Text-intensive (also known as *document-intensive*)
✔ Data-intensive

Although data-intensive XML documents such as financial records lend themselves easily to interaction with databases, text-intensive XML documents can also be configured to work with a database. For example, a database can store paragraphs of text; an XML document can then connect with the database to import a particular block of text information to add to the content of the XML document. When the information in the database changes, the content of the XML document changes, too.

In Chapter 18, you find out more about using XML with text-intensive content such as news feeds.

Data-intensive XML

Interacting with a database is "natural" for XML documents with data-intensive content. Businesses commonly use databases to store data-intensive content. This content can be imported from a database to populate XML documents with the most current version of the data. The XML document can then be displayed in print, on a Web page, in an online form, or on a mobile device.

Creating XML from Database Files

Using XML with databases is becoming easier and easier, thanks to software products that support XML. The particular product you choose depends, of course, on your data, the database you use, and your output needs.

In the following sections, we focus on using an Access database with XML documents in Microsoft Word 2003, Microsoft InfoPath, and Altova XMLSpy. You can download the Access database file (`bookstore.mdb`) from the Web site for this book: `www.dummies.com/go/xmlfd4e`. You don't need to be a database pro to do this — we provide any information you need as we go along.

The details of database structure and database management are beyond the scope of this book. For more information, see the *Access 2003 All-in-One Desk Reference For Dummies,* by Alan Simpson, Margaret Levine Young, and Alison Barrow (Wiley Publishing, Inc.).

Using Word 2003

All versions of Word 2003 can save documents in XML format. (The professional version of Word 2003 allows you to add external XML Schema documents to your Word XML documents.) You can download a 60-day free trial of the Standard Microsoft Office Suite (which includes Word 2003, Excel 2003, Outlook 2003, and PowerPoint 2003) at `www.microsoft.com/office/trial/default.mspx`.

To import database information into a Word 2003 XML document, follow these steps:

1. **Open Word 2003, choose File⇨New from the main menu, and then choose XML Document from the New Document task pane on the left.**

2. **Select View⇨Toolbars⇨Database.**

   The Database toolbar appears above the task pane.

3. **Click the Insert Database icon on the Database toolbar.**

   The Database dialog box appears.

4. **Click the Get Data button, browse to the** `bookstore.mdb` **file, and then click Open.**

   New options now appear in the Database Dialog box: Query Options, Table AutoFormat, and Insert Data.

5. **If you want to use Word's default table formatting options, move on to Step 6.**

   (Optional) If you want to select among Word's table formatting display options, click the Table AutoFormat button in the Database dialog box, choose a display style, and then click OK.

6. **Click the Insert Data button in the Database dialog box.**

   The Insert Data dialog box makes an appearance.

7. **From the Insert Data dialog box, choose All or a range of values for the Insert records option and then click OK.**

   Your XML file now displays the database information in a table, as shown in Figure 17-1.

If you don't want to display the `id` column, just select and delete that column of the table. The `id` column is the *primary key* in the `Book` database table. A primary key is used to uniquely identify a record (row) in a database table.

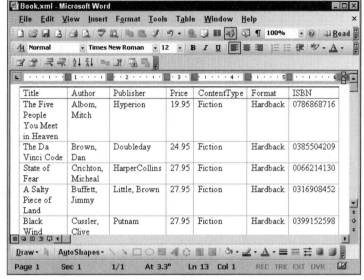

Title	Author	Publisher	Price	ContentType	Format	ISBN
The Five People You Meet in Heaven	Albom, Mitch	Hyperion	19.95	Fiction	Hardback	0786868716
The Da Vinci Code	Brown, Dan	Doubleday	24.95	Fiction	Hardback	0385504209
State of Fear	Crichton, Micheal	HarperCollins	27.95	Fiction	Hardback	0066214130
A Salty Piece of Land	Buffett, Jimmy	Little, Brown	27.95	Fiction	Hardback	0316908452
Black Wind	Cussler, Clive	Putnam	27.95	Fiction	Hardback	0399152598

Figure 17-1:
Book.xml
displays
data
imported
from book
store.
mdb.

Using InfoPath

InfoPath allows you to import database information into a blank InfoPath form. You can then design the form to make database queries and display the query results on the form page.

If you also want to use the form to add and edit records in the database, the database must be the primary data source for the form. In this case, you must start with a new InfoPath form — you can't modify an existing form to create a primary connection to a database.

You can order a free 60-day trial version of InfoPath on CD at www.microsoft.com/office/infopath/prodinfo/trial.mspx.

To import database information and create a new InfoPath form, follow these steps:

1. **Open InfoPath, and choose File⇨Design a Form to open the Design a Form task pane.**

2. **From the Design a Form task pane, choose New from Data Connection.**

   The Data Connection Wizard window appears.

3. **Choose Database from the Data Connection Wizard and then click Next.**

4. **Click the Select Database button in the next screen in the wizard, browse to the location of** bookstore.mdb**, and then click Open.**

   The Data Source window in the Data Connection Wizard now displays the column headers from the Book database table: ID, Title, Author, Publisher, Price, ContentType, Format, and ISBN.

5. **Click Next in the wizard screen and then enter a name for the data connection in the text field labeled "Enter a name for this data connection."**

   A summary of information about the connection is displayed beneath the name.

6. **Click Finish.**

   The form template opens with the Data Source task pane on the right. Query fields and Data fields are shown in the task pane.

7. **Insert the cursor in the Drag Data Fields Here box on the form template.**

   The text "Drag Data Fields Here" disappears, and a small gray box appears above the upper-left corner of the Data Fields box.

8. **Select the dataFields folder from the task pane and then right-click the folder.**

   A contextual menu duly appears on-screen.

9. **Choose Section with Controls from the contextual menu.**

   All of the Book table fields display as form controls. Notice that this is a Repeating Section, because the table holds more than one record (row).

10. **To format the display, right-click the Repeating Section label; choose Borders and Shading; use the main tab of the Borders and Shading dialog box to make your selections for border width, color, and size; and then click the Shading tab to choose a background color.**

11. **With your data fields out of the way, insert the cursor into the Drag Query Fields Here box on the form template.**

    The text "Drag Query Fields Here" disappears, and a small gray box appears above the upper-left corner of the Query Fields box.

12. **Select the queryFields folder from the task pane, and right-click the folder.**

    Another contextual menu makes an appearance.

13. **Choose Section with Controls from the contextual menu.**

    All of the `Book` table fields display as controls, but you can delete any fields that you don't want to include as query items. For example, we included only `Title`, `Author`, `Publisher`, and `ISBN`.

14. **Put the cursor in the Query box, and add a title for this box. Do the same in the Data box (we used `Book Query` and `Book Data` for our titles).**

    You can use the Font task pane to format the title text. Just click the downward-pointing arrow next to Data Source to see the task pane menu.

15. **In the area that says Click to Add a Title, enter a title for your form.**

16. **In the area that says Click to Add Form Content, add some instructions for form users.**

    For example, we used these instructions:

    ```
    To query the book database, type a value in one or more boxes in the Book
    Query table, and then click the Run Query button. To enter a new record in
    the book database, click New Record, then enter values in the Book Data
    table. Click the Submit button on the above toolbar to Submit the new
    information or changes to the database.
    ```

17. **Choose File➪Save and then click Save in the Microsoft Office InfoPath window to save the form design changes.**

    The Save As dialog box opens. Make sure that InfoPath Form Template (*.xsn) displays as the file type in the Save As Type box.

18. **Enter a name for your form (we used `Book.xsn`) and then click Save.**

    This saves your form as an InfoPath form template file.

19. **Choose File➪Preview Form➪Default to create a functional Preview file, and test out the form!**

Figure 17-2 shows the Preview version of the `Book` form.

When you create a form from a database table, InfoPath automatically creates a form with two layout tables and adds `queryFields` and `dataFields` to the Data Source task pane. After you add form controls to the tables, you can delete any field without affecting the underlying field in the database table.

If you're going to use the form for data editing and entry, you want to retain all the `dataFields` except for those that are automatically generated by the database, such as the `id` field in our database.

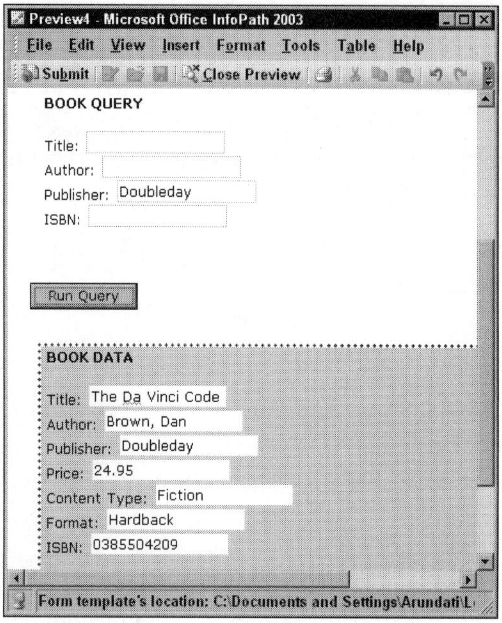

Figure 17-2:
InfoPath
form to
query a
database.

Clicking the Run Query button makes queries to the database based on the values in the `queryField` control fields. The database returns any records that match these values and displays them in the data entry part of the form. You can edit the returned values and submit them to the database by clicking the Submit icon on the toolbar.

Using XMLSpy

XMLSpy is a multifaceted XML tool, and we talk more about it in Chapter 19. In this section, you find out how to import and export XML to databases by using XMLSpy. You can download a free 30-day trial version of the full version of XMLSpy Enterprise or Professional Edition, or a free time-unlimited version of XMLSpy Home Edition, at `www.altova.com/download.html`.

Follow these steps to import information from a database and create a new XML file:

1. **Open XMLSpy, and choose Convert⇨Import Database Data from the main menu.**

   The Import Database data window appears.

2. **In the Import Database data dialog box, choose Convert Database Data into XML, and click OK.**

   The Select a Source Database window appears.

3. **Select Microsoft Access (ADO) from the Select a Source Database window and then click Next.**

   The Select a MS Access Database window makes an appearance.

4. **In the Select a MS Access Database window, click the Browse button and navigate to** bookstore.mdb; **then click Next.**

   The Import Database Data window appears.

5. **In the Import Database Data window, click the Choose Database Table button.**

   The Choose a Database Table window appears.

6. **In the Choose a Database Table window, select** Book **and then click OK.**

7. **In the Import Database Data window, go to the Import Settings section and choose the Compatible with Schema Data Types option, check the boxes for the Exclude Primary/Foreign Keys and the Create Empty Elements from Empty Fields options, and then click the Import button.**

   The XML file appears in XMLSpy in Grid view.

8. **Click the Text tab at the bottom of the file to see the underlying markup.**

   Note that the root element is Import and the data is contained in Row elements, as shown in Figure 17-3.

Here's how to export data from an XML file to a database:

1. **Choose File⇨Open from the main menu in XMLSpy. Navigate to your XML file in the Open dialog box and then click Open.**

2. **Choose Convert⇨Export to Text Files/Database.**

   The Export to Text Files/Databases dialog box appears.

3. **From the Export to Text Files/Databases dialog box, select Convert XML into Text Files or Database Data and then click OK.**

   The Export to Text Files/Database window appears.

4. **In the Automatic Fields section of the Export to Text Files/Database window, uncheck the Independent Primary Key Counter for Every Element box and then click the Export to Database button.**

   The Export to Database window appears.

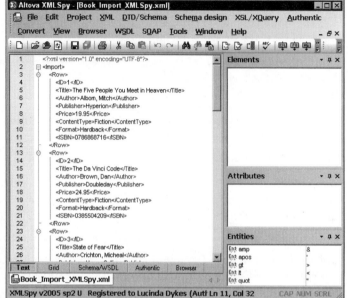

Figure 17-3:
Importing
database
information
to create an
XML file in
XMLSpy.

5. **Click OK in the next window (Export to Database) to create the database file.**

   The Save As dialog box appears. Enter a name for the database file and then click Save.

6. **Open the database file in Access and then click the Row table to view the table contents, as shown in Figure 17-4.**

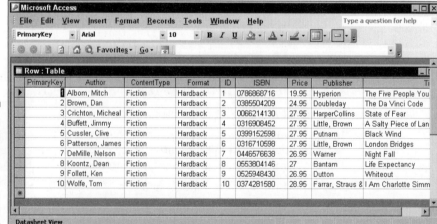

Figure 17-4:
Exporting
XML to
create an
Access
database in
XMLSpy.

As you have seen, all three of these software programs use database informa-tion in a different way to create XML files. Your choice depends on whether you want to create print documents for display of database information, searchable forms that directly interact with a database, or database files themselves.

Using XML with Access 2003

In addition to importing and exporting Access databases with other software, you can use Access 2003 itself to export XML data in several formats.

Using Access 2003, you can import data from an XML file as well as export data as XML files. The import and export methods in Access 2003 also allow you to import and export XML data, schema information, and/or presentation information to and from Microsoft SQL Server 2000 Desktop Engine, Microsoft SQL Server 7.0 or later, and the Microsoft Jet Database Engine. Access 2003 also supports the use of XSLT files when importing or exporting XML data.

Follow these instructions to import data from an XML file into Access 2003:

1. **Select File➪New to create a new database file.**

   The New File task pane opens on the right side of the Access window.

2. **Select Blank Database from the New list in the New File task pane.**

   The File New Database window appears.

3. **Enter a name for the database in the File New Database window and then click Create.**

   A Database window opens in the Access workspace.

4. **To get the import ball rolling, choose File➪Get External Data➪Import.**

   The Import dialog box makes an appearance.

5. **In the Import dialog box, choose XML from the Files of Type drop-down menu and then browse to the location of your XML file. Select your XML file and then click Import.**

   The Import XML dialog box appears.

6. **Click the Options button to show all the import options, as shown in Figure 17-5.**

   You can choose to import Structure Only, Structure and Data, or Append Data to Existing Table(s). If you import an XML Schema, the Options button is grayed out, because the only option is to import the structure only. You can also click the Transform button to add an existing XSLT stylesheet to the imported data.

Figure 17-5:
The Import
XML dialog
box in
Access
2003.

You must import the entire XML file to Access — you can't select a subset of the information for import. The fields in the database table will be the same as the names of the elements in the imported XML document.

Follow these instructions to export data from an Access 2003 table to an XML file:

1. **Open the database table in Access and then select File⇨Export.**

   The Export dialog box comes to the fore.

2. **In the Export dialog box, choose XML in the Save as Type drop-down menu and then click the Export button.**

   The Export XML dialog box appears, as shown in Figure 17-6. You can choose any or all of the options: Data, Schema, and/or Presentation. If you click the More Options button in this dialog box, you can choose additional features of the XML file, XML Schema file, or XSLT file.

Figure 17-6:
The Export
XML dialog
box in
Access
2003.

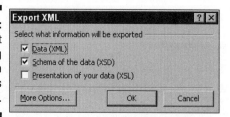

Depending on your choices in the Export XML dialog box, Access 2003 will create the following files:

✔ **An XML file:** Additional options include exporting all records or just the current record; applying an existing filter, sort, or XSLT stylesheet to the data; and choosing an encoding format.

✔ **An XML Schema file:** Schema options include creating a separate schema file, embedding the schema file in an XML document, and including primary-key and index information.

✔ **An XSLT file:** Access creates an XSLT file and also creates an HTML or ASP file from the transformation of the XML file with this XSLT document. Options include the choice of an HTML file or an ASP file and, if the data includes images, the choice to export images in these files.

In addition to exporting XML files from Access 2003 database tables, you can export Access 2003 database tables as RTF (Rich Text Format) files. This automatically displays the data in tabular form in a Word document, as shown in Figure 17-7. To transform your XML data for print, you can import the file to a database table in Access 2003 and then export the data as an RTF file.

Ready to distribute your Web site content? In the next chapter, you find out all about using RSS, an XML application, to create RSS feeds and syndicated content. RSS is not really a single thing; it's an acronym for Rich Site Summary, RDF Site Summary, or Really Simple Syndication, depending on the version of RSS you use — see Chapter 18 for all the details!

Figure 17-7:
Exporting
data as an
RTF file in
Access
2003.

ID	Title	Author	Publisher	Price	Co T
1	The Five People You Meet in Heaven	Albom, Mitch	Hyperion	$19.95	Fict
2	The Da Vinci Code	Brown, Dan	Doubleday	$24.95	Fict
3	State of Fear	Crichton, Micheal	HarperCollins	$27.95	Fict
4	A Salty Piece of Land	Buffett, Jimmy	Little, Brown	$27.95	Fict
5	Black Wind	Cussler, Clive	Putnam	$27.95	Fict
6	London Bridges	Patterson, James	Little, Brown	$27.95	Fict
7	Night Fall	DeMille, Nelson	Warner	$26.95	Fict
8	Life Expectancy	Koontz, Dean	Bantam	$27.00	Fict
9	Whiteout	Follett, Ken	Dutton	$26.95	Fict
10	I Am Charlotte Simmons	Wolfe, Tom	Farrar, Straus & Giroux	$28.95	Fict

Chapter 18

XML and RSS

*R*SS is an XML application for syndicating Web content and creating news feeds. It allows potential visitors to get a preview of the latest content on a site, and it's an economical and easy way to attract visitors. RSS feeds are used to distribute links to Web site content. Any time you want to retrieve the latest headlines from your favorite sites, you can access the available RSS feeds via a desktop RSS reader. You can also make an RSS feed for your own site if your content changes frequently.

RSS technology is in widespread use on the Web today for sites with dynamic content such as blogs (Web logs) and news sites. RSS is not limited to news, however — you can use it with any content that can be broken down into distinct items.

What does RSS stand for? Rich Site Summary, RDF Site Summary, or Really Simple Syndication — depending on which version of RSS you're referring to. You'll learn the details of the main RSS versions in the section "Sorting Out the Versions."

So get ready to rock. This is the chapter where you find out how to create RSS feeds and how to syndicate your RSS files. (You always wanted to go into syndication, didn't you? Now's your chance.)

Introducing RSS

RSS files include basic information about a site (title, URL, description), plus one or more item entries that include — at a minimum — a title (headline), a URL, and a brief description of the linked content. Your RSS files can be registered with an RSS registry to make them more available to viewers interested in your content area. You can also submit your RSS feeds to an aggregator. *Aggregators* filter a group of RSS feeds to create a feed that includes items from several different feeds in the same content area.

Visit O'Reilly's Meerkat service at www.oreillynet.com/meerkat/ for an example of an aggregator. Desktop RSS readers are also sometimes referred to as aggregators, but they don't include the capability of filtering and grouping feeds from different sites.

You can also download RSS feeds from other sites to display news items on your site, or use a desktop or online reader to access your favorite RSS feeds. The news content is dynamically updated as new RSS feeds become available, so it's always up to date — or at least as up to date as the last RSS feed!

Sorting Out the Versions

RSS development has been anything but a smooth and straight path. One of the main areas of contention is whether to use the W3C RDF (Resource Description Framework) data model for RSS. Two separate but parallel developments occurred in RSS: a version of RSS based on RDF (RSS 1.0) and a separate set of RSS versions that don't incorporate all the complexities of RDF (versions RSS 0.91, 0.92, 0.93, 0.94, 2.0, and 2.01).

You'll learn more about RDF in the "RSS 1.0" section in this chapter.

There are actually nine different versions of RSS, including both a Netscape and a UserLand version of some of the 0.9x series. We don't explore every detail of RSS history here — just the major versions — but if you're interested, you can learn more about all the details in Mark Pilgrim's article, "The myth of RSS compatibility," at

```
http://diveintomark.org/archives/2004/02/04/incompatible-rss
```

Different meanings for the term RSS came with the different forms of RSS: Rich Site Summary (RSS 0.9), RDF Site Summary (RSS 1.0), and Really Simple Syndication (RSS 0.9x, 2.0, and 2.01).

Four RSS versions are still in widespread use today. Statistics from Syndic8. com (`www.syndic8.com/stats.php?Section=rss#RSSVersion`), an RSS syndication site, show that RSS 2.0/2.01 is the most common version used today (61 percent of RSS feeds), followed by RSS 0.91/0.92 (22 percent) and finally RSS 1.0 (17 percent).

The good news is that you can usually use any RSS version for your RSS feeds. RSS validators, aggregators, directories, and readers generally support all RSS versions — at least so far!

RSS 0.9x

RSS 0.91 was originally released by Netscape and then modified by Dave Winer of RadioUserLand (`http://radio.userland.com`), who later released RSS 0.92, 0.93, and 0.94 — the last in the 0.9x series.

RSS 0.92, 0.93, and 0.94 were released after RSS 1.0.

RSS 0.9x syntax

An RSS file is an XML file and begins with an XML declaration:

```
<?xml version="1.0"?>
```

This is followed by the root element, `rss`, which contains one `channel` element that includes the rest of the document. It looks like this:

```
<rss version="0.91">
 <channel>
  ...
 </channel>
</rss>
```

There are five required child elements of `channel` in RSS 0.91:

- ✔ `title`: the name of the feed
- ✔ `link`: the URL of the Web site associated with the feed
- ✔ `description`: a description of the channel in plain text
- ✔ `language`: the code for the language (English, French, Chinese, what have you) the feed is written in
- ✔ `image`: an element to describe the graphic icon for the feed

The image element includes three required child elements:

- ✔ url: the location of the graphic icon file
- ✔ title: a description of the image
- ✔ link: the URL that the image links to (usually the same location as the link element in channel)

The image element can also include two optional elements:

- ✔ width: width of the icon (maximum 144 pixels; more common is a maximum width of 88 pixels)
- ✔ height: height of the icon (maximum 400 pixels; more common is a maximum height of 31 pixels)

There are also ten optional child elements of the channel element. Many of these elements have static content, so they don't need to be changed each time a new RSS file is created:

- ✔ copyright: copyright notice for the feed content
- ✔ managingEditor: e-mail contact
- ✔ webMaster: e-mail address
- ✔ rating: PICS (Platform for Internet Content Selection) rating
- ✔ pubDate: publication date of the feed content
- ✔ lastBuildDate: the date and time the feed last changed
- ✔ docs: URL that points to the RSS standard for this feed
- ✔ skipDays: specifies days of the week that the feed should not be retrieved
- ✔ skipHours: specifies hours of the day that the feed should not be retrieved
- ✔ textInput: text box and Submit button to a script for search features or e-mail

The heart of an RSS feed is the item element, a child of the channel element. Technically, it's optional — but without it, what's the point of a feed? The item element includes two required child elements:

title: the headline of the content item

link: the URL of the content item

It also includes one optional child element:

description: a plain-text summary of the content, up to a maximum of 500 characters

An RSS 0.91 file can include a maximum of 15 item elements.

Listing 18-1 shows a simple RSS 0.91 file with one news item:

Listing 18-1: An RSS 0.91 File (silkcreek.xml**)**

```
<?xml version="1.0"?>
<rss version="0.91">
 <channel>
  <title>Silk Creek News</title>
  <link>http://www.silkcreek.net/news.html</link>
  <description>Silk Creek News - By Lucinda Dykes</description>
  <language>en-us</language>
  <copyright>Copyright 2005, Lucinda Dykes</copyright>
  <managingEditor>editor@wiley.com</managingEditor>
  <webMaster>webmaster@wiley.com</webMaster>
  <pubDate>Sun, 20 Feb 2005 13:00:00 GMT</pubDate>
  <lastBuildDate>Sun, 20 Feb 2005 13:00:00 GMT
  </lastBuildDate>
  <docs>http://backend.userland.com/rss091</docs>
  <image>
  <title>Silk Creek Logo</title>
  <url>http://www.silkcreek.net/graphics/sc_logo.jpg</url>
  <link>http://www.silkcreek.net</link>
  <width>90</width>
  <height>67</height>
  </image>
  <item>
   <title>Attack update</title>
   <link>http://www.silkcreek.net/news.html</link>
   <description>
Just when you think it's safe . . .

    be sure to note that virus update renewal date!
    By Lucinda Dykes, Feb 20, 2005
   </description>
  </item>
 </channel>
</rss>
```

The text file can be saved with any file extension; the most common ones are
.xml and .rss. Regardless of the file extension you use, this is an XML file
and must follow XML rules; make sure your file is well-formed XML.

Some characters are illegal in XML; convert any illegal characters that show
up in your content to character entities *before* you validate your file. (For
example, a URL might include an ampersand or other XML-illegal character.)
For a list of character entities, see

www.webdevtips.com/webdevtips/html/special.shtml

RSS 0.92, 0.93, 0.94

The major changes to RSS 0.91 in later versions of RSS 0.9*x* included these:

✔ RSS 0.92

 • Any number of item elements can be used.

 • The description element can include HTML content, not just plain text.

✔ RSS 0.93

 • The optional expirationDate element is added.

✔ RSS 0.94

 • The expirationDate element is deleted.

 • The type attribute for MIME type is added to description element.

RSS 2.0/2.01

RSS 2.0/2.01 is very similar to RSS 0.9*x*, so we discuss RSS 2.0/2.01 first and then move on to RSS 1.0 in the next section of this chapter.

RSS 2.0/2.01 adds namespace modules and six optional elements to RSS 0.9x. The RSS 2.0/2.01 specification was written by Dave Winer of Radio UserLand. The copyright was later transferred to Harvard University.

Using namespaces in RSS 2.0/2.01

To use namespace modules in RSS 2.0/2.01, add the namespace declaration in the root element of the feed (rss), and use the correct prefix when using elements from this namespace. For example, to add the radioWeblogPost module, you could add the namespace as shown in the following code:

```
<?xml version="1.0"?>
<rss version="2.0"
  xmlns:radio="http://backend.userland.com/radioWeblogPostModule">
```

To see all currently available modules for RSS 2.0/2.01, visit

```
http://blogs.law.harvard.edu/tech/directory/5/specifications/
            rss20ModulesNamespaces
```

Options in RSS 2.0/2.01

The six new optional elements of RSS 2.0/2.01 are:

- ✔ `comment`: child of `item`; contains URL of comment page for the item.

- ✔ `generator`: child of `channel`; indicates which program was used to create the RSS file.

- ✔ `author`: child of `item`; contains e-mail address of author of content in the item.

- ✔ `ttl`: child of `channel`; specifies the number of minutes to wait before refreshing the feed.

- ✔ `pubDate`: child of `item`; gives the date the item content was originally published.

- ✔ `guid`: child of `item`; contains a string that uniquely identifies the item; *guid* stands for *globally unique ID*. (Not sure if it rhymes with *squid*.)

The `guid` element in RSS 2.0/2.01 is not necessarily the same GUID defined by the OSF (Open Software Foundation), which consists of a 16-byte integer generated by the OSF GUID algorithm.

The full RSS 2.0/2.01 specification, including sample files, is available online at `http://blogs.law.harvard.edu/tech/rss`.

RSS 1.0

RSS 1.0 (RDF Site Summary) is a W3C specification — based on the W3C RDF specification, to be more precise — and was released in 2000. RDF is a system for describing and interchanging metadata about resources on the Web. And while we're defining stuff, you should probably know that *metadata* is a special kind of data that describes and models other data. RDF is a framework for using metadata effectively for information search and retrieval on the Web.

There is currently very little metadata available on the Web; Search-engine strategy is still relatively crude because of this scarcity. For example, to search for a list of publications on the Web by a specific author, you could search on the author's name itself and hope that this query would find Web documents that included the author's name in the title, keywords, or text content of the page. It is not currently possible to search based on a category of metadata — say, a list of all authors of Web documents.

The RDF specification is complex and at the present time consists of six documents (Primer, Concepts, Syntax, Semantics, Vocabulary, and Test Cases) — whew! Luckily for us, RSS 1.0 is a relatively lightweight version of RDF.

How does an RSS 1.0 differ from an RSS 0.9x or RSS 2.0/2.01 file? Glad you asked; the upcoming steps convert the RSS 0.91 file to an RSS 1.0 file and, in the process, highlight those differences.

1. **Start with an XML declaration.**

   This line is the same for all RSS files:

   ```
   <?xml version="1.0"?>
   ```

2. **Replace the** `rss` **element with an** `rdf` **element, and specify the namespace.**

   This must be used exactly as shown here (except for adding more namespaces, if you choose):

   ```
   <rdf:RDF xmlns:rdf="http://www.w3.org/1999/02/22-rdf-syntax-ns#"
            xmlns="http://purl.org/rss/1.0/">
   ```

3. **Use the** `channel` **element and its** `link`, `title`, **and** `description` **elements as in the RSS 0.91 file (see Listing 18-1), but add an** `rdf:about` **attribute to the** `channel` **element.**

   The `rdf:about` attribute is required for each resource (channel, image, item, and text input). It associates a URI (Uniform Resource Identifier) with a resource. For the channel, the URI is our RSS 1.0 file itself (`http://www.silkcreek.net/silkcreek.rdf`). Note that the RSS 1.0 file is saved with a `.rdf` file extension:

   ```
   <channel rdf:about="http://www.silkcreek.net/silkcreek.rdf">
     <title>Silk Creek News</title>
     <link>http://www.silkcreek.net/news.html</link>
     <description>Silk Creek News - By Lucinda Dykes </description>
   ```

   A URI is a general class of identifiers that includes URL (Uniform Resource Locator) and URN (Uniform Resource Name). For more information about URIs, see the URI Syntax protocol at

   ```
   www.gbiv.com/protocols/uri/rfc/rfc3986.html
   ```

4. **Close the** `channel` **element.**

   Unlike RSS 0.91, the `channel` element does not include the rest of the document. You'll add some additional child elements to the `channel` element later, however.

   ```
   </channel>
   ```

5. Add the `image` **element as in the RSS 0.91 file (leaving out the** `height` **or** `width` **subelements) and then add an** `rdf:about` **attribute to the** `image` **element.**

The value should be the same as the value of the `url` element for the image, like this:

```
<image rdf:about="http://www.silkcreek.net/graphics/sc_logo.jpg">
<title>Silk Creek Logo</title>
<url>http://www.silkcreek.net/graphics/sc_logo.jpg</url>
<link>http://www.silkcreek.net</link>
</image>
```

6. Add the `item` **element as in the RSS 0.91 file and then add an** `rdf:about` **attribute to the** `item` **element.**

The value should be the same as the value of the `link` element for the item. Check it out:

```
    <item rdf:about="http://www.silkcreek.net/news.html">
<title>Attack update</title>
<link>http://www.silkcreek.net/news.html</link>
<description>
Just when you think it's safe . . .

    be sure to note that virus update renewal date!
    By Lucinda Dykes, Feb 20, 2005
</description>
</item>
```

Now, to tie all the pieces of the file together, Steps 7 through 9 add some further elements to the `channel` element . This is important, because aggregators may filter items from their parent `channel` elements.

7. Add an `image` **element within the** `channel` **element and then add an** `rdf:resource` **attribute to this** `image` **element.**

The value of the attribute should be the same as what you used for the `rdf:about` attribute in the `image` element in Step 5.

Use a closing slash (/); this is an empty element. Here's how it looks:

```
<channel rdf:about="http://www.silkcreek.net/silkcreek.rdf">
    <title>Silk Creek News</title>
    ...
<image rdf:resource="http://www.silkcreek.net/graphics/sc_logo.jpg" />
```

8. Add an `items` **element within the** `channel` **element and then add an RDF sequence to contain the item(s).**

In this case, our sequence contains only one item.

9. **Add an** `li` **element for each item and then add an** `rdf:resource`
   attribute to the `li` **element.**

   The value of the attribute is the same as the value of the `rdf:about`
   attribute for each item. Here's what you get:

   ```
   <items>
   <rdf:Seq>
   <li rdf:resource="http://www.silkcreek.net/news.html" />
   </rdf:Seq>
   </items>
   ```

10. **Close the** `rdf` **element, and save the file:**

    ```
    </rdf:RDF>
    ```

Make sure your XML file is well formed and doesn't include any illegal
characters.

Listing 18-2 shows the complete code for the RSS 1.0 file.

Listing 18-2: An RSS 1.0 File (`silkcreek.rdf`)

```
<?xml version="1.0"?>
<rdf:RDF xmlns:rdf="http://www.w3.org/1999/02/22-rdf-syntax-ns#"
        xmlns="http://purl.org/rss/1.0/">
 <channel rdf:about="http://www.silkcreek.net/silkcreek.rdf">
  <title>Silk Creek News</title>
  <link>http://www.silkcreek.net/news.html</link>
  <description>Silk Creek News - By Lucinda Dykes </description>
  <image rdf:resource="http://www.silkcreek.net/graphics/sc_logo.jpg" />
  <items>
   <rdf:Seq>
    <li rdf:resource="http://www.silkcreek.net/news.html" />
   </rdf:Seq>
  </items>
 </channel>
 <image rdf:about="http://www.silkcreek.net/graphics/sc_logo.jpg">
  <title>Silk Creek</title>
  <url>http://www.silkcreek.net/graphics/sc_logo.jpg</url>
  <link>http://www.silkcreek.net</link>
 </image>
 <item rdf:about="http://www.silkcreek.net/news.html">
  <title>Attack update</title>
  <link>http://www.silkcreek.net/news.html</link>
  <description>
  Just when you think it's safe . . .

   be sure to note that virus update renewal date!
   By Lucinda Dykes, Feb 20, 2005
  </description>
 </item>
</rdf:RDF>
```

The Semantic Web

The Semantic Web is a vision of Tim Berners-Lee and the W3C for automating data and information processing on the Web by adding *semantic* capabilities (okay, call it *meaning*) by using *metadata* (data about data).

Here's how it works: The key Semantic Web technologies are XML, RDF, and OWL (Web Ontology Language). That last one may be a bit unfamiliar: A *Web ontology* is a document that defines the relationships among terms as well as inference rules. For example, in the case of phone numbers, a specific value for `area code` infers a particular value for `city`, even though that is not a direct part of the area-code data. For more information on OWL, see the W3C specification at

`www.w3.org/TR/owl-features/`

Ontologies and metadata could improve Web searches by allowing precise searches rather than general (and often useless) searches using keywords.

At the time of this writing, the Semantic Web remains a vision that has a long way to go before it can be implemented. For an excellent introduction, see "The Semantic Web" by Tim Berners-Lee, and James Hendler on the *Scientific American* Web site at

`www.sciam.com/article.cfm?`
`articleID=00048144-10D2-1C7`
`0-84A9809EC588EF21`

For the latest news on the Semantic Web, see the W3C Semantic Web Activity page at `www.w3.org/2001/sw`.

If you're interested in delving further into RSS 1.0, check out "The W3C RSS 1.0 News Feed Creation How-To" at

`www.w3.org/2001/10/glance/doc/howto`

You can also view the RSS 1.0 specification at

`http://web.resource.org/rss/1.0/spec`

Validating an RSS Feed

When you're ready to validate your file, a couple of quick steps get the job done:

1. **Upload the file to your server so the validator can find the file.**

2. **Use an RSS validator such as** `http://rss.scripting.com/`.

   Just enter the URL of your RSS feed and then click the Validate button.

Once your file is valid (as shown in Figure 18-1), your feed is ready to be downloaded by RSS readers or added to a syndication site.

Atom is where it's at

The latest addition to the Web-publishing scene for blogs and news is the Atom syndication format. Atom is an XML document format *and* an HTTP protocol. Although already in use on the Web, Atom is still in development in the IETF (Internet Engineering Task Force) at the time of this writing.

Atom provides a format for feeds as well as a protocol for editing syndicated content. Atom is

sometimes called the successor to RSS. The Atom model supports any MIME (Multipurpose Internet Mail Extensions) type, can include non-XML content (such as HTML), and can handle binary content such as images.

For more information on Atom, see `www.atom enabled.org/` and `www.intertwingly. net/wiki/pie/FrontPage`.

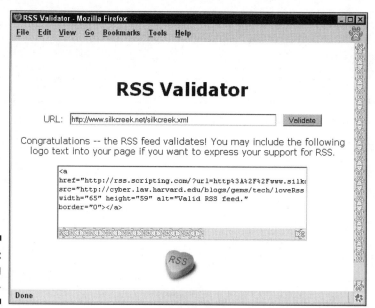

Figure 18-1:
Validating an RSS file.

Creating RSS Feeds

If you've been following along in the chapter, you've created two RSS files from scratch: an RSS 0.91 file and an RSS 1.0 file. Hand-coding is always an option for creating RSS feeds, of course, but consider: RSS feeds are really for content that changes frequently; they can be a good way to avoid having to hand-code a new RSS file every time your site's content changes. The easiest way to set up this timesaver is to use an *RSS feed template,* such as the one used for blogs created with Movable Type blog publishing software (www.sixapart.com/movabletype/). You can also use an RSS-module or class such as Perl's XML::RSS module (http://perl-rss.sourceforge.net/).

Get Syndicated!

If you want to make your RSS file widely available, register the feed with an RSS directory (also known as an RSS syndication site). The process is similar to registering a site with a search engine. The major RSS directory sites are:

✔ **Syndic8 (**www.syndic8.com**):** Syndic8 is the largest directory of RSS feeds. As shown in Figure 18-2, you can suggest a site at

> www.syndic8.com/suggest.php?Mode=data

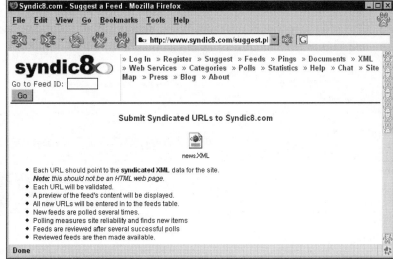

Figure 18-2:
Submitting
an RSS
feed for
syndication
by Syndic8.

✔ **Daypop (**www.daypop.com**):** Daypop is a large RSS search engine, where you can search the content of 59,000 RSS feeds. Daypop also features a Top 40 list and a Top News list. You can submit a site at www.daypop.com/info/submit.htm.

✔ **Feedster (**www.feedster.com**):** Feedster is another RSS search engine. You can add your feed at www.feedster.com/add.php.

Of course, it only makes sense to syndicate your content if your site changes frequently — which means you also have to update your RSS feed frequently. If you don't want or need to syndicate your content, consider adding a link on your site to your RSS feed so interested visitors can add your feed to their RSS readers.

If you want to create your own RSS aggregator and display RSS content from other sites on your site, you can use software such as zFeeder, available for free download at http://zvonnews.sourceforge.net/.

Using an RSS Reader

If you want to peruse headlines from your favorite news sites, you can use an RSS reader to check out the latest updates from these sites.

Feedreader is an easy-to-use and free RSS reader available for download at www.feedreader.com/. Add links for your favorite RSS feeds, and view the links and the content from Feedreader, as shown in Figure 18-3.

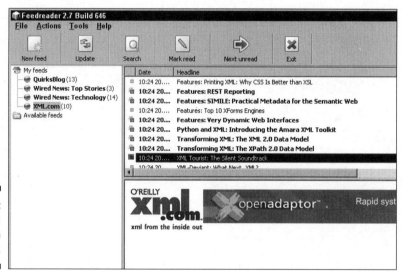

Figure 18-3:
Using a desktop RSS reader.

AmphetaDesk is another popular free RSS reader. Download the latest version at www.disobey.com/amphetadesk/.

If you use the Firefox browser (www.mozilla.org/products/firefox/), you can also create your own reader within Firefox by using Firefox Live Bookmarks. Using Live Bookmarks, you can view headlines from your favorite RSS feeds from the Bookmarks menu. For more information on adding a Live Bookmark to Firefox, visit www.mozilla.org/products/firefox/live-bookmarks.html.

Although RSS gives you a pretty nifty way to enhance your Web site's content, XML capabilities don't stop there. If you want to tinker with those capabilities, the next chapter presents our choices for the top XML tools.

Part VI
The Part of Tens

In this part. . .

This is the revered and traditional closing for all *For Dummies* books. With tongue planted firmly in cheek, this part of the book summarizes, epitomizes, and concentrates some of the most important content that appears in this book.

Chapter 19 covers a collection of useful and interesting XML software tools — from XML editors to XML document managers, XML-enabled Web browsers, and more such fiendish devices — many of which you'll find ready for your personal exploration on the companion Web site for this book (`www.dummies.com/go/xmlfd4e`).

Chapter 20 describes the ten most widely used XML applications on today's Web sites. Chapter 21 closes out this fiesta with the top ten resources for XML.

Chapter 19

XML Tools and Technologies

*N*obody tackles a lot of XML authoring without the help of some authoring tool or another, and no one should try to manage a collection of XML documents without using some software tools along the way. To help you, we offer here a list of some of our favorite tools for authoring, checking, viewing, and converting XML documents. If your resources or your time are limited — and whose aren't these days? — these are the essential tools that you absolutely must check out.

At the beginning of each section, you find a quick reference table (Table 19-1 through Table 19-5) that lists all the tools discussed in the section, along with the most pertinent of details: how much it costs and where to find out more. Also, we've included links to these sites on the Web page for this book at www.dummies.com/go/xmlfd4e.

Creating Documents with Authoring Tools

The first step in working with XML is to create a document, and you may have already gotten around to using your trusty old text editor to create your first XML documents. Don't feel like you have to go it alone, though, because we've found a few XML-specific editors that might change your habits. Table 19-1 introduces some heavy hitters among authoring tools.

Because many of the editors listed come at a hefty price, we recommend that you test-drive demo/trial versions when they're available. Demos or trial versions should be accessible on the product pages.

Table 19-1	XML Authoring Tools		
Product Name	**URL**	**Single-User Price**	**Free Demo Copy or Trial Version?**
Epic Editor 5.0	www.arbortext.com	$695	Yes
Turbo XML v2.4.1	www.tibco.com	$269.95	Yes
XMetaL Author 4.5	www.xmetal.com	$495	Yes
XML Pro v2.0.1	www.vervet.com	Free for non-commercial use	N/A
XML Spy 2005	www.altova.com	Free Home Edition	Yes

To help you get your documents under construction, the following sections list some of the best XML authoring tools available that we know of. Keep in mind that as long as XML continues to create a buzz, more tools will emerge on the scene. To keep up to date on the latest technology, be sure to read Chapter 21 for more on XML resources.

Epic Editor

Arbortext has built Standard Generalized Markup Language (SGML) editors for years — and has helped pave the way for XML tools. Epic Editor comes from that SGML background and has been adapted for XML.

Epic Editor, which has earned worldwide recognition for its power, performance, and capabilities, enables you to author and edit a medium-to-large volume of XML-based business documentation that needs to be disseminated in multiple forms (across the Web, on a CD-ROM, as PDFs, in print, and through wireless devices, for example). Use Epic Editor when you need to handle large document collections or documents with multiple authors.

This product is definitely designed for advanced XML creation. Although Epic Editor is expensive, it's complete and worth every pretty penny if you're building complex documents with XML or SGML. Visit the Arbortext site at www.arbortext.com to learn more about this tool.

Turbo XML v2.4.1

Turbo XML v2.4.1, from TIBCO Software, Inc., is an IDE (Integrated Development Environment) for XML that accelerates the creation and management of XML documents, DTDs, and schemas. It includes a toolset to help convert existing application and document structures to schemas, providing the base for well-formed and valid XML documents. In addition, it has import and output support for XML Schema, External Data Representation (XDR), Schema for Object-Oriented XML (SOX v2), RELAX (Regular Language Description for XML), and Document Type Definitions (DTDs).

Turbo XML v2.4.1 is well worth the money (only $269.95). We should add, however, that Turbo XML is definitely *not* designed for the beginner; a working knowledge of XML and an understanding of schema design basics are assumed. Turbo XML fully supports and extends the XML Schema specification. Read more about Turbo XML at www.tibco.com.

XMetaL Author 4.5

XMetaL, originally developed by SoftQuad Software, is now offered by Blast Radius (www.xmetal.com). XMetaL has expanded into a family of five products — with XMetal Author being the XML-authoring member of the family. It's not badly priced ($495 in the United States). Like many XML editors, XMetaL Author offers users a familiar word-processing environment that's easy to use. XMetaL Author supports both Cascading Style Sheets (CSS) and XSLT editing capabilities. XMetaL also supports both DTDs and XML Schema. It conforms to numerous standards, including SGML, XML, CALS tables, Document Object Model (DOM), CSS, and HTML. Find out more at www.xmetal.com.

XML Pro v2.0.1

A more basic product is XML Pro, developed at Vervet Logic. XML Pro sure can edit, but it doesn't claim to do much more. There's no support for document conversion, DTD creation, or stylesheet design.

You can create and edit XML documents while using a clean, easy interface. The newest release claims to be fully compliant with W3C XML 1.0, and is now open-source and free for individual and nonprofit use. You can read more at www.vervet.com.

XML Spy 2005

XML Spy 2005 Suite is one of the sweetest XML multitools around. Okay, maybe it can't slice, dice, chop, and pare, but it does handle XML and knows how to deal with XSLT, XPath, XQuery, WSDL, SOAP, and XML Schemas. But wait, there's more: It also supports graphical design, schema- or DTD-based validation, database connectivity, and so much more.

The XML Spy Suite includes three different software products:

- **XMLSpy:** A top-of-the-line XML editor that offers everything you need to create, debug, validate, and edit XML documents in a standards-based fashion.

- **MapForce:** A visual data-mapping tool that easily transforms data from one format into another.

- **StyleVision:** A visual interface for creating XSLT and XSL:FO stylesheets to transform XML documents; can also transform an XML document into HTML, PDF, or RTF (Rich Text Format) files.

XMLSpy Suite is available in an Enterprise ($1,499) and a Professional edition ($729)— it does an awful lot for the money. You can download a 30 day-evaluation copy of either the Enterprise or Professional edition.

Altova has now released a free version of XMLSpy — XMLSpy Home Edition. This is a great introduction to the XMLSpy family of products. You can request a free license for the home version at `www.altova.com/support_freexmlspyhome.asp`.

Be sure to check out Altova's StyleVision. It's a user-friendly WYSIWYG XSLT editor and creates clean, concise, valid XSLT markup. You can download a 30-day trial version at `www.altova.com/download_stylevision.html`.

Checking Documents with Parser Tools

Your XML document is a carefully crafted work of art and adheres to strict XML 1.0 compliance. You believe that you've followed the rules, and now you're ready to check your work. Luckily, you don't have to check each element by hand — parsers do that for you! Table 19-2 introduces some especially good ones.

Much of the software listed in this chapter is free for the downloading. The only payment you're asked to give is feedback. XML tools are still pretty green; this means you must watch out for bugs. Make sure that you report any bugs that you find to the responsible parties. They'll thank you for it!

Table 19-2		Parsers	
Product Name	**Validating?**	**URL**	**Single-User Price**
Ælfred v7	No	http://saxon.sourceforge.net/aelfred.html	Free
expat	No	http://sourceforge.net/projects/expat/	Free
Lark	No	www.textuality.com/Lark/	Free

Use a parser to ensure that your XML documents are well formed and, if linked to a DTD or schema, valid as well. (See Chapter 5 for more information on valid and well-formed XML documents.)

Parsing is a basic but important step in XML publishing. Errors can be the death knell to any XML document. Forget those old HTML days when browsers picked up your slack. An XML document must be well formed, and it must *also* be valid if it uses a DTD or schema. Parsers help enforce these requirements.

Some parsers check only to make sure that a document is well formed; others also check for validity. Make sure you examine the parser's capabilities when you're selecting one to meet your needs.

Ælfred

Ælfred is a Java-based parser available for free download at

```
http://saxon.sourceforge.net/aelfred.html
```

(Can't squawk about the price.) Ælfred is a nonvalidating parser, which means that it checks documents only for well-formedness. According to its designers, Ælfred concentrates on optimizing speed and size rather than error reporting, so it's most useful for deployment over the Internet.

Ælfred2 is a separate version of the parser that includes an optional valida-tor. Read more about Ælfred2 at

```
www.gnu.org/software/classpathx/jaxp/apidoc/gnu/xml/aelfred2/
            package-summary.html
```

expat

James Clark is a legend in the SGML community because of his amazing collection of tools that support all kinds of cool functionality — most of it in the form of freeware that works like the dickens. This James Clark contribution, expat v1.2, is a nonvalidating XML parser written in C. The 1.2 version was the last release by James Clark before he handed over the maintenance and further development of the software to a team of developers. You can download beta versions of the new expat releases on SourceForge at http:// sourceforge.net/projects/expat/.

Lark

Tim Bray offers the Java-based XML processor Lark, which he built as a way to sanity-check the XML design requirement so that ". . . it shall be easy to write programs that process XML documents." (What a concept.) Tim Bray has been a member of the W3C's XML Working Group since long before it operated under that name. (It all started as a special-interest group within the SGML cadre at the W3C.) His work on XML is widely recognized and deservedly renowned. Among other things, Tim was the coeditor of the XML specification.

Lark, a nonvalidating parser, could be useful for other programmers who seek to follow in his footsteps, but it's also a pretty great tool in its own right. The parser is solidly built and has been tweaked over time to meet most programmers' needs. The fruits of Tim's labor are available for download at www. textuality.com/Lark.

Viewing with XML Browsers

According to most Web developers, XML can revolutionize the way that people look at and transfer information across the Web — and that isn't just a caffeine-induced vision. Before XML can continue that revolution, however, browsers must provide their support. Netscape Navigator doesn't currently support XML fully. A few other browsers, however — such as Amaya, Opera, Mozilla, and Firefox — do provide such support. We find the browsers that we cover in this section (which Table 19-3 sums up) especially noteworthy.

Table 19-3	XML-Enabled Web Browsers	
Product Name	*URL*	*Single-User Price*
Amaya 9.0	www.w3.org/Amaya/	Free
Internet Explorer 6	www.microsoft.com/ windows/ie/default.asp	Free
Mozilla	www.mozilla.org	Free
Firefox 1.0	www.mozilla.org/ products/firefox/	Free
Opera	www.opera.com	Free

Amaya

Amaya is the W3C browser and authoring tool (software that's used to create Web content) that you can use to demonstrate and test many new developments in Web protocols and data formats. Amaya is versatile and extensible, which makes it easy to add new features. Along with support for XML, Amaya supports HTML, XHTML, MathML, and CSS 2. It also has limited Scalable Vector Graphics (SVG) support. (See Chapter 4 for more information on XHTML.) If it's good enough for the W3C, it should be good enough for you (hey, it's good enough for us)! Read more at www.w3.org/Amaya and then download the software for free.

Internet Explorer 6

The Microsoft king of browsers can't be left in the cold. Internet Explorer (IE) also offers XML support: Microsoft XML (MSXML) version 4.0 specifically. IE 6 also supports CSS 1, much of CSS2, and DOM 1. It also provides some support for Synchronized Multimedia Integration Language (SMIL). If you're using one of the current flavors of Windows, you probably already have it. Download the latest version of IE from

```
www.microsoft.com/windows/ie/default.asp
```

Microsoft has recently announced Internet Explorer 7 — though it's not yet known what, if any, changes in XML support this will include. Many observers expect no significant changes in Internet Explorer until the next version of the Windows OS is released.

Mozilla

Like many free XML tools, Mozilla is built around publicly available source code. Mozilla is fully compliant with standards for HTML 4.0, XML, CSS, and DOM. It includes expat for XML parsing (for more on expat, see the previous section on parser tools), supports CSS display for XML, and provides partial support for namespaces (Chapter 11) and simple XLinks. For more details about Mozilla's support for XML, see "Mozilla and XML" at www.mozilla. org/newlayout/xml/.

The Mozilla XForms Project is working toward the implementation of XForms 1.0 in Mozilla. A free XForms extension is available for Mozilla and Firefox at www.mozilla.org/projects/xforms/.

The folks at Mozilla.org are dedicated to debugging and updating this software, and you should be, too. Mozilla.org provides users an open forum to report bugs. To download this free software or keep up with changes, visit www.mozilla.org.

Firefox 1.0

Mozilla Firefox is Mozilla's award-winning new browser that supports XML, XPath, XSLT, and XForms. Firefox also offers a Live Bookmarks feature that enables you to read RSS feeds in Firefox. (See Chapter 18 for more details on RSS feeds.) Firefox can be extensively customized to meet your browsing needs. For more information, see www.mozilla.org/products/firefox/.

Opera

The brainchild of the markup gurus at Opera Software ASA in Norway, Opera is easily the most international and platform-friendly browser around. In addition to support for common operating systems such as Windows,

Macintosh OS, and Linux/Solaris, Opera also runs on BeOS, OS/2, QNX (a real-time version of Unix), and Symbian (a handheld device OS popular in Europe). This browser really gets around — and is much smaller, faster, and easier to customize than some other browsers we know. Opera also claims to provide " . . . full support for the XML 1.0 recommendation" and does a good enough job of delivering on that claim to be a part of our standard XML test environment.

You can get Opera for free (in which case you must submit to the small banner ads that support its "free" mode of operation), or you can buy it for a modest $39 or so per copy. Discover more about this fine tool at www.opera.com.

Using XML Parsers and Engines

XML parsers and engines provide tools that can ingest and interpret the contents of XML documents (with or without governing DTDs or schemas against which to validate). Most of the other tools we cover up to this point in this chapter have parsers and engines at the core; Table 19-4 sums up three.

Table 19-4	XML Parsers and Engines	
Product Name	*URL*	*Single-User Price*
XML C Library for Gnome	xmlsoft.org	Free
Java XML Pack	java.sun.com/xml/ download.html	Free
Xerces	xml.apache.org	Free

XML C Library for Gnome

Daniel Veillard's XML C Library for Gnome (libxml) is a collection of C-language routines that implement a validating XML parser. This parser is versatile enough to work with various XML document models (including the DOM and the so-called Simple API for XML, or SAX). It also implements support for XPath and XPointers, as well as lots of other goodies. (For more on XPath, see Chapter 13.) Check it all out at xmlsoft.org.

Java XML Pack

Sun Microsystems, Inc. offers a cornucopia of Java-based XML tools, APIs, and more. To find the Java XML Pack, visit the Sun Java Technology and XML page at

```
java.sun.com/xml/download.html
```

This site includes some of the most popular Java XML tools, including

- ✔ The Java Web Services Developer Pack
- ✔ **JAXM:** The Java API for XML Messaging
- ✔ **JAXP:** The Java API for XML Processing
- ✔ **JAXR:** The Java API for XML Registries
- ✔ **JAX-RPC:** The Java API for XML-based Remote Procedure Call

Of these elements, JAXP offers a reasonably complete XML processing engine, but the other tools will be of interest to those building distributed applications using Java and XML as well. Visit `java.sun.com/xml/download.html` for more information.

Xerces

The Open Source Apache project is famous for producing the world's most popular Web-server software — but that's just the barest suggestion of its large, intriguing collection of Web- and document-related software tools and technologies. Among the many Apache offerings, the Xerces-C++ Parser 2.0 offers a powerful (yet compact) XML parser to build your documents around. The Apache library of routines can handle a wide range of XML tasks — from parsing to generating, validating, and manipulating XML documents. The library is definitely worth your time. Discover more at `xml.apache.org/xerces-c/index.html`.

Originally developed by IBM as XML4J, Apache also offers a validating XML parser, Xerces2, that's written in Java. Xerces2 is a fully conformant XML Schema processor. It can also parse documents written in XML 1.1. Find more information about Xerces2 at `http://xml.apache.org/xerces2-j/index.html`.

Employing Conversion Tools

When it comes to making XML content as accessible as possible, consider using a tool to convert it from its native document format to something else. Many of these tools use XSLT (or implement similar capabilities) to do their thing. As you look at some of the conversion tools that we cover here, you should get a good idea that *something else* covers a lot of territory! Table 19-5 sums up two such tools; then you get a closer look at each one.

Table 19-5		XML Conversion Tools	
Product Name	*URL*	*Single-User Price*	*Free Demo Copy?*
HTML Tidy	`tidy.sourceforge.net`	Free	N/A
XPS	`www.softml.net/xps/index.html`	Free	N/A

HTML Tidy

W3C stalwart Dave Raggett created a wonderful tool called HTML Tidy that can validate against a whole slew of HTML, XHTML, and other DTDs. This conversion tool can even convert HTML to XHTML (or other forms of XML) as well. In fact, Dave's tool sits at the heart of numerous extremely good HTML tools — including HTML-Kit (available free from `www.chami.com`), a program that puts a friendly face on Tidy and adds lots of functionality. For more information on HTML Tidy, please visit `tidy.sourceforge.net`.

Extensible Programming Script (XPS)

SoftML Pte Ltd has created the powerful transformation tool *XPS* that can translate XML into other formats, or other formats into XML — and it's all based on an XML data-manipulation language. XPS supports easy transformations to — or from — databases that comply with Structured Query Language (SQL) or Open Database Connectivity (ODBC) — and it supports more text-intensive document types. For more information, please visit

`www.softml.net/xps/index.html`

The Ultimate XML Grab Bag and Goodie Box

All the other products that we list in this chapter have a focus on a particular piece of an XML solution — editing, validating, and so on. For those who want to collect the whole set of XML tools, some companies offer products that do it all. Here are a few of our favorites.

Microsoft does XML, too!

In its search to extend the reach and capability of its Internet software, particularly the Internet Explorer browser, Microsoft is an unexpected and ardent XML supporter, particularly for the Channel Definition Format (CDF) and the Resource Definition Framework (RDF) — among other XML applications. As Microsoft begins to add more XML support to its next release of Internet Explorer, it offers numerous other XML tools as well. To read more about the Microsoft view of XML, visit `msdn.microsoft.com/xml`.

webMethods automates XML excellence

webMethods, Inc., has constructed the core of its Web services toolkit (the webMethods integration platform) around XML and Java technology. This toolkit is marketed heavily for use in electronic commerce and related applications, and for automating access to a variety of Web-based data and services, both in HTML and XML. The webMethods integration platform has been well received in the marketplace and is worth investigating, especially if you're looking for a way to improve data access, data handling, and data security on your Web site.

To obtain an evaluation copy of the webMethods integration platform or for more information about the company and its products, visit `www.web methods.com`

A complete account of all the wonderful XML tools available would overflow our toolbox — and this book. To find a complete guide on XML software, check out `www.xmlsoftware.com`.

We hope you enjoy some of our favorite XML tools as much as we do. And don't overlook these two great tools: Consult the Web page for this book at `www.dummies.com/go/xmlfd4e` for links to download the XML tools covered in this chapter, and flip through this book's glossary for great help in decoding the sometimes-mysterious terminology and acronyms you're likely to encounter when you're canvassing the wild and wooly intellectual landscape of XML.

Chapter 20

Ten Top XML Applications

*B*y itself, any XML document contains nothing but plain, simple text. But when you look at XML the right way, or when you use various XML-based technologies together, its benefits can't be overstated. XML applications provide powerful tools to display and work with your XML documents.

Industry requirements drive most XML developments. That's the reason so many XML applications inevitably embody industry initiatives. Many applications are already available — for free! In this chapter, we highlight a few of the most interesting XML applications designed for specific uses.

This is a chapter on XML applications, yes, but that doesn't mean the applications listed here are the only ones worth investigating. To see a fairly exhaustive list, visit `www.oasis-open.org/cover/xml.html#applications` or `www.xml.com`. With a little elbow grease, you may find an application that's perfect for your needs!

XHTML = XML + HTML

As we've mentioned elsewhere in this book (particularly in Chapter 4), XHTML takes easy, familiar HTML markup and rationalizes it within a more rigorous and regular XML framework. Don't let that extra rigor stop you from using this excellent tool, though — in most respects, it's enough like HTML that even older browsers can't tell the difference as long as you follow safe formatting rules. (See Chapter 4 for more on these rules.)

Thinking about upgrading your HTML markup to its XHTML equivalent? Dave Raggett's wonderful HTML-Tidy tool is built into Chami.com's outstanding HTML-Kit utility and does most of the conversion work for you automatically. Just don't forget to validate the results (which HTML-Kit also does for you). Download HTML-Kit at www.chami.com.

XML Style Is a Matter of Application

The richest, most powerful ways to manage how XML data and documents are delivered to a Web browser involve the use of XML applications designed to read, organize, transform, and format XML into a variety of looks, feels, and formats. Possible forms of output include Rich Text Format (RTF), Adobe Acrobat's Portable Document Format (PDF), HTML or XHTML, plain text, and many more formats. To pull off this kind of magic, though, you need to find out about numerous XML applications, including:

- The eXtensible Stylesheet Language (XSL) and its relatives, XSL Transformations (XSLT) and XSL Formatting Objects (XSL-FO). For more details on XSLT, see Chapter 12.

- XML-based linking languages, especially XLink, XPath, and XPointer. For more information on XPath, see Chapter 13.

- And of course, you also need to understand how to grab XML content and reshape it into the exact form required to match your target format. For simple formats, such as plain text or XHTML/HTML, this is pretty easy; for more complex formats, such as PDF or RTF, you probably need help from special-purpose software tools such as the XMLSpy 2005 Suite (www.altova.com) or Office 2003 (http:office.microsoft.com).

Wireless Markup Language (WML)

As the name is meant to suggest, WML aims to support applications for wireless communications networks. It's part of an effort sponsored by leading telecommunications companies, including Ericsson, Motorola, Nokia, and the wireless communications specialist Unwired Planet. In essence, WML is designed to make it easier to use handheld, wireless communications devices *of all kinds* to access the Internet.

WML is an XML application designed specifically to meet constraints inherent in wireless devices. These constraints include a small display area with limited user-input capabilities (as on a cell phone), limited bandwidth (19.2 Kbps is typical for most handheld wireless devices), and limited CPU power and memory space. You might say that WML is a markup language designed with the phrase "small is beautiful" foremost in mind!

Read more about WML at `www.oasis-open.org/cover/wap-wml.html`. For general information on WAP (Wireless Application Protocol) and OMA (Open Mobile Alliance), check `www.wapforum.com/about_OMA/index.html`.

DocBook, Anyone?

DocBook is a standard SGML DTD designed to capture computer documentation and other types of lengthy, complex documents. DocBook already enjoys worldwide use in hundreds of organizations that manage millions of pages of documentation in a variety of print and online formats.

Visit Robin Cover's site at `www.oasis-open.org/docbook/` for more information on this subject. Also visit

```
www.oasis-open.org/committees/docbook/xmlschema/index.shtml
```

to view the experimental XML Schema-based version of DocBook.

Mathematical Markup Language (MathML)

Based on years of hard labor, the most recent version of the MathML 2.0 specification appeared on February 21, 2001. Before MathML came along, it was tricky to express mathematical equations inside Web pages. As an XML application, MathML supports mathematical and scientific markup for use on the Web. But it doesn't end there: You can also use MathML for computer algebra systems, mathematical typesetting, and voice synthesis.

Read more about MathML at its W3C home at `www.w3.org/Math/`. Robin Cover's site also offers a wealth of information on this application. Visit `http://xml.coverpages.org/mathML.html` for all the details.

Scalable Vector Graphics (SVG)

Scalable Vector Graphics (SVG) is a language for describing two-dimensional graphics in XML. SVG 1.0 is a recommended W3C standard — which means (heads up!) it's ready for production use.

SVG allows for three basic types of objects: vector graphic shapes (paths consisting of straight lines and curves), images, and text. The drive behind SVG is to develop a standard for the Web-based display of such objects.

Graphical objects can be grouped, styled, and added to previously rendered objects. What's more exciting is that these objects can be dynamic and interactive! The Document Object Model (DOM) for SVG, which includes the full XML DOM, allows authors to use scripting to create straightforward and efficient vector graphics animation for any SVG graphical object.

We wish we could outline all the fun ways to create graphics using SVG, but that would require its own book. To read more about SVG, visit the W3C at `www.w3.org/Graphics/SVG/`.

Resource Description Framework (RDF)

The Resource Description Framework (RDF) is a framework for metadata. RDF assures interoperability between applications that exchange application- or platform-specific information — you know, metadata — across the Web.

Why might this concern you? Because RDF helps increase the relevance of searches conducted in your XML documents. That fact alone gets us excited and might be a boon to you, too. (Okay, we admit it; we're really into the metasearch thing. Anything that saves us from wading through countless documents only to find irrelevant information on a two-headed reptile from New Guinea is okay in our book!) Briefly put, RDF provides a basis for generic tools for authoring, manipulating, and searching machine-readable data on the Web.

RDF is also the base for RSS (RDF Site Summary) 1.0. For more information on all versions of RSS, see Chapter 18.

For more information on RDF, see the W3C RDF page at `www.w3.org/RDF/`. To read more about RDF, visit Dave Beckett's excellent site on this subject at `www.ilrt.bris.ac.uk/discovery/rdf/resources/`.

Synchronized Multimedia Integration Language (SMIL)

We talked a little about graphics in the section on SVG, so now we turn your attention to multimedia. Ever since desktop computer systems started to include loudspeakers, multimedia has played a significant role on more than a few Web sites. If multimedia's your bag, you may want to keep up with the Synchronized Multimedia Integration Language (SMIL, pronounced, happily enough, "smile").

SMIL enables you to integrate a set of independent multimedia objects into a synchronized multimedia presentation. As stated by the W3C, you can use SMIL to:

✔ Describe the temporal behavior (or sequential behavior, such as the sequence presented in an animation) of the presentation

✔ Describe the layout of the presentation on a screen

✔ Associate hyperlinks with media objects

The bottom line is that SMIL enables authors to create television-like content for the Web and still avoid the limitations of traditional television. In addition, you don't have to worry about lowering the bandwidth requirements to transmit such content across the Internet. Yes, we mean that movies on the Web are theoretically possible — with no skimping on bandwidth (what a concept) — because producing audio-visual content is easy with SMIL. The best part is that using SMIL doesn't require you to learn a programming language; you can create it with a simple text editor.

To keep track of SMIL progress, stay tuned to `www.w3.org/AudioVideo/`.

Servin' Up Web Services

An interlocking collection of XML applications is under development to support so-called Web services (which we cover in more detail in Chapter 15). A *Web service* is a tool or capability that you use your Web browser to access; it doesn't reside locally on your own desktop, and it isn't saved on your hard drive. Web services permit users with just about any kind of computer (using any operating system) to run the same database access programs, read or send faxes, manage bank accounts or financial portfolios, and so on, without a care in the world. (We shudder to think of all the possibilities — today the server, tomorrow the universe. . . .)

The Web services infrastructure includes a bunch of pieces and parts designed to make it easier for service providers to create and advertise such services and for would-be end users to identify and access such services. These pieces and parts include the following elements:

- **Simple Object Access Protocol (SOAP):** This is an XML-based technology that permits senders and receivers to easily exchange self-describing, XML-based messages. SOAP enables arbitrary service providers and service consumers to communicate directly. For a super collection of SOAP resources, visit `http://xml.coverpages.org/soap.html`.

- **Universal Description, Discovery, and Integration (UDDI):** This XML-based technology is designed to permit service providers to describe the services they offer, to permit those services to be discovered by those seeking same, and to establish how providers and consumers can interact with each other should a consumer decide to request services from a provider. Think of it as a kind of Yellow Pages that also brokers direct connections between those who list themselves therein (the providers) and those who use them (the consumers) as a way to locate potential providers. A good place to start further investigations regarding UDDI is Robin Cover's pointers at `http://xml.coverpages.org/uddi.html`.

- **Web Services Description Language (WSDL):** An XML-based technology that permits Web services — and the message formats and contents necessary to interact with them — to be formally described and advertised. Those message formats are, in turn, based on SOAP. Thus, WSDL provides the ways to integrate the providers and consumers between whom UDDI acts as a broker. For more information on WSDL, see Robin Cover's Web site at `http://xml.coverpages.org/wsdl.html`.

XQuery

The goal of XQuery is to provide an interaction between XML and databases so that XML documents can be accessed and queried like databases. XQuery and XPath are closely related; many features of XQuery are seen as so important that they will be incorporated into the next version of XPath — XPath 2.0.

Several XQuery and XPath documents have been very recently released by the W3C, including a Working Draft of the XQuery 1.0 specification. For more information on XQuery and XPath specifications, see

```
www.w3.org/XML/Query
```

An XQuery tutorial is available at

```
www.yukonxml.com/articles/xquery/
```

Create XML Applications with Zope

Although this chapter focuses on applications used with XML, we'd also like to point you to software that enables you to create your own XML applications. Zope 2.7.4 is a free, open-source application server that does just that. Created by Digital Creations and written mainly in Python, Zope runs on both Windows and UNIX platforms.

Zope works in an *object-oriented* environment. More plainly, Zope views a Web application in terms of objects, which define not only types of data, but also the kinds of operations (called *methods* in object-oriented programming lingo) that may be performed on those objects.

Zope enables you to combine objects to create powerful and flexible ways to acquire, manage, and manipulate all kinds of data. As you'd expect, these object collections can respond to Web requests dynamically — which makes building interactive, Web-based applications a relative breeze. The result is dynamic content and a happy content creator (that would be you).

If you can't find the right XML application for your needs, you might want to create one yourself using Zope. Read more about this open-source treasure at www.zope.org.

Chapter 21

Ten Ultimate XML Resources

*Y*ou can find information on just about any XML topic online, in addition to other more "real" (or at least, less virtual) locations. If we had to boil this entire chapter down to a single tip, it would have to be: "When looking for XML information, search the Web first and foremost." Chances are eXtreMeLy good that you can find what you seek! Allow us to demonstrate. . . .

XML's Many and Marvelous Specs

For XML itself, and for standard XML applications, the place to start your search for descriptions, metadata, and other details is the World Wide Web Consortium (W3C) site:

```
www.w3c.org/XML/
```

Check the left-hand column listing for the acronym you seek or visit the W3C XML page. And when you visit the home page for an XML application at the W3C's site, you find a plethora of pointers to other resources on the same subject, so it's a good place from which to mount broader searches as well.

An XML Nonpareil

Nonpareil isn't just a chocolate candy covered with sprinkles. No, the XML nonpareil (which is just a fancy-schmancy word for unparalleled) on the Web is Robin Cover's XML Pages site. Here's how you get to it:

```
www.oasis-open.org/cover/
```

At this site, you not only find pointers to relevant specifications and other related documents, but also see brief descriptions of the markup or application itself, as well as pointers to numerous other useful resources. If you're into XML, you may want to add this one to your bookmarks or favorites. (*Note:* Robin's last name rhymes with "over" or "clover.")

Top XML Tutorial Sites

We dare you to type ***application* tutorial**, (substituting the name or acronym of your favorite XML application, of course) in your favorite search engine. Go ahead. See? Your search produced a plethora of results. If you'd like to come out from under it, we've found the following sites to be unusually useful when seeking sources for XML tutorials:

- ✔ www.zvon.org: A crazy, quirky, but incredibly competent Czech XML collective, Zvon offers some of the best XML tutorials we've seen anywhere. Czech them out! Also, be sure to look up the original meaning of the term "zvon" in Czech; you'll never think of these guys as anything other than humble forever afterward. (For those of you too busy to look it up, it means "bell" or "ding-dong.")

- ✔ www.xml.com: An O'Reilly & Associates Web site devoted to covering XML news, applications, tools, and technologies, this site also offers a plethora of tutorials on everything from namespaces to SOAP (212 tutorials total during our last visit there, in fact).

- ✔ www.w3schools.com/xml/: World Wide Web Schools has its own XML School, which you can enter here. Check it out for a well-organized collection of information about basic XML, and important XML applications.

Try them; we think you'll like them!

XML in the Mail

Although mailing lists on the Internet are neither terribly interactive. nor do they always address your questions without some effort on your part, they can be wonderful sources of information — and they provide a superb way for you to seek answers to particular, detailed questions that may not be addressed elsewhere on the Internet (at least, not without a long, complex, tedious search)

Once again, XML master and maven Robin Cover scores big with a massive collection of SGML- and XML-related mailing lists (70 in all). Visit his site to see what we mean; don't overlook the annotated listings on each list:

```
www.oasis-open.org/cover/lists.html
```

Excellent XML Examples at zvon.org

So simple, so useful:

```
www.zvon.org
```

Although assiduous digging and careful reading of XML-related specifications can produce examples galore, example collections created specifically to instruct and demonstrate XML applications are quite worthwhile. Clever searches turn up lots of potential sources, but we've found those crafty Czechs at `www.zvon.org` to be a peachy source for well-organized and explained XML examples.

For a great collection of XML examples, please visit Zvon's Example Respository at `www.zvon.org/HowTo/Output/index.html`.

XML News and Information

Numerous trade publications are available in print and online. We've looked at most of them but have found the following to be especially interesting, useful, or informative. In many cases, you can read them online and, if you like what you see, qualify for free delivery of the printed versions.

✔ `www.xml.com`: This O'Reilly Web site covers the topic pretty darn well and is usually worth reading. XML.com is not only a good source of information on topics you want to research, but it's also a good bell-wether for topics you might not know exist! They also provide an RSS 1.0 feed at `www.oreillynet.com/meerkat/?_fl=rss10&t=ALL&c=47`.

- `www.xml-zone.com/`: Fawcette Publications' DevX includes an "XML Zone" that's chock-full of late-breaking XML news, information, tutorials, how-tos, and more.

- `www.fawcette.com/xmlmag/`: Fawcette also publishes XML & Web Services Magazine, which operates online. The XML & Web Services Magazine is also worth regular visits.

- `www.oasis-open.org/cover/sgmlnew.html`: Robin Cover — who else? — also provides regular news updates and information. This Web page is more newsy and less technical or how-to than the other items mentioned here, but it's still worth following.

- `www.ibiblio.org/xml/`: Elliotte Rusty Harold's Café Con Leche XML News and Resources isn't just a great source for XML news and musings, it's also a wonderful XML resource in its own right (and you see his name later on in the "Building a Bodacious XML Bookshelf" section in this chapter; he's a real XML star, too). Visit the Café Con Leche XML News and Resources site and see for yourself!

- `comp.text.xml`: In the Usenet newsgroup hierarchy, this newsgroup is a great source of XML news and discussion, although you sometimes have to blow a lot of chaff off the wheat. You can now access this group at `http://groups-beta.google.com/group/comp.text.xml`.

XML Training Options

When it comes to training, you can find as much about XML offered online as you can in various classrooms in the real world. If you're interested in XML training, try to find offerings that best fit your learning style — and although it's undoubtedly cheaper to learn through self-study, computer-based training, or Web classes, sometimes the opportunity to interact with a real, live instructor in a real classroom is worth the extra time and expense.

The following training companies, among many others, offer classroom training on XML:

- **Global Knowledge:** `www.globalknowledge.com`
- **SkillBuilders:** `www.skillbuilders.com`
- **Zveno:** `www.zveno.com/courses`

Also, don't overlook offerings from local community colleges, colleges, and universities, many of which also offer classroom XML training.

When it comes to XML training via computer-based training (CBT) or online, check with your favorite online training company for more information — many, if not most of them, now offer online introductory and advanced XML classes. Everybody from DigitalThink (www.digitalthink.com/dtfs/) to SmartForce (www.smartforce.com/smb/) has jumped on this bandwagon!

Commercial classroom training normally costs upwards of $250 per person per day (sometimes $500 or more); computer- or Web-based training seldom costs more than $700-800 per class (and prices at half that amount or lower are common). Be sure to pick XML training offerings that meet your education needs but that also stay within your training budget!

Building a Bodacious XML Bookshelf

A quick hop to Amazon.com or your favorite online bookstore and typing **XML** as a title element or keyword choice produces hundreds of hits (827 hits in Amazon as we write this, in fact). XML has no shortage of reference, tutorial, introductory, or advanced material. If reading helps you feed your brain, or you're like us and enjoy the heft and easy access to information that a good reference book can provide, you'll probably find it worthwhile to amass at least a small collection of XML books.

To begin with, we urge you to look for competitive reviews (like the customer reviews posted on Amazon and at other online bookstores or published book reviews that you can find in abundance on the Web) and let them guide you to prospective purchases. At the bookstore, be sure to use your own judgment before buying anything; if you purchase online (and you can get some fabulous deals if you do), be sure you can get your money back if you return a book that you decide you don't like later on.

All that said, here is our top-five list of XML books, any or all of which are well worth their purchase price:

- Elliotte Rusty Harold: *XML: Extensible Markup Language,* Wiley, Indianapolis, IN, 1998. ISBN: 0-6745-3199-9. List Price: $39.99. The best technical introduction to XML around, period. Now out of print but available used for a great price on Amazon.com.

- Elliotte Rusty Harold: *XML 1.1 Bible,* Wiley, Indianapolis, IN, 2004. ISBN: 0-7645-4986-3. List Price: $39.99. A great general reference and how-to book, chock-full of useful examples, and updated with XML 1.1 information.

✔ Elliotte Rusty Harold and W. Scott Means: *XML In a Nutshell, 3rd Edition,* O'Reilly & Associates, Sebastopol, CA, 2001. ISBN: 0-596-00764-7. List Price: $39.95. The best compact all-around reference on XML and key applications available in print.

✔ Steven Holzner: *Inside XML,* Pearson Education, Boston, MA, 2000. ISBN: 0-7357-1020-1. List Price: $49.99. A great all-around reference on XML and key applications, leavened not only with great examples, but also with implementation considerations and details.

✔ Erik T. Ray and Christopher R. Maden: *Learning XML, 2nd Edition,* O'Reilly & Associates, Sebastopol, CA, 2003. ISBN: 0-596-00420-6. List Price: $39.95. An excellent step-by-step guide to learning and using XML for building basic documents.

Well, yeah, Elliotte Rusty Harold's name does pop up a lot in our short list of XML Great Books. Coincidence? No way! He does good work.

Studying XML for Certification

For further proof that XML is making the big time, numerous groups and organizations are starting to offer exams to warrant the knowledge and skills of those with the moxie to take and pass such tests. Although this particular market is still in its infancy — by which we mean we've not begun to see the total range of XML certifications by any means just yet — you can already choose among a surprising number of options to demonstrate your knowledge, skills, and expertise.

Here's a list of organizations that offer XML certification at present (at least, ones that we can find), with pointers to more information about their programs and credentials:

✔ IBM's Certified Developer program includes an XML specialization. For more information, visit

```
www-1.ibm.com/certify/certs/xm_index.shtml
```

✔ Global Knowledge has created an XML Developer Certification that combines training in basic XML terms, concepts, markup, and applications with coverage of ASP or Java programming to warrant individuals who can build XML-based systems and solutions. For more information, point your browser to

```
www.globalknowledge.com/training/certification_listing.asp?PageID=
        12&certid=215&country=United+States
```

✔ Learning Tree International has yet another XML Development Certified Professional program that covers a broad range of topics, skills, and XML applications, supported by a collection of 3 core courses and 10 elective course topics. It's one of the more comprehensive XML-certification programs currently available; read more about it at

```
www.learningtree.com/us/cert/progs/7062.htm
```

✔ U2test, a Pakistani-based skills-and-competency-testing outfit, has an XML exam (and certificate) available. To find out more, visit

```
www.u2test.com/avtestn.asp
```

✔ BrainBench offers exams on XML and XSL that are warranted by the International Webmaster's Association (a Web-oriented professionals' association). For more information, check out their exam offerings under the general heading of "Web Design and Development" at

```
www.brainbench.com/xml/bb/homepage.xml
```

By the time you read this book, more XML certifications may be offered. To find out about certifications not in the list given here, check out general certification resources online, such as www.gocertify.com or www.it certmag.com.

Serious Searches Lead to Success

What we've presented in this chapter is only the merest suggestion of the enormous trove of resources, publications, news, information, examples, tutorials, and other useful XML resources available to you. Don't forget that the power of the Web — when viewed through your favorite search engine (be that engine Yahoo!, Ask Jeeves, Google, AltaVista, or whatever) — can lead you to just about any XML-related information. The sooner you start searching, the sooner you start finding what you need. Good luck!

Glossary

● ●

ADO (Active X Data Objects): A Microsoft interface for data objects.

aggregator: In RSS, software that filters a group of RSS feeds to create a feed that includes items from several different feeds in the same content area.

ASCII (American Standard Code for Information Interchange): A coding method to translate characters, such as numbers, text, and symbols, into digital form. ASCII includes only 127 characters and is only useful for English (okay, and Latin, but nothing else really).

ATOM: A syndication format and a protocol for editing syndicated content.

attribute: In XML, a property associated with an XML element that is a named characteristic of the element. An attribute also provides additional data about an element.

attribute declaration: In XML Schema and DTDs, an attribute declaration is markup that defines the name of an attribute and its properties.

attribute group: A collection of attributes in an XML Schema document.

attribute-list declaration: In DTDs, a declaration that defines the name, datatype, and default value (if any) of each attribute associated with an element.

axis: In XPath, an axis identifies a family relationship. For example, child, parent, or preceding-sibling are XPath axes.

binary: A numbering system (base 2) based on the two digits 0 and 1.

bit: A 0 or a 1; the basic computer storage unit.

byte: A collection of 8 bits.

CDF (Channel Definition Format): An XML-based file format, developed by Microsoft.

CGI (Common Gateway Interface): A standard that allows external programs of various types to interact with Web servers, usually to provide interactive responses or services related to user input from a browser.

channel: Information about organized content on an intranet or the Internet. Channels enable Web developers to categorize and describe Web site content and make that data available to users on demand.

character data (CDATA): In XML, a string of characters.

character entity: A string of characters that represents other characters. For example, `&lt;` and `&Egrave;` show a string of characters (`lt` and `Egrave`) that stand for other characters (< and È).

character set: When referring to script, a collection of values that maps to some specific symbol set or alphabet.

child element: An element that occurs within some parent element and is therefore part of that parent's content model.

choice group: In XML Schema, a method that allows you to make either/ or choices between two elements, in addition to choices among several elements.

closing tag: XML elements that contain content must begin with an opening tag and end with a closing tag. XML syntax for a closing tag is `</element-name>`, where `element-name` is a placeholder for the element's name.

CML (Chemical Markup Language): An XML language with specific extensions for describing molecules and compounds.

comment: An SGML markup construct that permits authors to insert documentation, notes, and remarks into documents that are ignored when an XML document is parsed or processed. Comments begin with the markup string `<!--` and end with the markup string `-->`.

complex type definition: In XML Schema, a definition of an element that can contain other elements and/or can contain attribute declarations.

component: A part that is essential to the operation of a larger system.

compositor element: In XML Schema, an element that specifies order and occurrence constraints. XML Schema compositors include `sequence`, `choice`, and `all`.

content analysis: The process of identifying the properties of a collection of information.

content identifier: A token that can be used to uniquely identify any piece of data or content.

content model: Defines the order in which components (usually, child elements, but also datatypes such as #PCDATA or #CDATA) may or must appear within an XML document.

CSS (Cascading Style Sheets): A method of markup that allows Web developers to define how certain HTML, DHTML, or XML structural elements, such as paragraphs and headings, should be displayed using style rules instead of additional markup. The versions of CSS are CSS1, CSS2.1, and CSS3, with CSS2.1 being the most recent recommendation and CSS3 under development (as of March 2005).

CSV (comma -separated values): A format for tabular data where fields are separated by commas.

data intensive: Describes text content that includes many additional constraints, such as patterns of content.

datatype declaration: In XML Schema, markup that tells the processor the valid format for the content of an XML Schema element or attribute.

declaration: In programming languages (and metalanguages such as SGML DTDs and XML Schema documents), a declaration is a way to identify some kind of variable or data structure and to associate a specific name with one or more specific attributes to indicate what kind of value or values should be associated with that name. In DTDs, the ELEMENT declaration is associated with a specific name, and other characteristics, to identify and describe valid document components.

diacritical mark: An accent mark added to a letter.

DocBook: A heavy-duty DTD designed and implemented by HaL Computer Systems and O'Reilly & Associates. DocBook is used for authoring books, articles, and manuals, particularly those of a technical nature.

document element: In XPath, the document element node is a single node that contains the entire contents of the document except for any processing instruction nodes or comment nodes that are children of the root node.

DOCTYPE: See *document type declaration.*

document prolog: The portion of an XML document or DTD that occurs at its very beginning and defines the document's content, and may reference external and/or internal DTDs, XML Schemas, stylesheets, namespaces, and other sources for context or definitions for content.

document type declaration: A declaration that tells the processor where a DTD is located that may also contain additional new or custom declarations for the particular document in which it appears. Also known as a DOCTYPE declaration.

DOM (Document Object Model): A platform- and language-neutral programming interface that allows programs and scripts to access and update the content, structure, and style of documents in a standard way.

DOS (Disk Operating System): The original PC operating system, first introduced in 1982. DOS has been largely supplanted by Microsoft Windows on most desktops.

DSSSL (Document Style Semantics and Specification Language): A superset of XSL. DSSSL is a document style language used primarily with SGML files.

DTD (Document Type Definition): A statement of rules that specifies which elements (that define markup tags) and attributes (that define values associated with specific tags) are allowed in your documents.

e-commerce (electronic commerce): The exchange of money for goods and services between businesses, or between businesses and consumers, across the Internet or another public network.

EDI (Electronic Data Interchange): A standard for the electronic exchange of basic business information.

element: A named section of a document that may be either the root element or some child element that is normally defined by start and end tags that enclose document content or an empty tag that includes no content. In the bookstore DTD and Schema, `books` is the root element, and `book` is the element within which individual recipes may be defined.

element content model: A way to include a specification regarding children in element declarations. For example, you can specify that an element may contain only child elements.

element declaration: In XML Schema and DTDs, markup that defines the name of an element and its properties, including what child elements the element may include.

element type: A specific — or named — element defined within an SGML DTD or an XML Schema, such as `books` or `title`.

element type declaration: Provides a description of an element type and its content within the DTD.

empty element: An element used in markup languages that does not require a separate closing tag. In XML, an empty element is identified with a slash (/) before the closing greater-than sign (>), as in the ⟨br/⟩ element used in HTML and XHTML. When expressed as markup, an empty element may also be called an empty tag.

encoding: A technical term for how many bits you use to describe characters.

entity: A named object in an SGML DTD that represents a string of characters; thus the entity &Addr; could stand for "2207 Klattenhoff Drive, Austin, TX, 78728-5480". Entities provide useful shorthand when they're used to represent strings (like the preceding address) that appear in multiple or numerous locations in a document.

entity declaration: Defines a named set of text information that can be referenced by its name within a document or DTD. As the document or DTD is processed, every time the entity name is encountered, it's replaced by the set of information associated with that name. Thus, it provides useful shorthand for text that appears repeatedly in a document or DTD.

external parameter entity references: A string of characters that refers to information that appears in a separate file from the DTD or document prolog in which it appears.

external subset: A portion of a DTD that's stored in an external file. Also called an *external DTD* or an *external DTD subset.* Not all DTDs have external subsets, but any XML document or DTD that references another DTD does have an external subset.

FAQ (Frequently Asked Questions): A collection of questions and answers related to a specific topic. FAQs are most commonly found on Internet newsgroups.

font: A collection of bitmaps for a character set.

formatting object: In XSL, a piece of a document (which may be a single document element or a parent element and its various children) to which some particular formatting operation is applied. Thus, the children elements of the books element, book, might be associated with a formatting object that produced a numbered or bulleted list when processed.

freeware: Software available for use at no charge.

FTP (File Transfer Protocol): An Internet file-transfer service based on TCP/IP protocols. FTP provides a way to copy files to and from FTP servers elsewhere on a network.

GedML (Genealogical Markup Language): An XML language used to describe genealogical data.

general entity: An entity created in a DTD but used in an XML document; this differs from an internal entity, which is defined in a DTD and used only in that DTD (not in documents based on that DTD).

glyph: An individual bitmap in a font.

GUI (Graphical User Interface): As opposed to the plain text of a DOS command line, a computer interface designed for users to use a mouse (or trackball) to interact with (by clicking) graphics, windows, and menus to get information.

hexadecimal: A numbering system (base 16) using the symbols 0–9 and a–f.

HTML (HyperText Markup Language): One of the document-description markup languages used to create Web pages.

hypertext: A way of linking document locations so that clicking a particular hypertext element takes the user's browser from one document to another document.

IANA (Internet Assigned Numbers Authority): An organization that oversees IP (Internet Protocol) addresses, as well as character set numbering.

InfoPath: A visual XML forms editor, part of Office 2003.

inheritance: The result of an element (a child or sibling) having taken on the characteristics assigned to a higher-level element (parent).

inline style: A style rule that appears within the same XML document that contains the element to which the rule applies. This might involve writing XSLT instructions or CSS directives in a document prolog as a separate text block.

internal entity: In DTDs, an entity that contains the definition for its content (or substitution value) directly within the declaration itself, instead of referring to such content within some other, external file.

internal subset: The portion of the DTD that appears within the document. Also called an *internal DTD subset* or *internal DTD*. Not all DTDs include an internal subset; those that refer only to external DTDs may properly be said to contain no internal subset.

intranet: A private network within a company or organization that uses the same protocols as the Internet but that can't be accessed by Internet users.

ISO (International Organization for Standardization): The most popular computing- and communication-standards organization. It is comprised of standards bodies — such as ANSI, IEEE, EIA/TIA, CCITT, and so forth — from all over the world.

ISO-Latin-1: Also known as ISO 8859-1 (the numeric equivalent), ISO-Latin-1 is the default character set for HTML and XHTML; modern XML implementations are more likely to use the ISO 10646 character set, also known as Unicode, but can also use ISO-Latin-1 (where Web browsers may be involved, this can help avoid potential display difficulties).

Java: An object-oriented programming language used for Web application development. It was created by Sun Microsystems.

JavaScript: An inline scripting language often used with HTML or XHTML (and only infrequently with XML) to add dynamic behaviors or interactive capabilities to Web pages and related documents.

kilobyte: Equal to 1024 bytes.

linking element: An element that contains a hyperlink. In HTML, `img` and `a` elements are examples of linking elements.

locator: Data that identifies a resource to which a link may be made using some kind of linking elements. Such resources may include documents, special display formats (such as Adobe's Portable Document Format, or PDF) or binary files (graphical images, executable files, and so forth).

macro: A text or code script that performs an action when called, usually used to automate repetitive activities, such as combinations of keystrokes, a series of mouse-click sequences, or both.

markup language: A language that uses tags to label, categorize, and organize information in a specific way.

MathML (Mathematical Markup Language): An XML language that provides a way of representing mathematical and scientific content on the Web, especially where complex formulas or arcane notation are used.

metadata: Within a document, specially defined data elements that describe the document's structure, content, or rendering, or that use external references to describe these features of the document. (*Metadata* literally means *data about data.*)

metalanguage: A language used to communicate information about language itself. Many experts consider both SGML and XML to be metalanguages because they are used to define other markup languages, such as HTML and XSL.

MIME (Multipurpose Internet Mail Extension): Extensions that allow e-mail messages to carry multiple types of data (such as binary, audio, video, and graphics) as attachments. MIME types are also used to identify document types during transfers over the Internet. XML documents are text/xml or application/xml.

mixed content: A type of content model that permits XML elements or child elements to contain character data.

MSXML (Microsoft XML): The Microsoft Internet Explorer XML parser.

multimedia presentation: A presentation that involves two or more forms of media (text, audio, and video, for example).

namespace: See *XML namespace.*

nested: Used in XML to denote something that's contained within something else. For example, an element may be nested within another element — contained within the opening and closing tags of another element.

node: Used in XML to denote a piece of a document's tree structure, as generated when the document is parsed or processed (as according to the Document Object Model [DOM] or some other processing model).

notation declaration: Associates a notation name with information that can help find an interpreter of information described by the notation. Thus, to permit an external program to handle some kind of multimedia format in an XML file, a notation could be defined to associate the file extension .mov with some kind of multimedia player.

numeric entity: A string of numbers that represents a character. Numeric entities are identified by an ampersand followed by a pound sign (#). For example, < and È show a string of numbers (60 and 200) that stand for characters (< and È). More commonly called *character entities.*

OASIS (Organization for the Advancement of Structured Information Standards): A global consortium for developing e-business standards.

object: A unit of meaning or value in a programming or markup language, where objects have names and associated values called properties or attributes. Objects are like maps or descriptions of specific sets of values, called object instances, in that they define a name and structure for information but don't define specific sets of values that follow such definitions. Only object instances contain actual values and have some correspondence to "real data." Objects are also associated with specific operations or transformations called methods that create, manipulate, or destroy specific object instances.

object-oriented programming: A method of programming in which data is defined in terms of objects and where objects may be acted upon by operations called methods. In contrast to other programming techniques (such as procedural programming, where code acts directly upon data values and variables), objects are much more self-describing in terms of their attributes or properties and in terms of the methods that apply to them. In many ways, XML is an object-oriented markup technology.

occurrence indicator: A symbol, such as ?, *, and +, that's included in a DTD element declaration to further provide structural guidance about how elements are to be applied within a document. For example, an occurrence indicator may say how many times a portion of a content model may appear within a document.

ODBC (Open Database Connectivity): A software interface for connecting to database management systems.

OFX (Open Financial Exchange): A specification that provides a standard way of describing financial data and transactions in a way that banks, Web protocols, and your personal financial software can understand.

OSF (Open Software Foundation): An industry consortium for creating standards for software engineering.

operating system: The underlying program that enables computer-system hardware to run other applications. Macintosh, Windows, UNIX, and DOS are common operating systems.

OWL (Web Ontology Language): A W3C specification for defining the relationships among terms as well as inference rules. For example, in the case of phone numbers, a specific value for area code infers a particular value for city, even though that is not a direct part of the area code data. One of the technologies for the Semantic Web.

P3P (Platform for Privacy Preferences): A W3C specification that enables browsers to automatically understand a Web site's privacy practices.

Packaging/Extensions layer: In Web services, a data management or handling layer primarily concerned with establishing, managing, securing, and packaging information for exchange between service consumers and producers. See Chapter 15 for more information about the Web services model.

pagination: The process of dividing a document into pages.

parameter entity: An entity created and used within a DTD, where the value associated with that entity occurs in an external file or definition in a way that's easy to change. The value of this entity may then be used to alter or guide the processing of the document, so that one value might cause the document to be processed for print output and another value might the document to be displayed on a screen.

parent: In a content model, an element that contains one or more other elements is called a parent or parent element; the contained elements are called children or child elements.

parsed character data: Also called *PCDATA,* this is text that the document processor actually looks at.

PDF (Portable Document Format): A graphics file format created by Adobe Acrobat. To view a PDF file, you must download Adobe Acrobat Reader or have access to another Adobe application, such as PageMaker or Photoshop.

PICS (Platform for Internet Content Selection): A W3C specification that uses labels to categorize Internet content, P3P was originally created to help parents control what Internet content children could access.

POST method: A means by which users return information to a Web server using an HTML form. Posted data returns to the server as directed by a CGI script. Often, such data is analyzed or processed in some way by an application that then returns a new Web page, often generated on-the-fly, to the user's browser.

primary key: An identifier that's used to uniquely identify a record in a database.

processing instruction: Similar to the prolog, a special directive in an XML document that provides a way to send instructions to computer programs or applications, not humans.

processor (also XML processor): A special software program that knows how to read, interpret, and internalize the structure and contents of an XML document. Any time that a program reads and handles an XML document, an XML processor is involved in that activity.

property: A named value associated with a data object. For XML elements, attributes play the same role that properties play for objects.

pull technology: Technology that enables users to retrieve information from a Web server (using a Web browser). Servers that offer news or entertainment channels may be accessed by configuring Web browsers to read and update information at regular intervals ("pulling" those updates from the server). Client initiation of activity represents pull technology; server initiation of activity is what represents push technology, as noted in the following definition.

push technology: Technology that initiates delivery of material from a server to a properly equipped client (Web browser). Some kinds of software update services (such as Windows Update, as implemented in Microsoft Windows XP Professional) automatically deliver updates to registered clients as soon as they become available. Also called *push publishing.*

query: A request for information. In databases, queries are often formulated using SQL (Structured Query Language).

RDF (Resource Description Framework): A W3C specification for an XML language and metadata model used to describe resources.

regular expression: A specific pattern for a group of characters.

RELAX NG (Regular Language for XML Next Generation): A schema language for XML that specifies a pattern for a valid document.

reserved character: In XML, characters that can't be used in XML documents unless they are part of a CDATA section or unless they're escaped with a character entity. For example, to include a <, it must be replaced by <. Other reserved characters in XML include >, &, ', and ".

resource: Any resource that can be retrieved over the Internet — for example, a document, image, sound file, or even a list generated automatically in response to a query.

restriction constraint: In XML Schema, a limit applied to a built-in datatype that can be narrowed as needed.

root element: A single top-level tag that contains everything in an XML document except the XML declaration and processing instructions.

root node: In XPath, a single node that is the root of the document tree and contains the entire document. This is not the same as a root element. The root node contains the document element node and can also contain processing instruction nodes and comment nodes.

RSS: An XML language used for news feeds and Web logs (blogs). RSS stands for Rich Site Summary, RDF Site Summary, or Really Simply Syndication, depending on which version of RSS you're referring to.

schema: In general, a pattern that represents the data's model and defines the elements (or objects), their attributes, and the relationships between the different elements. A schema can also be a language written in XML that defines the rules for the structure and the content of an XML document.

Schematron: A schema language for XML that uses patterns and document trees for validating XML documents.

scripting: A simple method for including programming or processing instructions within a Web page, usually to facilitate user interaction or changing displays or behavior. See *JavaScript*.

scripting language: A specialized language used to create sequences of simple instructions that, when inserted into a Web page, control various elements of the page, such as the user interface, styles, and HTML markup. JavaScript and VBScript are the primary scripting languages.

selector: In CSS, the part of a style rule that identifies the element (or elements) to which that rule applies.

semantics: The science of describing what words mean; it's the opposite of syntax. In XML, semantics are conveyed in various ways: through element names, content models, and through value restrictions and occurrence indicators.

Semantic Web: A vision of Tim Berners-Lee and the W3C for automating data and information processing on the Web by adding semantic capabilities (meaning) using metadata (data about data).

SGML (Standard Generalized Markup Language): A metalanguage used to construct markup languages, such as HTML and XML.

SGML declaration: A declaration that acts separately from a DTD to provide specific instructions to an SGML parser.

SGML parser: A text-handling program that interprets SGML markup in a document and builds a model of the document's structure and contents. Normally, an SGML parser then passes that model to some other program for further action so that it may be edited, displayed, or archived.

sibling (also **sibling element):** Two document elements that are both child elements of the same parent element are sibling elements to one another. Thus, in our `bookstore` XML document, `title` and `author` are siblings, and share the same parent, `book`.

simple type definition: In XML Schema, a definition of an element that can contain only text; by contrast, complex type definitions can contain simple types, fixed values, and even parameters.

SMIL (Synchronized Multimedia Integration Language): An XML language that allows the integration of a collection of multimedia objects that follow a schedule, which is laid out by the developer.

SOAP (Structured Object Access Protocol): An XML-based protocol for exchanging messages.

SQL: Either of two database-management programming languages from Sybase and Microsoft.

SQL server: A database server that uses the Structured Query Language (SQL) to accept requests for data access.

standalone: In XML, a standalone document isn't dependent on any other document to be complete.

style: To apply formatting instructions.

style rule: A rule in an XML document that identifies a style pattern specifies an action that must be applied when the pattern is found. Such rules can result from the application of CSS or by the application of XSL.

stylesheet: A file that holds the layout settings for a certain category of a document. Stylesheets, like templates, contain settings for formatting features such as headers and footers, tabs, margins, fonts, columns, and more.

substitution group: In XML Schema, this is a technique that allows you to define one element that may be substituted for one or more other elements of the same type (or derived from the same type).

SVG (Scalable Vector Graphics): An XML language for describing vector graphics.

syntax: The rules that govern the construction of intelligible markup language documents or markup fragments, similar to the grammar rules used in spoken languages, such as English.

tag: In markup languages, the term *tag* refers to the ways in which document elements appear within documents. They generally take one or two of the following forms: `<element-name/>` (a single form for empty elements) or `<element-name>` and `</element-name>` (opening and closing forms for elements that contain content).

taxonomy: A hierarchical classification scheme.

TCP/IP (Transmission Control Protocol/Internet Protocol): The family of formal rules and formats for networked communications, called protocols, used on the Internet. This family of protocols (also known as a protocol suite) takes its name from two of its most important members: the Internet Protocol (IP) used to carry individuals packages of data from a sender to a receiver, and the Transmission Control Protocol (TCP) used to provide reliable transport of messages between a sender and a receiver.

template: The instructions in an XSLT stylesheet that control how an element and its content should be converted. A template identifies which element in a document should be changed and then specifies how the element should be changed.

text intensive: Content that does not need to be in any specific format other than text strings.

Transport layer: In Web services, a layer that acts like the highway that carries messages from senders to receivers across the Internet. For Web services, the most commonly used protocol to provide this capability is the HyperText Transfer Protocol (HTTP).

traversal: The result of clicking a link. By clicking a link, a Web browser *traverses* from one resource to another.

tree: A diagram of an XML document that is constructed as the document is processed with a structure that corresponds to the order of and relationships among the elements that the XML document contains. The general name for such diagrams is a *parse tree;* for XML documents, that name may be used, or it may also be called the *document tree.* This diagram may be queried, navigated, or manipulated as a way of acting upon the contents and structure of the related document to which the diagram corresponds.

UDDI (Universal Description, Discovery, and Integration): UDDI is an XML language used as a method for finding Web services.

Unicode character set: A 16-bit character encoding scheme, defined in ISO/IED 10646, that encompasses standard Roman and Greek alphabets, plus mathematical symbols; special punctuation; non-Roman alphabets, including Hebrew, Chinese, Arabic, and Hangul; and other ideographic character sets.

UNIX: One of the most powerful multiuser operating systems around, designed by a hacker in 1969 as an interactive timesharing operating system to play games on.

URI (Uniform Resource Identifier): A character string that identifies the type and location of an Internet resource.

UTF (Unicode Transformation Format): A mapping method for associating a number with a character. The two most common UTFs are UTF-8, an 8-bit Unicode character encoding, and UTF-16, a 16-bit Unicode character encoding.

valid: When an XML document adheres to a DTD or schema.

validating parser: A software utility that compares an XML document with a declared DTD or XML Schema; if the document includes no violations of the rules that a document description states, that document is said to be valid. But if errors or violations are detected, that document is said to be invalid.

vocabulary: In XML, a set of names and definitions for XML elements, attributes, and datatypes. A vocabulary is defined in an XML Schema or a DTD.

W3C (World Wide Web Consortium): An organization that develops standards for the Web (and the Internet), including markup languages, communication protocols, and XML applications too numerous to mention.

Web service: Remote applications that carry out specific tasks or functions. They can be accessed through the Web rather than being run locally on a desktop. They allow different applications from different sources to communicate with each other by using XML.

Web standards: A group of technologies for creating and interpreting Web-based content, includes W3C specifications as well as specifications from other standards organizations.

well-formed document: An XML document that adheres to XML's syntax rules.

white space: Nonprinting characters such as spaces, tabs, carriage returns, or line feeds.

WIDL (Web Interface Definition Language): An object-oriented, SGML-based markup language that helps designers create powerful, intuitive, Web-based user interfaces.

WSDL (Web Services Definition Language): An XML language used to describe what kinds of information and services a Web service provider has to offer.

WYSIWYG (What You See Is What You Get) interface: Any interface or application that allows users to enter and see information as it will appear in the final document, as opposed to an interface or application that shows markup or other content obscuring a document's appearance.

XDR (XML-Data Reduced): A Microsoft schema language.

XForms: A W3C specification for an XML language for creating forms.

XHTML (eXtensible HyperText Markup Language): The reformulation of HTML 4.0 as an application of XML 1.0.

XLink (XML Linking Language): An XML language that provides a simple set of instructions to describe the links among objects.

XML (eXtensible Markup Language): A system for defining, validating, and sharing document formats so that they are well formed.

XML declaration: The markup at the very beginning of an XML document that specifies which version of XML the document is written in as well as other information. (As of this writing, declarations must refer to XML 1.0 because that's the only version available.)

XML Encryption: An XML language for secure exchange of encrypted data.

XML entity: A string of characters that lets a text viewer (such as a browser) display a symbol but prevents the viewer from interpreting the symbol as markup. An entity often enables a viewer to represent a larger range of characters than might otherwise be possible, yet keep character sets small.

XML namespace: A namespace is a vocabulary, a collection of names and definitions of elements, attributes, and types. A namespace declaration associates a specific namespace (vocabulary) with a document. A unique identifier (attached through a prefix) links an XML markup element to a specific DTD or schema. For example, in XML Schema, you add the prefix xsd or xs to an XML Schema element to indicate that it belongs to that namespace: `<xsd:element name="books">`.

XML notation: A form of XML markup designed to accomplish some specific objective. Examples include the mathematical and chemical notations supported by MathML and CML (both of which are XML applications), respectively.

XML prolog: An XML prolog is part of an XML document and may include an XML declaration, a DOCTYPE declaration, comments, processing instructions, and white space.

XML Query (XQuery): An XML language designed to query a collection of XML data.

XML Schema: A W3C language that defines the rules for the structure and the content of an XML document. The resulting document specifies the overall structure of an XML document and identifies all the components of the XML document, as well as how they can be validly used.

XML Schema document: A document written in the XML Schema language, according to rules defined by the World Wide Web Consortium (W3C).

XML Signature: An XML language for digital signatures.

XPath: An XML language that describes directions for how to get from one place in an XML document to another. XPath is used by XSLT, XPointer, and XQuery.

XPointer: An XML application that provides a method for accessing specific locations within a document, even though you may not have edit privileges for that document.

XSL (eXtensible Stylesheet Language): An XML language that defines the specification for an XML document's presentation and appearance.

XSL-FO (XSL Formatting Objects): Defines how XML documents should be displayed or converted into various forms of output, such as the Adobe Acrobat Portable Document Format (PDF).

XSLT (XSL Transformations): An XSL conversion tool that provides a set of rules to convert documents described by one set of elements to documents described by another set of elements.

Index

• J •

• Z •